D0759326

Liberty and Property

The Johns Hopkins University
Studies in Historical and Political Science
105th Series (1987)

1. NOBLES IN NINETEENTH-CENTURY FRANCE
The Practice of Inegalitarianism
By David Higgs

2. LIBERTY AND PROPERTY
Political Economy and Policymaking in the New Nation, 1789–1812
By John R. Nelson, Jr.

Liberty and Property

Political Economy and Policymaking in the New Nation, 1789-1812

JOHN R. NELSON, JR.

The Johns Hopkins University Press

BALTIMORE AND LONDON

This book has been brought to publication
with the generous assistance of
the Andrew W. Mellon Foundation.

The Johns Hopkins University Press,
701 West 40th Street,
Baltimore, Maryland 21211
The Johns Hopkins Press Ltd., London

The paper used in this publication
meets the minimum requirements of
American National Standard for
Information Sciences—Permanence of Paper
for Printed Library Materials,
ANSI Z39.48-1984.

Library of Congress Cataloging-in-Publication Data

Nelson, John R., 1952–
Liberty and property.

(The Johns Hopkins University studies in historical and political science;
105th ser., 2)
Bibliography: p.
1. United States—Economic policy—To 1933. 2. United States—Politics and
government—1789-1815. 3. Liberalism—United States—History. 4. Laissez-faire—
History.   I. Title.   II. Series.
HC105.N45   1987   338.973   86-21373
ISBN 0-8018-3440-6 (alk. paper)

For Doris, Alex, and Katie

Contents

Acknowledgments

I have several debts. Phi Alpha Theta—the National Honorary Society—and Northern Illinois University provided me with fellowship aid to research this study. E. James Ferguson was kind enough to read and comment on two significant sections of it in different form. Through discussions and lectures, Carl P. Parrini has informed my method of analysis and assisted me greatly in understanding political economy. Martin J. Sklar was helpful in drawing my attention to several important issues through his unpublished essay, "Some Questions Relating to the Hamiltonian-Jeffersonian Conflict in Early United States History" (University of Wisconsin, 1955).

My greatest scholarly debt is to my advisor and friend Alfred F. Young. His patient criticisms and unequaled erudition guided my research with skill and empathy. I attribute whatever merit it has to his guidance.

Throughout the painstaking task of doing this study, my wife, Doris M. Nelson, has been an unfailing source of encouragement, good humor, and perspective.

In slightly different form, Chapter 3 appeared as "Alexander Hamilton and American Manufacturing: A Reexamination," *Journal of American History*, 65 (March 1979), 971–95.

Introduction

There was no subject, Thomas Jefferson once remarked, about which Americans knew less than political economy. In this instance, he was speaking of political economy in the sense of academic economics. Political economy as a practical matter could not have been more central to the politics and policies of the third president and his contemporaries. More than an academic theory, they conceived of political economy as a composite of commercial activity, government policy, and individual psychology. Adam Smith, the preeminent economist of their era, understood three dimensions of political economy: a scientific inquiry into the nature and origins of national wealth, a theoretical basis for policies to increase national wealth and power, and a mode of intelligibility to uncover the political, economic, and social dynamics of progress. Political economy cut a wide conceptual swath along the cognoscenti of the late eighteenth century in America. Precisely how wide a swath and with what impact on policymaking are the central questions this study seeks to answer. To narrow its scope I have chosen to focus on two principal leaders of the early national period: Alexander Hamilton and Albert Gallatin. James Madison and Thomas Jefferson, because of their virtually inseparable political relationship with Gallatin—Henry Adams called them a triumvirate—also receive appropriate attention. This study deals with three aspects of the political economies of these men: their world views, the interest groups within their political constituencies, and the historical context in which world view and interest interacted.

In large measure this study is an analytic essay, a commentary on and an interpretation of events and decisions. Its main sources are the papers of Hamilton, Gallatin, Jefferson, and Madison. It draws extensively on the ongoing accomplishment of collecting in print and on microfilm all the papers of the major national leaders. For the first time, scholars have access to a complete edition of the extant correspondence, incoming and outgoing, and the writings, published and unpublished, of these men. In many respects these editions supersede biographies and enrich our understanding of the concerns that moved these leaders. The editions are also valuable sources for the political opinion of the various interest groups. Through them and numerous petitions, I have been able to reconstruct the demands and perceptions of these groups, particularly merchants and manufacturers. I also marshal economic data and link these data with key interest groups and policy decisions to establish an economic context for the politics of the period. And for political activities and issues within each state, I have synthesized the large body of specialized research on the states into an interpretative overview of the period.

Chapter 1 begins with an analysis of classical liberal thought in the Anglo-American tradition as the conceptual paradigm of the four leaders. It is a selective, almost impressionistic, survey of the way in which the principal actors of the subsequent quarter-century viewed the new Constitution and the federal government. It is not a comprehensive social portrait of America in 1789 or a detailed recounting of the formation of the union. It is a stage-setting device: a survey of the liberal intellectual tradition inherited by the leadership groups in America, the economic situation of the new nation and federal government, and the definition of political objectives of important interest groups. Chapter 2 explores Hamilton's political economy in theory and practice. Chapters 3 and 4 take up its effects on domestic manufacturing and foreign policy. Chapter 5 analyzes the decision by Jefferson and Madison to split with Hamilton and assume the leadership of an opposition party. Chapter 6 examines the origins and composition of the Republican political coalition. Chapter 7 details Gallatin's role in the opposition leadership between 1796 and 1800, and the Republican victory in the election of 1800. Chapters 8 and 9 explore Republican domestic and foreign policies while the Republicans were in office. Chapter 10 presents an overview of the relationship of the Republicans to manufacturing throughout the period. In a concluding chapter some observations are offered on the overall relationship of political economy to policymaking in this era.

Both Hamilton and the Republican triumvirate have accumulated an interpretative crust in historiography. Hamilton is portrayed as the harbinger of American nationalism, industrialization, and economic development. The triumvirate, particularly Jefferson, is often portrayed as advocating a laissez-faire agrarianism that was modified, once they came to power, under the pressures of actual governance. These stereotypes skew efforts to produce a coherent overview of the politics and policies of this era. They tend to reify the categories of analysis by removing fundamental issues from reconsideration and reinterpretation. Instead, the basic positions of these leaders on fiscal policy, federal intervention into the economy, development of manufacturing, and other crucial issues are assumed. The results of new historical research are either placed in procrustean interpretative beds or, more commonly, simply not assimilated into any overarching analysis.

This volume offers a new interpretative framework which builds on both the insights of past scholars and a growing body of new data — particularly about the political allegiances of various interest groups. The nexus of this new framework is the concept of political economy. Political economy conveyed several meanings to the early national leaders. One involved their concept of the nature and purpose of the individual in a social context. A second centered on how they believed government policy should respond to human nature and human society. The third meaning linked the other two in that it established the limits of individual conduct and political activity. These parameters were the boundaries of their world views — a combination of ideological assumptions, material interests, and historical events. An interpretation of the political economies of these leaders is an analysis of their politics, policies, and conflicts as expressions of their political economies. The conflicts generally revolved around the definition of socioeconomic problems and the political solutions devised by those in conflict. The resolution of these conflicts was a multifaceted process confined neither to intellectual debate nor naked self-interest. To analyze the politics and policies of this era as expressions of conflicting political economies is less an interpretative imposition than a systematic inference based on the world view of the principal policymakers. The issue is not that of an economic interpretation versus a political, religious, or ideological interpretation; the issue is how the leaders making much of the period's history understood what they were doing and why. If, as I argue, political economy was fundamental to their understanding, then it is logical to pursue an analysis of their history through this medium.

The basic argument of this work is that two divergent political economies, Hamilton's and the Republican triumvirate's, were at the root of the political conflicts over federal policy in this area. The cornerstone of this argument is the concept of stabilization — a modern term generally applied to fiscal policies which seek to deal with social and political disruptions wrought by economic changes. Consequently, stabilization policies have political and social implications. Common to the founders was the assumption that economic disruption portended political unrest and social upheaval. Stabilization is the

active element in political economy, its policy arm. Stabilization policies make a world view operational. They expose that view to a reality
of change and conflict. Such policies seek to control social change,
mediate social conflict, and direct social progress—in a word, stabilize
a society.

The achievement of economic and political stability, I shall argue,
was the goal of both Hamilton's and the triumvirate's political economies. They advanced or opposed federal policies insofar as they believed that such policies would contribute to this end. To insure stability and secure the new government Hamilton relied on a handful of
powerful merchants, the mimetic tradition of prerevolutionary colonial politics, and the coercive powers of the state: force and patronage.
In practice, Hamilton's method of achieving stability retarded comprehensive economic development, particularly manufacturing. The
triumvirate—Gallatin in particular—recognized and opposed this aspect of Hamilton's stabilization policy as destructive to the essential
purposes of a liberal polity. In its place the triumvirate proposed other
policies which promised comprehensive economic development, more
government participation in this development, and less overt political
manipulation through power and patronage. They sought to integrate
all economic interests, not only a handful of merchants, into a political coalition to support their stabilization policies.

This book maintains that their primary instrument for social stability was a national market system. The triumvirate believed that the
integration of all propertied citizens into a national market system
(with international connections) would generate economic prosperity,
political unity, and social stability—the essential attributes of a powerful and independent nation. The market system would replace the
often corrupt and coercive stabilization policies of Hamilton, which
threatened all three attributes of national independence, hence jeop-
ardizing independence itself. The triumvirate wanted a strong nation
and supported a strong central government only insofar as it strengthened the market system. Hamilton believed a powerful central government was essential to a strong nation, whereas the triumvirate relied
on the market system to create a strong nation which would create a
stable, hence powerful, government. The market system was in effect
the centripetal force counterbalancing the centrifugal forces of section, interest, and faction. The market system was the triumvirate's
method of eliminating the twin dangers posed by the democracy of the
Confederation and the oligarchy of Hamilton's rule to a republican
government and a liberal polity. While the extended political sphere,
articulated by Madison in his Tenth *Federalist,* was prophylactic
against the political causes of social and economic turmoil, the market

system, most clearly developed in Gallatin's reports on manufactures, internal improvements, and banking, was the seminal agent for stability—the active instrument for political cohesion and economic progress.

An analysis of this scope requires limits to the detail and the number of areas explored in depth. While I propose a new interpretative framework for a large period of history, much remains to be worked out, modified, and refined by further studies. I do not pretend to answer all questions. In many instances, I seek only to suggest the proper directions for further exploration and analysis. A great deal of research is required to clarify the interest-group coalitions within each party during this period, especially in the early nineteenth century. The domestic and international trade patterns of each urban area have not been adequately explored. The same is true for the rural marketing patterns of the nation, particularly the extent to which small farmers were integrated into the market economy and the effect of such integration on their political behavior. The lack of more solid empirical data in many places compels me simply to suggest underlying patterns and speculate about their significance. Nevertheless, I hope this concentration on political economy will contribute to resolving a number of important interpretative problems that have long plagued scholars of this period and will stimulate further research into political economy.

Liberty and Property

CHAPTER ONE

America in 1789

An Overview

I

America was heir to a liberal intellectual tradition already a century and a half old at her founding. This tradition and the ideas it contained constituted the liberal world view that was the ground, the substance, and the very language of the early American leaders. These leaders comprehended the world through the assumptions, definitions, and goals of liberal thought. The structure of their thought represents an intellectual paradigm, visible to them only as specific ideas and perceptions. The whole of it they could not comprehend, for it was their very mechanism of comprehension. Only through historical analysis can it be identified as an integrated world view and its essentials discussed.[1]

The starting point of Anglo-American liberal thought was an intrinsically self-interested individual living in a social context. Politics was the collective reason of society attempting to deal with individual self-interest. It was a means toward an end and could not be divorced from that end in practice. Property originated in the nature of man as the social expression of self-interest. It was an ontological attribute of political society. Property protection defined social relations as civilized. Virtue was self-interest disciplined by an enlightened reason. Vice or licentiousness was undisciplined or misdirected self-interest. No political faction or leader could violate property without destroying civil society and contradicting human nature. Men created government to realize their collective self-interest. Government insured that man's "passion" for immediate objects did not subvert the essential condition for the social realization of the most basic passion, self-interest. This condition was the preservation of individual property acquired according to the rules of justice, which bound all men. In another respect, the realization of self-interest required active effort by government to facilitate the exchange and accumulation of property through economic programs and commercial policies. Political economy synthesized the dual purpose of government to secure and advance collective self-interest—private property.

What became the liberal intellectual tradition in Anglo-American thought originated with Thomas Hobbes over a century before the American Revolution. He was the first philosopher to break away from the dominant scholastic tradition of medieval society and broach a modern epistemological method. Amid the massive social upheavals of seventeenth-century England, which Thomist categories could not comprehend much less explain, Hobbes created a new methodology to understand what was happening to the English world. Institutions and traditions appeared no longer capable of subsuming the vicissitudes of the present. Hobbes came to assume that society was reverting to a prepolitical state in which the traditional forms of social relations had ceased to define activity. Confronted with what were now discrete, almost atomistic, individuals, he developed a sociology rooted in the epistemology of the New Science. This epistemology took each datum as a particular observation from which the faculty of reason could construct, in conjunction with other observations, explanations of reality. The crucial step here was the recognition that scientific thought through the agency of reason was the constituent of the real world.[2]

This recognition unleashed two divergent but related developments in modern thought. On the one hand, by admitting that phenomena could not be understood in themselves, the New Science made human apprehension of phenomena the sole basis of knowing. What man discovered in the world was absolutely wedded to the psychological tools with which he examined the world. Ultimate reality was unknowable. On the other hand, man—more precisely human psychology—became the key to epistemology. The human mind stood under all understanding of the world. Man created the knowable world through the conceptualization of sensations and ideas into knowledge. Thus, individual psychology, in the sense of the observation and analysis of the process of perception, held the information necessary for understanding why the world was what it was.[3]

Hobbes seized the new epistemology to build his political sociology. During the radical dissolution of English society he could observe man without the rigid hierarchy of medieval law and custom. In this "natural" (prepolitical) state Hobbes saw a lonely, solitary creature driven by greed, by violence, and above all by fear—fear for his life, his property, and his liberty to enjoy them. Building from discrete observation he concluded that political society was born of this fear. Its very purpose derived from the inability of the individual to secure his life and property from his neighbors' unscrupulous avarice. Only the political state vested with the collective unmitigated power of all individuals in the society could secure each from their fear of each other. Hobbes's etiology of political society remained the tacit assumption of all liberal philosophers to follow. They would refine his psychology and add the crucial distinction between authority and power, but they would never forget his political sociology.[4]

It was not John Locke but William Petty who first took up the Hobbesian gauntlet on the issue of power and authority. Petty accepted Hobbes's genesis of political society, but he balked at the absolute, unchecked power Hobbes accorded the sovereign state. How could life, property, and freedom from fear be insured if the state could arbitrarily incarcerate or kill citizens? Why replace the *bellum omnes contra omnes* with the war of one possessing irresistible force against all the rest? While retaining the effective power of the state over life, liberty, and property, Petty qualified it with the provision that the authority to exercise such power be granted and directed by bodies representative of the nation's citizens. In this regard the state still possessed sufficient power to maintain social order, but was circumscribed by its purpose of preserving life, property, and the free enjoyment of these.[5]

Under Locke's skillful guidance Petty's addition of representative authority to Hobbesian sociology evolved into a doctrine of natural rights. Locke subsumed the attributes of life, liberty, and estate under the general rubric of property. Property was natural because it developed out of the nature of man; it was a right because it both preceded and defined political society. Civilized social relations were impossible without government. And what made relations among individuals civil and social was property. The attributes of man, which Locke defined as property, were inseparable from a social context. By its contrast the social context gave substance to the concept of the individual and his property. Yet, as it provided the situation necessary to their realization, society threatened the individual and his property with other individuals who also desired to possess property. The passion of each individual to preserve his property led him to create an authority with the power to protect property. This political artifact was the final step toward civilized social relations and civil society.[6]

In integrating the basic tenets of early modern thought Hume developed all the essential elements of what would become the European Enlightenment.[7] "We cannot," Hume wrote, "go beyond experience; and any hypothesis that pretends to discover the ultimate original qualities of human nature, ought at first to be rejected as presumptuous and chimerical." Observation and reasonable inference were the chief components of "experience." Observations of discrete phenomena led to reasonable inferences about their origins. The human mind possessed certain inherent, universal "propensities" by which it inferred causality. These propensities, themselves merely universally observable forms into which sense data were poured, were the foundation of understanding. Hume's concept of mental propensities rescued his philosophical method and the whole epistemology of the New Science from hopeless skepticism. It allowed him to increase the breadth of human knowledge while circumscribing its depth. Man could see only so far into the noumenal world, but he could deal in a more rational scientific way with what he did see. This phenomenal world of human society and human nature was defined by universally observable, therefore "natural," attributes of man.[8] The proper study of the physical world became the way in which mankind's understanding acted to constitute the world; and the proper study of mankind's understanding became the irreducible, discrete phenomenon of man himself.

For Hume, as for all liberal thinkers, man was a creature of passions. "A passion," he explained, "is an original existence." It constituted the subject's "reflective impression," which proceeded from "original impressions or impressions of sensation" due to external stimuli. The passions distinguished subject from object and constituted the very individuality of being. The "direct," or primary, passions were pain and pleasure, from which came the other passions: pride, humility, ambition, love, hatred, envy, fear, and security. These passions were the wellsprings of all human activity. In the social maelstrom of these passions property arose.[9]

Property and political society developed through the agency of reason. "Reason," Hume argued, "is, and ought to be the slave of the passions, and can never pretend to any other office than to serve and obey them." Passion could not contradict reason because any conflict of reason "consists in the disagreement of ideas," and passions were not ideas. Reason was the mediative agency among the various passions and their objects. It was a means to attain the objects of the passions. Since reason was neither causal nor purposeful in itself, those qualities of substance in man and society had to be rooted in the passions. The pillars of civil society, morality and justice, were rooted in the passions. Virtue and vice were the individual expressions of morality and justice and corresponded to the passions of pleasure and pain.[10]

Morality existed only in the relationships "betwixt internal actions, and external objects, and must be applicable either to internal actions, compared among themselves, or to external objects, when placed in opposition to other external objects." With respect to morality, good and evil "are nothing but *particular* pains or pleasures" writ large. Within a social context, morality became justice; its rules became laws. Justice was "artificial" in that, unlike morality, it was a social contrivance lacking an immediate origin in individual passion. Nonetheless, the rules of justice were common to and inseparable from all civilized societies and, in this respect, could be properly called "Laws of Nature."[11]

For Hume, justice was at bottom the rules governing the property system of a society—a system stemming from the passionate nature of man. "The origin of justice," he wrote, "explains that of property. A man's property is some object related to him. This relation is . . . moral, and founded on justice." Self-interest—an individual's passion—was the origin of property and justice. In reality no "state of nature" had ever existed; man had always lived in a social context. A social context enhanced his abilities to realize his passions. Passions, however, sought external objects for their satisfaction. Individuals vying for these objects engendered conflicts. Thus, to retain the advantages society accorded to the satisfaction of passions while avoiding civil conflict, reason enlightened individual self-interest and enabled it to establish justice and secure property. "This can be done," Hume concluded, "after no other manner, than by a convention enter'd into by all the members of the society to bestow stability on the possession of those external goods, and leave every one in the peaceable enjoyment of what he may acquire by his fortune and industry."[12]

Reasonable restraint of the passions was possible only insofar as it served to realize the true objects of the passions and curb "their heedless and impetuous movement." Indeed, if this restraint were "contrary to these passions," it "cou'd never be enter'd into, nor maintain'd." The social contract stabilized the property system, established justice, insured domestic tranquility, and secured the right of possession. "No one can doubt," he maintained, "that the convention for the distinction of property, and for the stability of possession, is of all circumstances the most necessary to the establishment of human society." Man's passion for objects could be restrained only through enlightened reason, which revealed "that the passion is much better satisfy'd by its restraint, than by its liberty, and that in preserving society, we make much greater advances in acquiring possessions, than in the solitary and forlorn condition, which must follow upon violence and an universal licence."[13] Through a century of revision and development in liberal thought, Hobbes's etiology of political society remained intact.

Hume also expounded on the republican aspect of liberal thought. Though the power of the government was absolute in that it could confiscate life, liberty, and property, only the law, made by representative bodies, could authorize the exercise of such power. A government of laws, he explained, became necessary because "'tis impossible for men to consult their interest in so effectual a manner, as by an universal and inflexible observance of the rules of justice, by which alone they can preserve society, and keep themselves from falling into that wretched and savage condition, which is commonly represented as the *state of nature.*" Through elected magistrates whose "immediate interest" [is] in the interest of any considerable part of their subjects," government could act to promote those interests. As the self-interest of individuals had created political society, the self-interest of political leaders insured that government served the fundamental interests of its citizens. "Thus," Hume concluded, "bridges are built; harbours open'd; ramparts rais'd; canals form'd; fleets equip'd; and armies disciplin'd; every where, by the care of government, which, tho' composed of men subject to all human infirmities, becomes, by one of the finest and most subtle inventions imaginable, a composition, which is, in some measure, exempted from all these infirmities."[14]

Representative governments, however, were subject to two serious afflictions: corruption and faction. Corruption was generally the power of the executive to influence citizens, particularly legislators, with patronage. Used properly, Hume believed it to be a necessary increment to the maintenance of law and order. In a mixed government—the form liberal thinkers generally advocated for representative systems—influence was the chief check the executive imposed on the two houses of the lawmaking body. The lower house represented those of small and increasing property, the upper house those of large property and prestige. Each body advanced the interests of its constituents, while the executive endeavored to balance the two with a view to the aggregate interest of society. Only when executive influence threatened to subvert the role of a legislative body did it portend political unrest. The greater threat to representative government, however, was faction.[15]

Since the purpose of government was to aid its citizens in the realization of their passion for pleasure and happiness through their property, "the greatness of a state and the happiness of its subjects . . . are commonly allowed to be inseparable with regard to commerce." Commerce encompassed all aspects of economic activity that allowed individual accumulation of property. The state acted to enhance, expand, and protect commerce. The benefits were reciprocal: "As private men received greater security in the possession of their trade and riches from the power of the public, so the public becomes powerful in proportion to the opulence and extensive commerce of private men."[16] In a government whose purpose was to advance the commercial interest of its citizens, a problem arose when the interest of one group (or faction) of citizens seriously conflicted with the interest of another or with the aggregate interest of society.

Hume divided factions into three kinds: "those from *interest,* from *principle,* and from *affection.*" All factions stemmed from the passions, for they were the activating forces of all human movement. Religious fanaticism, charismatic leaders, and imagined fancies generated factions of principle and affection. Rarely tied to the most powerful passion, self-interest, they could be subdued by force or mediated by reason. Factions stemming from self-interest were "the most reasonable and most excusable." These factions had the character of "parties" and expressed the various economic interests of the citizenry. "The only dangerous parties," Hume warned, "are such as entertain opposite views with regard to the essentials of government." In other words, as long as a party did not question the "essential" purpose of government to preserve and increase property—that is, as long as the property system was not challenged—the abolition of party distinction was not "practicable" and "perhaps not desirable in a free government." What statesmen had to do was control factions and direct them toward the public good.[17]

Hume looked on a mixed republican government as the ideal means to check parties and factions. The charismatic appeal of the executive, the wisdom of the upper house, and above all, the diversity of the popular house served to blunt, redirect, and defuse the dangers of factions without tyranny. Factions "arise most easily in small republics," where "the force of popular tides and currents [are] very sensible." In addition to adopting a mixed government, a republic could best resist dissolution into factions through expansion. In an extensive republic "the parts are so distant and remote that it is very difficult, either by intrigue, prejudice, or passion, to hurry them into any measures against the public interest." Hume's concept of the imperial republic completed the edifice of liberal political thought.[18]

Perhaps the *Federalist* essays reflect most cogently the extension of Hume and the liberal tradition into America. Most scholars regard these essays as the epitome of American political thought in this era. Written for the most part in a collaboration between the two great allies, then antagonists of the early national period, James Madison and Alexander Hamilton, these essays embodied the basic beliefs of those who would rule America over the next decades. They were conservative essays in that they sought to reaffirm the basic purpose of government, of the Revolution, and of political society. For the most part Madison and Hamilton dealt with the form of the newly constituted government, but of necessity they also touched on the fundamentals of all governments seeking to administer a private property system. In doing so Hamilton and Madison reached deeply into liberal thought, revealed their absolute kinship with it, and established the framework which both shared, despite their bitter partisan struggles. Undeniably, their essays reflect the intellectual milieu of 1789 and after.

The essays affirmed the liberal concepts of man's "passion" and the function of political society. "Government is instituted no less for the protection of the property, than of the person, of individuals."[19] The exchange and accumulation of property followed from man's passion of self-interest, expressed in social terms as the desire for property. "The prosperity of commerce," their phrase for this accumulative interchange, was "a primary object of [the] political cares" of "all enlightened statesmen."[20] Morality itself rested on the "foundation of property and credit."[21] In political society individual morality—the natural passion for the accumulation of wealth and the retention of life and liberty—expressed itself as "justice." Justice "is the end of government" and "of civil society."[22]

The country, they argued, was in the midst of a crisis. A conflict had developed in American society between immediate self-interest and enlightened self-interest. Immediate self-interest expressed itself as factions. Like all human institutions and endeavors, factions were rooted in the passions. Unenlightened by reason, these factions conflicted with the "permanent and aggregate interest of the community." They could not be eliminated because they had originated in self-interest, the wellspring of man's activities. Political stability could not be attained at the expense of destroying the very interest that it was meant to secure. The only solution, then, was to control factions by preventing them from seizing political power to further their own ends and by actively advancing all the interests of the society. The authors offered their solution in the form of a new central government presiding over an extensive republic and responsible to all economic interests in the society.[23] In this government "all authority . . . will be derived from and dependent on the society," but the collective reason of the community would control passions of faction.[24] They concluded: "It is reason, alone, of the public, that ought to control and regulate the government. The passions ought to be controlled and regulated by the government." The *Federalist* was an owner's manual for government based on liberal thought.[25]

The propertyless had no place in liberal thought. Generally, women, children, tenants, nonwhites, and wage laborers were not citizens in republics, ancient or eighteenth-century. They were neither independent in livelihood nor in possession of significant property, but were the dependents of white adult male property owners. The liberal world view held property to be an ontological attribute of political society and civilization. Despite their importance to the economic system, the propertyless existed in the pores of the political system. They were bound to a propertied citizen by familial ties, involuntary servitude, or wage employment.[26] Since the wage laborer and slave had no property, little liberty, and a life dependent on an employer or owner, they commanded little attention from liberal thinkers.

The propertyless were beyond the liberal world view because they lacked virtue, individuality, and liberty—in short, all the qualities of a civilized citizen. The dearth of any mention of their political role despite their proportion of the population reveals more about the attitude of liberal thinkers toward them than volumes might otherwise. It was not so much that liberal political philosophers were unaware of the existence of the propertyless; rather they had no place for them in their philosophy, until and unless they acquired property. They excluded the propertyless from political participation through the requirement that voting be restricted to those owning a certain amount of property. Thus, for example, were three-quarters of the adult white male population of Britain divorced from the formal political process.[27]

In the America of 1789 the *permanently* propertyless were even less of an issue. Most adult white males owned property and could participate in the political process. Those who owned none had a fair chance of acquiring some in their lifetimes.[28] However, the propertyless wage laborer did become a concern during the 1790s and early nineteenth century, especially in the coastal cities, where immigration nearly doubled the urban population between 1790 and 1800. Although their presence influenced urban politics, the principal political issues arose from conflicts among different propertied interests and their tendency to form factions, not from conflicts between those with property and those without. The question of the political role of the propertyless per se never arose in this period. Even with the economic and demographic changes in the era the problem of a permanently propertyless majority still remained largely in the future. After all, from the liberal viewpoint the continent to the west was empty.

II

The American Revolution was an economic as well as a political upheaval. The war itself cost some $160 million—a sum greater than the
total federal government expenditures during its first twenty years.[29]
Though estimates vary, per capita war casualties were probably larger
than in any other American conflict involving a foreign nation. When
adjusted for population size, the American Revolution generated five
times the émigrés and confiscated 83 percent of the property of the
French Revolution.[30] The national government and the states incurred
$75 million in revolutionary debts. After three-quarters of a century of
rapid economic growth the American economy stagnated during the
Revolution and the 1780s.[31] Trade faltered. In a mercantilist world of
closed empires, the United States stood alone. American ships, once
the mainstay of the British empire, carried little more than half the
trade they had.[32]

Although the statistics on American commerce at the close of the
1780s are sparse, the evidence does indicate that trade patterns were
relatively stable between 1787 and 1792. An average of 43 percent of
American exports went to the British empire over these years. American ships carried only a little more than half of the nation's foreign
commerce; British ships carried over 85 percent of the remainder. With
the exception of agricultural staples such as coffee, tea, sugar, salt,
and liquor, 90 percent of imported goods were made in Great Britain.
Of the staples perhaps one-half came from the British empire. Over 60
percent of American foreign commerce—the lifeblood of its urban
areas, where great political and economic power resided—was with
Britain and its colonies. On a given day in any American port three of
every five ships entering or departing would be going to or arriving
from the British empire. Britain was not America's only trading part-
ner. Over these five years, the French empire received 25 percent of
American exports, the Netherlands 10 percent, the Spanish empire a
little over 8 percent, and the Portuguese 6 percent. The remaining 8
percent was scattered among the Germanic towns, Italy, and elsewhere. Somewhat over 1 percent of American exports went to Asia. As
a rough approximation, however, it is safe to assume that the vast
majority of American merchants traded within the British empire on
either their outbound or return voyages. This situation remained substantially unaltered from the time of the Constitutional Convention
through Washington's first term.[33]

Led by Robert Morris, the nationalists in the 1781 Confederation
Congress attempted to incorporate the power of taxation into the central government. They pressed for federal assumption of state war

debts, funding of the national debt through a revenue tariff, and establishment of the Bank of North America to support federal fiscal programs. Unsuccessfully, they sought to turn the rumbling of a coup
d'etat in the army officer corps to their advantage in forcing these
changes. Their plans were thwarted by the unanimous consent requirement for constitutional amendments and a satisfactory provision
for army claims. The states also defeated John Jay's efforts to enlist
Spanish support in removing the British from the northwest forts in
American territory. Crippled by its lack of revenue, the Confederation
government faltered fiscally. In 1786, the states began assuming federal
debts. The following year the government defaulted on its debt payments to France and Spain. Finally, the Board of Treasury proposed a
total transfer of federal debt to the states.[34]

The severe depression of the mid-1780s both highlighted the Confederation's inability to deal with economic crises and placed the onus
of responsibility on the states. The postwar flood of British goods on
easy credit had depressed prices and invited heavy indebtedness. When
the credit bubble burst in 1785, depression followed. Many states acted
forcefully to reduce their debts and revive their economies. Some, in
the manner of Massachusetts, contracted the money supply by withdrawing paper currency to curb inflation and preserve the real value of
contractual debts. Others, like Rhode Island, expanded their money
supply through large injections of fiat currency which devaluated
debts and inflated commodity prices. Five states, including Pennsylvania, New York, and Massachusetts, imposed protective tariffs to thin
the flow of British manufactures and satisfy their manufacturer-
mechanic constituencies, grown strong during boycotts of British
products just prior to the Revolution and the wartime demand for
domestic goods. The diversity and efficacy of these efforts to confront
the economic crisis raised very disturbing questions in the minds of the
wealthy and powerful throughout the union.[35]

Ruling elites throughout the country detected a political crisis in
the nation. The depression only underscored its severity. In and of
itself, the depression was not a cause of great alarm; neither was the
breakdown in debt service. More fundamentally, the economic problems, the breakdown in debt service, and the political upheavals revealed the failure of the present political system to protect property,
particularly in the form of contract. The issue was not simply the fears
of wealthy creditors for their bond holdings. Creditors wanted assur-
ance that the political system could and would uphold the inviolability
of contract.[36] The elite sought to restore the mimetic politics of deference which had been severely shaken during the Revolutionary upheaval. Symbolically and in fact, Rhode Island and Massachusetts

represented to the ruling elites the dual problems of either entrusting the sanctity of contract to democratic state governments or relying solely on the ability of any single state government, even one under little popular control, to secure property.

In May 1786 the newly elected Rhode Island legislature passed a bill authorizing $100,000 in fiat money to ease the financial strains of the depression and tight credit. The money was made legal tender for all private and public debts. This legislation reflected the interest of Rhode Island's debt-ridden farmers. When the creditors, mostly merchants, refused to accept the money in fulfillment of purchases and contract, riots and legal sanctions ensued until they relented or fled. The creditors sued in state court, seeking to have the currency law declared invalid. The judges abjured jurisdiction in the matter, but they voiced their belief that the law was unconstitutional. For their temerity the legislature hauled them into the statehouse and demanded an explanation of their opinion. Though the judges were released without punitive sanction, the legislature defeated very narrowly a bill mandating a loyalty oath from all state officials on this issue. Without a senate, without an executive veto, and without judicial review the popular assembly of Rhode Island had passed and enforced a law repugnant to the sanctity of contract and security of property. Six other states had created some kind of fiat money, much to the horror of the men of great property throughout the nation. It was a slide into a legal "Shaysism," the elites throughout the nation feared. This tyranny of the majority—an "elective despotism," as Jefferson called it—was not what they had fought for.[37]

As Rhode Island symbolized the horrors of legal infringements of property rights, Massachusetts raised the fearful spectre of extralegal attacks on property and order. Unlike Rhode Island, Massachusetts had a bicameral legislature, an executive veto, and strong judicial controls. Working through the government, creditors obtained legislation retiring paper money and raising taxes for debt service. The contracting money supply coupled with the depressed market to lower agricultural prices and reduce farm income. Debtors defaulted; creditors foreclosed and sold farms. In response, the farmers of western Massachusetts, most affected by these foreclosures, rose en masse to block judicial proceedings and interrupt the collection of debts. Fearful of losing their property to creditors, Daniel Shays and other desperate farmers resisted violently. Western creditors were unable to muster a local force against Shays. Thus, the governor had to dispatch the Boston militia into the west to restore order and end the rebellion. Among the ruling elites in America the fact remained that, despite all the proper republican checks on popular passions, the people had revolted and for a time appeared capable of disabling the legal process securing property and contract.[38] To many of the elite something drastic was needed to avoid the abyss of licentiousness.

The rebels of Massachusetts and the voters of Rhode Island were not indigent wage laborers or black slaves. Although they were not the propertied gentlemen with great estates and businesses, they did own land. Though hopelessly in debt, they were not wage laborers. They had property sufficient to vote, if not to govern. Their interest in the protection of property was real, but skewed. They depended on the ownership of landed property sufficiently productive to sustain their livelihood. That property gave them the freedom to participate in the political process and the independence to do so with a regard to their economic interests. Their economic interests, however, did not extend to the unmitigated enforcement of contractual obligations if those obligations meant loss of livelihood. The political conflict of the 1780s was not between the propertied and the propertyless, but between those whose property was a means of livelihood and those whose property was a means of accumulation. On occasion, for polemical reasons, a spokesman for a ruling elite might speak of rights of property versus the rights of persons. In reality he knew that the issue was property used principally to accumulate more income-producing property versus property used principally to sustain an independent livelihood.[39]

Small property owners posed a threat to those of large property. The threat was political where majorities produced laws contrary to contract; it was social where large factions rebelled against law and order; and it was economic wherever political or social movements upset the stability required for investment, credit, trade, and commercial development. The movement to create a new central government came not from a desire to garner a speculative windfall in the securities market nor to foreclose farms for debts, but from a desire to restore stability to political society in America. In the wake of recession, inflation, and rebellion, the nationalist movement sought to bring such stability through a new central government better insulated than state authority from popular passions.

The two principal leaders of the constitutional movement, Madison and Hamilton, embodied its essentially national character. James Madison grew to political maturity and prominence in the most closed and class-conscious ruling group of America, the slaveholding planters of the South. Inculcated from birth with an awareness of the unending effort required to maintain hegemony over a hostile labor force, the planter class produced most of the early national leaders.[40] Taught to think in terms of a system of dominance, these southern leaders never overlooked the murderous consequences of instability and revolt. As Washington, Jefferson, Madison, and Monroe demonstrated, it was easy for a man who always thought in terms of social stability to extend his horizon from the slave system of the South to the property system of the nation.

Surveying the national scene in 1788 Madison believed "that the real danger to American and its liberty lies in the defect of *energy & stability* in the present establishments of the United States."[41] This instability was caused by the "acts in which the Government is the mere instrument of the major number of constituents."[42] America had witnessed the "turbulence, violence, and abuse of power, by the majority trampling on the rights of the minority . . . which, in republics, have more frequently than any other cause, produced despotism."[43] Madison conceived and brought to fruition the Constitution to secure life, liberty, and property for all citizens and end the despotic rule of the majority.

Like his southern compatriot, Alexander Hamilton moved within the highest circles of New York mercantile wealth. Though not born into this class, his brilliance and his marriage enabled him to stand as spokesman for the great commercial interests of the northern cities. Hamilton, too, believed the "American empire" was sinking into "disunion anarchy and misery."[44] The "impudence of democracy" and its "turbulent and uncontrouling disposition" required powerful "checks." The "late Govermt.," he continued, "had entirely given way to the people." He supported the new Constitution "to attain stability and permanency." From all parts of the nation, the convention delegates affirmed a loss of balance in the Confederation government. Roger Sherman of Connecticut argued that "the people . . . immediately should have as little to do as may be about the Government." Elbridge Gerry of Massachusetts blamed "the evils we experience" on "the excess of democracy" and "the levelling spirit." George Mason of Virginia agreed "that we had been too democratic." Edmund Randolph of Virginia summarized the "general object" of the convention: "to provide a cure for the evils under which the U.S. laboured" which "every man had found in the turbulence and follies of democracy."[45] Indeed, democracy so worried Hamilton that in the Constitutional Convention he proposed a stronger, less representative government than the one agreed on.[46] It is significant, however, that Hamilton's plan was rejected. The convention delegates realized that the Revolution had forever altered American politics. While they agreed on a stronger government to curb democracy, they still produced a constitution that ultimately rested on popular rule.

Hamilton and Madison epitomized the national consensus on a

new central government between the two most powerful political and economic interests in America—the planters and the merchants. They carried the arguments for a new government to the public forum in their *Federalist* essays, which linked the liberal world-view to the specific crisis america confronted. Their essays held majority infringements on minority rights to be the essence of the crisis of the 1780s. Conflicting economic interests were endemic to a free society, where different abilities and circumstances yielded competing "classes." When these classes sought to use government to further their interests, they became "factions" that introduced instability to political society and lessened the security of property. Without absolute security for all property, economic growth faltered, intensifying the conflict over political aid to each interest. When political relief was not forthcoming, violence often ensued, as in Massachusetts. When it was forthcoming, minority rights were often violated, as in Rhode Island. Either case unsettled political society.

Their solution was the 1787 Constitution, which gave the central government the power to secure property and regulate economic growth. It also extended the sphere of the republic to prevent any faction from easily turning the government to its own ends. The new leaders would administer American society with regard to the public good alone. They would secure property and all legitimate interests. Economic growth would ensue, and the dangerous pressures of factions would abate. As in all republics, the ultimate authority would rest with the people, but the checks of distance, of representation, and of wisdom would prevent popular passions from undermining the purpose of political society. In the minds of Hamilton, Madison, and their allies the new government would realize the promise of the Revolution.[47]

III

Though created by the elite, the Constitution of 1787 was adopted by the people. Not all the people, but enough of them to make it a genuine expression of popular will. The Constitution was a republican document which sought to balance popular rule and property rights within the liberal world-view. Perhaps as much as to the elites, it was the fulfillment of the Revolution to many mechanics and farmers. In speculating about the chances for adoption Hamilton captured this coalition of interests that would support it. First of all it had the backing of George Washington and most of the other leaders of the Revolutionary movement. The Constitution possessed "the good will of the commercial interest throughout the states which will give all its efforts to the establishment of a government capable of regulating protecting and extending the commerce of the Union." Hamilton also counted on "most men of property . . . who wish a government of the union able to protect them against domestic violence and the depredations which the democratic spirit is apt to make on property." He did not forget the most infamous interest, "the Creditors of the United States," who hoped "that a general government possessing the means of doing it will pay the debt of the Union." In broad terms he expressed confidence that all those citizens "anxious for the respectability of the nation" and preservation of the union would support the Constitution.[48] Hamilton, as usual, was not mistaken.

A brief survey of nationwide support for the Constitution can substantiate and somewhat deepen Hamilton's "conjectures." In Virginia the agricultural interests divided on the constitution according to their perceptions of the benefits of a central government.[49] Declining soil productivity and tobacco prices had led many Virginia planters to turn to wheat and other grains. This shift relocated the markets for their products from Britain to the West Indies and southern Europe. Confronted with the severe restrictions of European empires they supported the new government in the hope that it could open these markets through an aggressive foreign policy. On the other hand, tobacco planters saw little to gain from the constitution. Their markets were firmly established in Britain and France. Tobacco demand in other areas was negligible, and no political entity could remedy the enervating problem of soil exhaustion. They had little reason to forsake their political power rooted in the state government and risk federal enforcement of the 1783 Treaty of Paris provision for recovery of their pre-Revolutionary debts to British creditors.[50]

In the western part of Virginia smaller farmers supported the Constitution. They hoped for better protection from Indian attacks and military aid in their encroachments on Indian lands. Unlike their tidewater brethren, the western tobacco planters perceived in federally supported westward expansion a cure for the declining productivity of their soil. The western grain farmers, like their eastern counterparts, wanted more foreign markets for their crops. Some opposition, in east and west, originated in a fear of federally mandated emancipation. Patrick Henry played long and loud to this dread. This threat, however, carried little weight, since the Constitution strongly ensconced slavery and property in its articles.[51]

Much the same pattern existed throughout the south. In Georgia and the Carolinas the desire for federal protection from Indians determined much of the support for ratification. Land speculators in North Carolina wanted the Indians cleared to enhance their western holdings. Southern merchants, particularly in Charleston, sought wider market and security for their ships. Charleston's mechanics and manufacturers voted for ratification in hopes of tariff protection from imports and navigation laws to stimulate domestic shipbuilding. Lawyers in North Carolina voted to ratify under the assumption that British creditors would employ their services for recovering planter debts in federal courts. Opposition came from many small subsistence farmers, who feared losing what little political influence they had to a distant and alien government.[52]

Each major Middle Atlantic state possessed a commercial city, generally the center of political and economic activity, and a hinterland, apart from and often alien to the commercial center. In Maryland, Baltimore spearheaded support for the Constitution. Both its merchants and its manufacturers sought to end the inflationary spiral of paper money. As creditors, the merchants opposed the inflationary depreciation of fixed debts. The manufacturers wanted to lower interest rates, pushed very high by the glut of depreciated currency. Coinage, regulated by federal statute, would answer both their needs. Manufacturers desired protection from imports and discrimination in favor of American-built ships. Merchants carrying grains sought to open the West Indies and southern Europe to their ships. In April 1788, these Baltimore groups managed to stage a demonstration of a thousand citizens in support of ratification.[53]

In Maryland's hinterland a division among planters similar to that in Virginia characterized the conflict. Planters, who had turned to grain production, supported the Constitution in the hope of a federal expansion of their West Indian and southern European markets. Tobacco planters anticipated little federal aid for their established markets in Britain. Plagued by soil exhaustion and declining prices, they feared federally enforced payment of their debts to British merchants. In western Maryland along the Potomac River the prospect of federal aid for internal improvements engendered some support for ratification among farmers. Not surprisingly, speculators in confiscated Tory estates and debtors absolved from specie payments by paper money opposed the Constitution. Hard money and federally mandated compensation for Revolutionary expropriations promised only financial difficulties to them.[54]

In Philadelphia the serious trade imbalance of 1785–87 created a mechanic-merchant alliance. A decline in international commerce, the dominance of foreign shipping, and a flood of British manufactures had disenchanted both groups with the Confederation government. Merchants sought commercial discrimination; manufacturers sought protective tariffs. The wealthy, such as Robert Morris, lacked political power in the state government because of its radical constitution. They looked toward the new national government to restore their political status. Both rich and poor were threatened by the inflationary conditions of the 1780s. Only the middle classes, entrenched in state government, found the inflation a salve for their debts. These classes included small farmers in eastern Pennsylvania, but not their western brethren, who hoped for federal protection on the frontier. Land speculators split over the salutory effects of the inflation on land values and the need of security for their western holdings. The nationalists triumphed, particularly in Philadelphia, and massive demonstrations hailed their victory. Momentum from the federal Constitution carried them to another victory in overturning the state's radical constitution and replacing it with a document more to their liking.[55]

New York City followed Philadelphia's and Baltimore's patterns of support for ratification. Manufacturers and mechanics pushed vigorously for ratification. Their chief economic concern was British dominance in the form of imported manufactures and foreign-built ships. They hoped for tariff protection and navigation laws to aid their enterprises, weakened by foreign competition and the 1786 depression. New York's mechanics and manufacturers exhibited a strong sense of patriotism, support for national economic development, and a democratic ideology. The first two were essential to their prosperity as manufacturers; the last was essential to their ability to affect political decisions as small property owners. This combination appeared in all five major commercial cities and accounted for the support of manufacturers and mechanics for the Constitution. Throughout New York State the wealthy, established merchants, and manor lords supported ratification. They anticipated direct economic benefits in the funding of federal debts, federal promotion of trade, and the security for their property promised by the central government. Hamilton had expressed their desires and fears in his speeches and essays on behalf of the new Constitution. In large measure under the control of these manor lords, most subsistence farmers and tenants who could vote voted for ratification. Although they often had little choice in the matter, there were small farmers who resisted ratification because the manor lords they hated supported it. As in other states, there were those New Yorkers from all classes who simply disliked the powers given the new government and preferred to keep them in local hands.[56]

The commercial centers of Massachusetts encountered many of the same problems as New York, Philadelphia, and Baltimore. The depression of the mid-eighties coupled with British economic incursions to produce a decline in shipbuilding and local manufacturing. The affected groups of manufacturers and mechanics placed strong pressure on the state for protective tariffs in the form of specific duties on imports or foreign tonnage. The latter method, a navigation law, was in effect a protective tariff for shipbuilders. When the manufacturers decided that the General Court was incapable of affording effective protection, they voiced their support for ratification. They were joined by commercial farmers seeking federal help in security new markets and most of the lawyers. [57]

Although there was strong support for ratification among Massachusetts' merchants, their support arose from significantly different motives. One group of merchants looked toward the new government to end high state tariff rates and curb discriminatory legislation. These merchants traded principally with Britain, profited by and large from imports instead of the carrying trade, and did not wish to risk their British trade for manufacturing or the carrying trade. In addition this group sought federal funding of the national debt and the stability of a strong central government. The other group of merchants were smaller businessmen who had been precluded from the British trade and sought new markets in Europe and the West Indies. They sought discrimination in favor of their carrying trade over that in foreign vessels. And they too looked toward the central government to provide new markets and navigation laws. Membership in either mercantile group was not hard and fast, but there were important distinctions among merchants supporting ratification. [58]

Throughout the nation the one distinguishing characteristic of those groups supporting the Constitution was that they had a significant business interest in government economic policy. Their support depended on how they anticipated the federal government would affect their economic interests. For manufacturers and mechanics, there was the hope of protective tariffs and navigation laws to stimulate shipbuilding. For merchants, there was the hope of new markets and navigation laws favoring American-owned ships. For commercial farmers and planters, there was the hope of new markets for their surplus produce, higher prices, and better transportation facilities. For frontier settlers, land speculators, and planters with exhausted soil, there was the hope of federal troops to protect their expansion into Indian lands. For creditors and potential borrowers, there was the hope of sound money to halt the depreciation of debts and lower interest rates. For the wealthy, there was the hope of more security for their property in a less democratic central government. For the burgeoning entrepreneur, there was the promise of economic nationalism to stimulate new enterprise. For the established entrepreneur, there was the promise of stability for his business.

The supporters of the Constitution cannot be categorized by ideological predilections. They included the most democratic elements of the population in the mechanics and frontier farmers, and the most antidemocratic in the largest landowners and merchants. The antidemocratic tenor of the authors of the Constitution and the role of creditors should not be overemphasized in explaining ratification. Many democrats, including Thomas Paine, supported the document. It accorded small property holders both the promise of economic advantage and continued political representation, though at a more mediated level. The very fact that such great concern for popular intrusions on elite prerogatives were expressed in the convention indicate the elite's recognition of the power of the people in political decision-making. That Hamilton's very conservative plan for a new government was rejected suggests that the power of popular volition was sufficiently acknowledged by the delegates to induce them to ignore so undemocratic a proposal. There had, after all, been a revolution against British tyranny only a decade before. The support of small property holders for the Constitution cannot be reduced to economic interest any more than can the support of larger property holders.

Jackson Turner Main in his exhaustive studies of the nationalist and antinationalist coalitions has divided them into "cosmopolitan" and "localist" in their world views.[59] Main's division conforms to the many state and local studies of social origins of the nationalists and antinationalists. This division is rooted not in wealth, although the wealthy were cosmopolitan, nor in political ideology, since both aristocrat and democrat voted for ratification, but in the manner one's economic interest coincided or failed to coincide with the anticipated impact of the new government on the national economy as a whole. The localists opposed the Constitution because they anticipated little or no benefit from the central government. Those without significant stake in commerce generally opposed ratification because they believed a dynamic economic program might disrupt their way of life. (Frontier farmers who sought the new government's aid in removing the Indians were an exception.) Those few with a significant commercial stake who opposed ratification believed the new government could do little or nothing to improve their fortunes. Neither antinationalist group thought the sacrifice of political power worth the benefits of central government. They were not so much men of little faith as men of little hope.

This localist-cosmopolitan division between antinationalists and nationalists was portentous for the political struggles of the 1790s. Those with a localist outlook in the political sense, whose position in state government led them to resist any diminution of their power by a federal government, persisted in their political activity and often became Republicans. Those whose localist views were economic in origin because of their nonintegration in the market economy remained conservative and often became Federalist. Over the decade, however, the war boom enticed many of these into the national and international market system. As their commerce broadened, so too did their political outlook. The nationalists, on the other hand, were consistently concerned with federal politics and, by the very nature of their cosmopolitan interest, were bound to be satisfied or dissatisfied with federal programs. Owing to the diverse and often conflicting hopes of the nationalist coalition, the politics of the new government would inevitably engender political opposition within nationalist ranks. Thus, it is *within* the constitutional coalition and not outside it that the interest group origins of the political and party conflicts of the 1790s must be sought.

The efforts of some historians to trace the party conflict of the nineties to the constitutional conflict of the eighties under the ambiguous rubrics of "agrarian versus capitalist" or "democrat versus aristocrat" appear misapplied. They neglect the fact that in numbers too large to be ignored, agrarians and capitalists, aristocrats and democrats supported the Constitution. Indeed, although to a much lesser extent, persons from all four of these categories opposed the Constitution as well. Any analysis of the interest-group conflicts, which evolved during the 1790s into political struggles, must begin with the constitutional coalition and its leadership. There lie the seeds of the partisan battles to come. They are as plain as a banner carried by Baltimore manufacturers in a parade three-thousand strong celebrating adoption of the Constitution. Displayed among the throngs of mechanics, manufacturers, merchants, and farmers, it read: "NO IMPORTATIONS AND WE SHALL LIVE!"[60]

CHAPTER TWO

The Political Economy of Alexander Hamilton

Theory and Practice

The three great objects of government, *agriculture, commerce and revenue,* can only be secured by a general government.
—Hamilton speaking in the Constitutional Convention (Yates version), June 19, 1787

Politics contains two parts, very different the one from the other. The one, containing the original of societies, and the use and extent of political power; the other, the art of governing men in society.
—John Locke

In one form or another Alexander Hamilton's fiscal politics and political beliefs have been described, discussed, lauded, or condemned numerous times. That he sponsored some form of reverse Keynesianism to create a *rentier* class of government supporters is a truism in historiography. In recounting some familiar facts, tone and emphasis, particularly an idea of the priorities Hamilton set among his integral programs, are not without significance for subsequent discussions of his relationship to domestic manufacturing and his foreign policy concerns. Moreover, a careful reconstruction of the precise context of his decisions is necessary to avoid anachronistic inferences from his policies. This final point requires elaboration.

Hamilton's biographies, though numerous and occasionally excellent, must juggle their presentations of his political economy as a coherent system to move their narratives through the events in his life. This narrative progression tends to segment, sometimes formally in chapters and subsections, his political economy. Indeed, rarely in these biographies are Hamilton's economic program and political beliefs discussed as a coherent political economy. Political economy possesses an atemporal character whose coherence is not easily maintained in chronological narratives. At best there emerges a topical-eventful approach arranged according to time sequence which, although satisfactory for purposes of exposition, truncates analysis of his political economy.[1] An alternative is the progress-of-economic-thought-and-policy approach. Such presentations contain very helpful studies of Hamilton's economics, but they tend to draw it too far from both the political milieu and the intellectual tradition. There remains the need to integrate Hamilton's economics and the politics into a political economy.[2]

Presenting Hamilton's policies and programs in the context of his political economy shows how each part fits with the other and in their interaction recasts the others. A detailed reconstruction of his policies and programs as an interrelated political economy can shed a new light on the Report on Manufactures and the Society for Establishing Useful Manufactures, in which they come to be seen as particular responses to the demands of the times and not elements of a grand scheme to industrialize America. In this new context the author of the most famous affirmation of industrial development can be shown to have effectively opposed the expansion of American manufactures. Its implications extend to the overall political conflicts of the 1790s. Clarifying Hamilton's methods and objectives enlightens by contrast the political economy of his chief antagonists. It is, then, for a variety of reasons necessary to present in a different manner another historical analysis of Hamilton's policies and program.

I

Hamilton was a statesman, not a philosopher. He wrote no comprehensive tome of politics, economics, or psychology. Yet, during his thirty years of public life he revealed in his many letters and pamphlets a coherent theory of political society. His tactics were malleable, but his fundamental goals and assumptions were fixed. To understand his political economy, ideas expressed over a lifetime must be compressed and analyzed into a comprehensive whole. This approach abstracts from temporal vicissitudes his assumptions and goals, which are by their very nature a priori. They lack an existential character and serve rather to characterize existence. Theory is by no means unrelated to events; indeed, it is their essence expressed. Theory extracts from events their essence in a form which permits an understanding of and a meaningful responses to events. Hamilton's political economy in theory and practice developed out of a coherent, relatively immutable world view.

His world view was not unique. It reflected what Hegel called the *Zeitgeist,* which in the late eighteenth century was encapsulated in liberal thought. Consonant with David Hume, whom he often cited as an authority on political society, Hamilton grounded his political economy in the psychology of man. In 1775, in his first major political disquisition, "The Farmer Refuted," he wrote: "Self-interest [is the] most powerful incentive of human actions. . . . By this interest we must govern him, and by means of it *make him co-operate to public good,* notwithstanding his insatiable avarice and ambition." Again in the Constitutional Convention he reaffirmed that "our prevailing passions are ambitions and interest; and it will ever be the duty of a wise government to avail itself of those passions, in order to make them subservient to the public good."[3]

"The true politician," he argued in 1795, referring, of course, to himself, "takes human nature (and human society its aggregate) as he finds it, a compound of good and ill qualities of good and ill tendencies—endued with powers and actuated by passions and propensities. . . . With this view of human nature he will not attempt to warp or distort it from its natural direction . . . but he will seek to promote his action according to the byass of his nature, to lead him to the developpment [*sic*] of his energies according to the scope of his passions, and erecting the social organization on this basis . . . taking care to infuse in each case all the ingredients which can be devised as preventive or correctives of the evil which is the eternal concomitant of temporal blessing." And in the twilight of his political career, Hamilton restated what he had believed for three decades of public life. "Nothing," he lamented to James Bayard in April 1804, "is more fallacious than to expect to produce any valuable or permanent results, in political projects, by relying merely on the reason of men. Men are rather reasoning than reasonable animals for the most part governed by the impulse of passion."[4]

Passion generally manifested itself as self-interest. It was an essential aspect of human nature and the ineluctable problem of political society. Self-interest was the origin of property, industry, and commerce—the "temporal blessing" Hamilton lauded. Men had constructed government to protect property and insure the liberty to pursue one's self-interest, usually property. The "essential ends of political society" were "the security of private property and personal liberty."[5] Government, he explained, "is the POWER by which individuals in society are kept from doing injury to each other and are bro't to cooperate to a common end."[6] This regulation of harmful individual passions must itself be regulated to avoid the destruction of liberty and the violation of property. Hamilton advocated a republican form of government, by which he meant "the *equality* of political rights exclusive of all *hereditary* distinctions"; popular elections at some point in the political process of choosing rulers; and an absence of constitutional barriers to individuals seeking office.[7] The "end and intention of this right [of republican rule] is, to preserve the life, property and liberty of the subject, from the encroachments of oppression and tyranny."[8]

If all men were governed by "an enlightened sense of their interests," republican government would present no problems to "the order and happiness of society."[9] Men, however, were not so governed. As early as 1775, Hamilton feared the disruption of social order by the "passions" of "the multitude, who have not a sufficient stock of reason and knowledge to guide them." For him the "excess of popularity" engendered by the Revolution became in the 1780s a "general disease which inflicts all our constitutions." Democracy portended anarchy, the "road to *despotism*."[10] Whether in the chaos of anarchy or the oppression of despotism, political society would dissolve as life, liberty, and property lost the unmitigated protection of government.

Sitting in the Constitutional Convention Hamilton perceived two crises in the United States: one immediate and very serious, the other distant and probably fatal. His analyses of these crises are crucial to any understanding of his future political and economic programs. All his policies were directed toward solving the immediate crisis and forestalling on the final one. He began his analysis of the immediate crisis with a simple statement: "In every community where industry is encouraged, there will be a division of it into the few & the many. Hence separate interests will arise. There will be debtors & creditors etc."[11] Hamilton traced the origin of these interests to this economic division, rooted in the nature of a private property system. His use of the debtor-creditor example indicated that he was speaking of individuals and groups who possessed some property. Obviously, the creditor had property of some substance. The debtor, too, had some property which served to secure the debt. With the possible exception of bond servitude, a debt could be secured only by a marketable asset, which among adult white males did not include their persons.

Still addressing the immediate crisis, Hamilton pointed out that vesting "all power" in the many or the few would allow the vested group to oppress the other. Since the Revolution, the "many" had held sway. Owing to the basic conflict between their interests and those of the "few," they had become the oppressors. An end to this oppression was the immediate object of the Constitutional Convention. In a subsequent speech he again explained the origins of the political crises confronting the country, but with a new twist which portended a

future, more serious crisis in the nation. By piecing together the three
versions of this speech a sense of both what Hamilton said and what
his fellow delegates understood him to mean can be ascertained.

In Madison's version Hamilton asserted "that nothing like an equality of property existed; that an inequality would exist as long as liberty
existed, and that it would unavoidably result from that very liberty
itself." The Yates version of this speech recorded him as saying that the
"differences of property is already great amongst us. Commerce and
industry will still increase the disparity." The only other version of his
speech, recorded by Lansing, quoted Hamilton as saying, "In the ordinary Progress of things we must look to a Period as not very remote
when Distinctions arising from Property will be greater."[12] Thus, the
term "liberty" became "commerce and industry" and finally "the ordinary Progress of Things." These phrases are not so much three
different meanings drawn from his speech as three expressions of the
same concept—that is, the temporal ontology of political society in
liberal thought.

To Hamilton's mind there was in the very being of political society
certain immutable laws that accorded with the nature of men. The
pursuit of property stemmed from the dominant passion of self-
interest. The protection of property through political institutions originated in the social context through which man acquired and accumulated property. Government insured the "liberty" for the pursuit of
property and prevented licentious assaults on property so acquired.
The pursuit of property assumed the advanced social form of "commerce and industry." They were extensions of the nature of man in
political society and thus assumed the character of "the ordinary Progress of Things." Since the pursuit of property was essentially materi-
alistic, it was reified in liberal thought to reinforce its natural
character—that is, its origin in the nature of things.

From this ontology of political society Hamilton extrapolated certain social changes over time. The progress of political society would
lead to ever-growing disparities in property holdings. An inner logic in
the dynamic of economic development would create a society of a rich
few and a poorer multitude. The immediate crisis affirmed this dynamic, but it remained a crisis of those with large property and those
with little. The present crisis was only a harbinger of a far more
serious one in which those few with all the property would confront
the vast majority without any—as in England. Indeed, some forty
years later Madison wrote of this very crisis. In his version, however, it
would await another century to appear. When the continent was fully
populated, then, Madison believed, America would need a king.
Hamilton's empire ended at the Mississippi, not the Pacific, and he

adjusted his advocacy of monarchy accordingly. Hamilton and Madison's disagreement was over time, not principle.[13]

Hamilton continued his oratorical analysis. Since "this inequality of property constituted the great & fundamental distinction in Society," he warned that "your government must meet this state of things; or combinations will in process of time, undermine your system." More prosaically he explained that "you must devise a Repository of the Rights of the wealthy."[14] He addressed his plan for a new government to this problem. There were five "great & essential principles necessary for the support of Government": interest, utility, habit, force, and influence. Interest was the degree to which a government could attract the support of particular economic groups. Utility indicated the ability and determination of a government to satisfy the demands of interest groups and individuals with its programs. Habit meant the traditional authority of government to command the loyalty of its citizens, a mimetic form of nationalism. Force was the coercive power of the state through its military to command obedience. Influence subsumed the offices, honors, and emoluments which a government dispersed to citizens to retain their support. Hamilton believed that a central government must employ these five principles to gain national support and reduce the political power of state governments.[15]

He modeled his proposal on the government of Britain, "the best in the world." Britain's constitution had dealt with the inevitable crisis over the distribution of property which America faced now in a subdued form and would face again in the future. His plan included a bicameral legislature composed of a popular assembly elected for a three-year term and lifetime senate elected by popularly chosen electors. Chosen by electors twice removed from the people, the supreme executive served for life and could exercise an absolute veto over legislative acts. A supreme court of twelve judges appointed for life would have appellate jurisdiction in all cases of federal revenue laws. The central government would appoint all state governors and vest them with absolute veto power over state laws. The central government would also appoint all militia and military officers throughout the nation. Hamilton acknowledged the awesome power of his British-modeled government, but he "doubted whether any thing short of it would do in America."[16]

Those in the convention sympathetic to his plan knew that the states would never acquiesce in their virtual abolition as political entities. Those opposed to such extreme centralization sat in a stunned silence. History, too, might have ignored Hamilton's rather eccentric and draconian plan had he not become the "First Lord of the Treasury" in the new government or had he not been articulating the views of a large segment of the northern ruling elites.[17] Although the delegates agreed on a constitution somewhat different from the one Hamilton proposed, he promoted its ratification cogently. Throughout his public life, he never ceased to believe that the Constitution was a "frail and worthless fabric." Only experience, he believed, could determine "whether it be consistent with the *stability* and *order* in Government which are essential to public strength & private security and happiness." As he told Jefferson, "It will probably be found expedient to go into the British form."[18] Nevertheless, he would give the new government every chance of succeeding. The method he chose to promote its success plunged his country into bitter partisan struggle, undermined its independence, destroyed his career and his party, and, ultimately, led to his death.

In late 1792, when the great cries of battles to come were only whispers, Hamilton wrote his own epitaph in an anonymous essay. "Whatever may be the good or ill qualities of that officer (Hamilton), much flexibility of character is not of the number. He is not therefore liable to the suspicion of having disavowed any principle which he really entertains, because it may have excited a degree of clamour." The essay was appropriately titled "Fact."[19]

II

When Hamilton assumed control of the new Treasury Department, two concerns overrode all others: to strengthen the new government and to restore fiscal stability. Both concerns were rooted in property. The new government would secure it more strongly than before, and fiscal stability would abet commercial prosperity. "Commerce," Hamilton said, "leads to an increase of individual property." The new government needed to protect liberty in its truest form, economic activity. "True liberty by protecting the exertions of talents and industry and securing to them their justly acquired fruits, tends more powerfully than any other course to augment the mass of national wealth." Indeed, the very measure of a successful government was the prosperity of the economy. It acted as one of "those constant moral causes, which include [a government's] general results, and . . . assist in bringing it back to its natural course."[20] To Hamilton's mind the economy in general and the nation's credit in particular were the barometers of good government.

The first test of the new government involved the Revolutionary debt (Graph 1; see Appendix C for all graphs). In itself the debt was a contract between the nation and individual creditors. The "established *rules of morality and justice,*" Hamilton insisted, "*are applicable to nations as well as to Individuals.*" Governments, he continued, "are bound *to keep their promises, to fulfill their engagements, to respect the rights of property* which others have acquired under contracts with them." The payment of the debt was an issue of "right and wrong justice or injustice." Without discharge of this obligation, "there can be no such thing as rights—no such things as property or liberty."[21] To anyone who believed in the rights of private property, contract, and liberty, the payment of the debts held the highest mandate. Knowing this, Hamilton defended his funding program in terms of property and contract. Yet, he also knew that the debt could be used as a powerful means of strengthening the new government. The funded debt could serve not only as an affirmation of the government's commitment to property and contract, but also as an explicit financial link between the government and the wealthy creditors throughout the nation.

What would become government policy in the 1790s took shape in Hamilton's mind a decade earlier. Under the leadership of Robert Morris, the head of the Confederation's treasury board, the nationalist elements had assumed control of the continental government in 1780.[22] The fiscal problems confronting Morris and other financiers were similar to those Hamilton faced with the inauguration of the Constitution: depreciating government securities, specie shortages, inadequate revenues, and a national debt in arrears. Despite nuances, the leaders of the American financiers developed a more or less common solution to this crisis: induce the "monied men," those dealing in species and commercial paper, to support government stock and reward them for their cooperation.

No one man formulated this program; rather, it was a shared conclusion within enlightened financial circles. Morris tried unsuccessfully to implement it through a provision for federal revenues independent of state assessments, funding of a consolidated debt, and use of a national bank. The attempt was significant; in its wake Hamilton articulated in his correspondence and essays virtually all of what would become the fiscal program of the new government. Indeed, it was Morris's failure to establish such a program within the framework of the Confederation that prompted Hamilton to examine the possibilities of a new constitutional framework to realize a viable stabilization program.

A central government with the power to tax, regulate commerce, coin money, conduct foreign affairs, and administer fiscal policy was the prerequisite of Hamilton's specific stabilization program.[23] If such powers were forthcoming, the government could move with authority to stop the depreciation of the currency and restore credit. "The only plan that can preserve the currency is one that will make it in the *immediate* interest of monied men to cooperate with government in its support."[24] Hamilton would accomplish this through a bond issue backed by government revenues and subscribable in outstanding government debentures or fiat money. The interest and principal would then be payable in specie. The "monied men" would "contribute the whole or part of the stock" and receive "the whole or part of the profits."[25]

He advocated a national bank to link "the interest of the state in an intimate connexion with those of the rich individuals belonging to it [so] that it turns wealth and influence of both into a commercial channel for mutual benefit."[26] The national bank would support government credit, provide loans, and discount the notes of merchants. They would reap the benefits of interest on the national debt, dividends from bank stock, and more profits from a larger trade. A restored credit and a prosperous mercantile establishment would have a beneficial effect throughout the economy. The national government would itself be strengthened as its credit rose and the economy stabilized. It would command with certainty the loyalty of the wealthiest merchants and their associates. Thus, Hamilton concluded in a letter to Morris, a "national debt if not excessive will be to us a national blessing; it will be a powerfull [sic] cement of our union." Morris agreed, but could not consummate the plan in an enduring form.[27]

Throughout the long struggle of 1780s to create a new constitutional framework capable of supporting his plans, Hamilton stressed the role of the merchants. They had the most liquid capital in specie and commercial paper. They were the conduits of interstate and international trade, the vessels of the market system through which flowed the life-blood of credit, specie, and commercial paper. Morris had once reminded him that the credit instruments the merchants accepted, the shopkeepers accepted; and what the shopkeepers accepted, the farmers, mechanics, and manufacturers also accepted. Hamilton agreed, but speculated further. "Mechanics and manufacturers," he wrote, "will always be inclined, with few exceptions, to give their votes to merchants . . . as the natural representatives of all these classes of the community."[28] Economic dependence always begat political allegiance. "This is a principle of human nature, on which all political speculations to be just, must be founded."[29]

To the merchants, he promised "moderate duties" for government revenues. High duties acted as prohibitions, while low duties increased the "quantity of commodities" traded. In return for their support of public credit and a national bank, he would offer them "immediate advantages analogous to those they receive by employing their money in trade."[30] Hamilton aimed at a relatively small group of rich and powerful men. By 1790 only 2 percent of the adult white population held securities. Less than 0.5 percent held a fourth of all the nation's stock.[31] Yet, this handful of merchant-creditors constituted enough political and economic might to insure success to a new government.

When he took office as Treasury secretary, Hamilton implemented his long-planned program for political economic stabilization. In the Report on Public Credit of January 1790, he restated his basic supposition: "If all the public creditors receive their dues from one source, distributed with an equal hand, their interest will be the same. And having the same interests, they will unite in the support of the fiscal arrangements of the Government."[32] The following year his plan for a national bank became law. Like the funding and assumption, the roots of the bank lay in the early 1780s. Its basic purpose was to "interweave itself into the *monied* interest of every State" and "by its notes [to] insinuate itself into every branch of industry and [to] affect the interests of all classes of the community." With its economic muscle, the bank would serve the political end of insuring "the firm establishment of the National Government."[33] Beyond commercial utility and political attachment the Bank of the United States had another purpose: to raise government stock prices, a purpose discussed in detail below.

Funding and assumption were political and economic acts. They were political insofar as they drew crucial support to the central government after a bitter struggle over ratification. They were economic insofar as they restored government credit and stabilized the monetary system after a decade of chaos. Beyond any strictly political or economic action, they reaffirmed the moral foundations of the republic: property and contract. Among those who ruled American society, regardless of their personal profits from these acts, "the maxims of public credit" were "of the essence of good government, as intimately connected, by the analogy and sympathy of principles, with the security of property in general, and as forming an inseparable portion of the great system of political order." These were Hamilton's words, but any leader of either party would have agreed. Despite the disputes over how much should be paid to whom at what profit for which partisan purpose, Jefferson, Madison, Gallatin, and the others would have concurred in Hamilton's conclusion: "The cause of credit and property is one and the same throughout the states." A ruined credit meant a ruined government, a shattered union, and morally bankrupted society.[34]

Since Hamilton believed the Constitution to be woefully inadequate to the task of national administration, all his activities as Treasury secretary were directed towards enhancing the effective power of the government. He used the debt as a means of influence, a form of what his critics called corruption. Consistently, he advocated the use of government revenues and offices for political ends. Only two years after Yorktown he recommended creation of an English-style corps of customs collectors, independent of the states, "to introduce the influence of officers desiring their emoluments from & consequently interested in supporting the power of Congress." In the Constitutional Convention he again explained that "influence . . . was necessary to support a good government." Government must "present objects sufficiently interesting to the human mind."[35] Whether through interest payments and offices or the more subtle secondary influences of the commercial elite over the metropolitan mechanics and farmers, Hamilton strove to link by any and every means citizens to the central government. Those he could not pay, he would coerce with the army, whose officer cadre belonged to the Society of Cincinnati.[36] Religion, too, was a legitimate expedient to exact loyalty. "The Government," he advised James McHenry, "will be very unwise, if it does not make the most of the religious pre-possessions of our people—opposing the onest [sic] enthusiasm of Religious Opinion to the phrenzy of Political fanaticism."[37]

Against Hamilton's unending efforts to enlarge the actual power of the government, despite the authoritative circumscription of that power in the Constitution, his opponents directed their attacks. He believed the structural weaknesses of the Constitution would cause the dissolution of the political union and subject property to the abuses of local democracy. This belief lay at the heart of his political economy. The national debt and its attendant measures were the means by which the central government would augment its power through the informal, but very real, attachment of large property holders and their economic dependents. His political economy secured the accumulation of property through central government, central government through debt service, debt service through a particular fiscal program, the fiscal program through tariff revenues, tariff revenues through imports, and imports through trade with Great Britain. No block could be removed or allowed to crumble under the weight of the others without endangering the entire edifice. After his fiscal program became law, Hamilton played the busy mason for the next decade.

III

From a political perspective the funded debt would strengthen the new government; from an economic one it would stabilize the monetary system of the nation and serve as a basis for commercial growth.

Hamilton explained its latter function in his Report on Public Credit. "Trade is extended by it, because there is a larger capital to carry it on, and the merchant can, at the same time, afford to trade for smaller profits; as his stock . . . brings him interest from the Government, [and] serves him also as money . . . in his commercial operations." Agriculture and manufacturers would also be beneficiaries of the greater capital the merchant had to invest. Interest rates would decline in proportion to the increase in the quantity of money circulating as federal securities. "But," he cautioned, "these good effects of a public debt are only to be looked for, when, by being well funded, it has acquired an adequate and stable value; till then, it has rather a contrary tendency." As long as the stock remained an insecure and fluctuating commodity, "all the money applied to it is so much diverted from the more useful channels of circulation, for which the thing itself affords no substitute." In this state the debt "contributes to the scarcity of money" and acts as "a pernicious drain of our cash from the channels of productive industry." As a result of this monetary scarcity, land values declined, interest rates rose, and all the beneficial effects of a stable stock were lost.[38]

Hamilton argued that funding would cure these evils, but he warned that benefits would not be "instantaneous" and "it might require some time to bring the value of stock to its natural level." Then investor confidence would allow it to substitute for money.[39] In other words, he recognized that the economic benefits of funding would accrue only if he could stabilize the value of government stock at or near par. If not, if speculation made stock prices volatile, then all the economic problems of an unfunded debt would persist and intensity. Since its benefits would not extend beyond speculative profits and interest payments to those relatively few foreign and domestic holders, the funded debt would become a political issue. What might have been an economic asset to the whole community would become instead a windfall gain to a few speculators at the community's expense. What might have been a political anchor for the new government would become an invidious progenitor of factions and partisan politics.

The international rate of interest on loans to America varied between 5 and 6 percent. Based on the market rate and the fact that American stock was selling at about 50 percent of face value, financier Stephen Higginson advised Hamilton to fund the debt at 2 or 3 percent interest.[40] The effective yield would be then between 4 and 6 percent. Hamilton, however, planned to fund most of the debt at twice that rate, 6 percent, which at current prices would mean an effective annual rate of 10 to 12 percent. At this higher interest rate, he hoped to draw sufficient capital from domestic and foreign sources to increase stock prices to par. Then, as stock prices increased, the effective rate of interest would decline and approach the nominal rate of 6 percent. Selling near face value and providing a steady interest income, the stock could serve as a monetary instrument.

To realize what enormous problems Hamilton confronted before and for several years after the funding legislation passed, one must understand the techniques of foreign and domestic speculators. A speculator would, for example, buy 6 percent government securities at 75 percent of face value providing an effective yield of 8 percent per annum. He would then pledge these securities as collateral for a loan at 6 percent interest to purchase more securities. The 8 percent interest would pay the 6 percent due on the loan and yield 2 percent profit. When the market rose, the speculator could sell at the higher price and realize a capital gain plus the interest differential between his loans and his yields on the securities. There were numerous variations on this basic scheme, particularly stock options, which divided speculators into bull and bear groups.[41]

The profits on speculations depended principally on the price of the stock relative to its face value. If the stock were selling at par, then little or no interest rate differential would exist between international loans and U.S. bonds. By the same token, if stock prices were stable and near par, then little or no capital gain could be realized. The stock would no longer drain loan funds or capital from productive areas into security speculation, but would instead provide such funds. Moreover, a stable, par-value stock would improve U.S. credit in international markets. Foreigners would not command interest payments on the debt issue above market rates.

Hamilton recognized the serious nature of this speculation. He was particularly anxious to eliminate the stock as a cause of specie dearths, which paralyzed commercial transactions, raised interest rates, and at times increased discount rates to 50 percent.[42] To achieve this goal he had to raise the prices of government securities to par value. Employing five distinct methods—the funding itself, foreign loans, a sinking fund, the Bank of the United States, and the Society for Establishing Useful Manufactures—Hamilton directed his enormous energy to this end. The funding program provided regular interest payments at a high effective rate. The higher yield was designed to attract capital into the stock and raise its price. Next, he created a sinking fund supported by government revenues to retire prescribed portions of the debt and use the interest payments on the fund's stock to purchase more stock. The fund could borrow foreign capital at 6 percent or less to intervene in the stock market and support price levels. In effect, Hamilton adopted the speculators' technique of borrowing at a low rate of interest to purchase securities yielding a higher interest rate and raise stock prices. His purpose, though, was not windfall gains, but a stable, par-value stock. As he explained to Customs Collector Benjamin Lincoln, one of the government agents in these transactions, "Be liberal, rather than to manifest a disposition unfavorable to the Creditor . . . one of the objects of the act is to raise the [prices of the] funds."[43]

Hamilton had stressed the role of a national bank in credit stabilization since 1780. When he finally presented his plan in December 1790, his conception reached full maturity. The Bank of the United States would have an initial capital of $10 million, 80 percent from private subscriptions and the rest from the government. Three-quarters of the private subscriptions would be in 6 percent government stock and the rest in specie. That alone would draw some $6 million of federal securities out of the speculative market and boost prices. through its notes and discounts on bills of exchange, the bank would increase the supply of money and lower interest rates. Apart from the commercial benefits accruing from lower rates, the higher effective yields of government securities converted to bank stock would attract much of this additional money into the stock market and boost prices further.[44]

Faced with a potential presidential veto of the bank, Hamilton naturally presented to Washington the most compelling reasons for enactment. He stressed its power, already demonstrated in the market, "to enhance the value of the public stock by a prospect of greater advantage." Merely the anticipation of the bank "has been a main cause of the rise in the public Debt. It operated upon it like a charm." After recounting to Washington the various commercial benefits of a bank, he moved to the crux of the issue. "The raising of the public Debt is a circumstance of immense importance in the affairs of the Country. *It is tantamount to the establishment of public credit.* No man can be in credit whose Bonds are selling for one third or one half their value: the same thing in respect to a Government." Foreign acquisitions at these low prices are "so much loss to the Country." If the debt passed to them at only a portion of its true value, then, he concluded, "the existence of a public Debt would have been truly a curse."[45] Washington signed the bill.

The passage of the funding legislation and his bank proposal finally began to produce good results in Europe. America's agent in Amsterdam, William Short, reported that "our new constitution & the confidence which its present administration has inspired at this place are the real & efficient causes of the prosperous situation of the credit of the U.S." He added that a million dollar loan for the government had been fully subscribed by Dutch financiers. A few days later he wrote Hamilton that news of the proposed national bank had inspired further confidence in America and that the bank would attract foreign investment.[46] Hamilton's ability to obtain foreign loans was vital to his fiscal program. Europe was his major source of specie, a commodity dear in the United States. Foreign loans provided the funds for government intervention in the securities market and bridged the perennial gap between federal revenues and expenditures. The impact of events and government policies on America's position in international capital markets was something Hamilton could not ignore.

Despite his efforts to stem it, speculation persisted. Merchants faced with European empires not yet opened by world war saw their trade decline throughout 1791. Many turned to the stock market, where high interest rates and speculative profits abounded.[47] The consequent instability and unproductive drain on capital resources were damaging to Hamilton's program. They harmed the economy, weakened American credit, and incited political opposition to him throughout the nation. What he needed was a productive outlet for the capital that would not interfere with a slow, steady rise in security prices. If the stock could be turned to an immediate productive use, instead of awaiting its monetization, then the economy would benefit and political criticism subside. Moreover, the additional utility of the stock would enhance its value and make it less vulnerable to random fluctuations. It was in this context and under these circumstances that Hamilton first turned his attention to manufacturing.

CHAPTER THREE

Hamilton and Manufacturing

A Reexamination

A degree of illusion mixes itself in all the affairs of society. The opinion
of objects has more influence than their real nature.
—Hamilton, c. January 1780

Perhaps no other facet of Hamilton's political economy has been so
greatly lauded as his advocacy of domestic manufacturing. There is a
major problem in these expositions: the failure of their authors to
integrate his Report on Manufactures and the Society for Establishing
Useful Manufactures (SEUM) into the overall context of Hamilton's
political economy and the circumstances under which he presented
them. The question of Hamilton's relationship to manufactures involves three areas: the Report on Manufactures, the SEUM, and foreign economic policy, specifically commercial relations with Great
Britain. This chapter reexamines the first two areas and integrates
them into his fiscal program. Equally important is the foreign policy
area, discussed in the following chapter. This third area involves the
crucial issues of tariff rates, tonnage duties, and trade agreements with
the chief competitor to domestic manufacturers, England. Of these
areas, foreign economic policy is perhaps the most indicative of Hamilton's position on American manufactures. In the report and the
SEUM, he evinced an ambivalence toward manufacturers that was
transformed, under the pressures of the stock market, into active support for manufacturing in one form at least. In foreign policy, Hamilton acted in a manner unquestionably hostile to domestic manufacturers in that he surrendered by treaty America's ability to protect its
manufactures from English imports. Although analyzed in separate
chapters, the three areas are integral to a coherent picture of Hamilton
and manufactures.

I

In 1791, Hamilton faced a highly protean security market on which rested his whole economic stabilization program. Speculation threatened his program by generating political opposition and fiscal instability. Constantly, he sought new ways to lessen market fluctuations and raise stock prices. In early April 1791, Hamilton decided on another means toward these ends, the Society for Establishing Useful Manufactures. Working closely with Tench Coxe, his assistant secretary, Hamilton seized on Coxe's long-standing scheme for a large manufacturing society. He chose a location in New Jersey near New York City, the center of stock speculation, and designed the financial apparatus for the society.[1] His original proposal was for a capitalization of at least $500,000. Ninety percent of the SEUM stock would be subscribed in 6 percent government stock or bank stock and the remainder in 6 percent deferred stock. A foreign loan at 5.5 percent would then be obtained using the government and bank stock for collateral and interest payments.

Although Coxe sought a broad range of manufactures, including cotton, iron, glass, and wool, Hamilton narrowed it to cotton goods. He believed that "the operation must favour the holders of the public debt and Bank Stock by creating a new object for them, and taking large sums out of the market."[2] With this in mind he wrote William Duer, future chairman of the society, "The more I considered the thing, the more I feel persuaded that it will equally promote the Interest of the Adventurers & of the public and will have an excellent effect on the Debt."[3]

Involved in the final passage and execution of the national bank, Hamilton put aside the SEUM plan until August 1791. As Graph 2 (see App. C) illustrates, the bank had stimulated a long summer upswing in stock prices. In early August, the market faltered. Unchecked speculation had led Rufus King, a close ally, to write Hamilton of "mechanics deserting their shops, Shop keepers sending their goods to auction, and not a few of our merchants neglecting the regular & profitable commerce of the City." Although he believed some readjustment in prices useful in restoring sanity to the New York commercial community, Hamilton hoped desperately to preclude "a bubble," the "most formidable" of his "enemies." He instructed the local government broker, William Seton of the Bank of New York, "to keep the Stock from falling too low" by purchases, which, if at all possible, should aid "any Gentlemen who support the *funds*" not those "who *depress* them." Finally, he told Duer, the prince of the speculators and the great bull in the market, of his fervent hope that Duer could maintain the price of the bank stock against strong selling trends. "The acquisition of too much of it by foreigners will certainly be an evil."[4] Hamilton feared the transfer of bank dividends abroad and the political repercussions of foreign ownership of the already controversial institution.

The moment appeared ripe to release SEUM's formal prospectus, and in late August Hamilton did so. In exalting the enterprise, the prospectus foreshadowed many of the arguments he would use in his Report on Manufactures. Women, children, immigrants, and machinery would mitigate the scarcity and cost of labor. Foreign and bank loans, secured by government stock, would supply needed capital. The initial capitalization would be $500,000 with the option, at the directors' discretion, of increasing it to $1 million. Naturally, all subscriptions to SEUM stock were required to be in government securities. As a "means of public prosperity and an instrument of profit to adventurers in the enterprise, it, at the same time, affords a prospect of an enhancement of the value of the debt; by giving it a new and additional employment and utility." Hamilton merely repeated the same justification he had included in his Report on a National Bank. SEUM, too, operated on the debt like a charm.[5]

The stock market rose and continued its rise into the winter of 1791. New Jersey's legislature, weighted with investors and directors of the society, granted a charter of incorporation in late November.[6] On the final day of the month Hamilton canceled a previously planned loan in Holland. "The prices of the public debt here," he explained to Short, render "it questionable whether it be any longer the interest of the United States to prosecute the idea of purchases [of stock] with monies borrowed at 5%."[7] Prices were high enough to make any Treasury intervention in the market superfluous. Effective interest rates on the 6 percent stock neared 5.5 percent and were dropping. Then, as if to christen the SEUM three weeks after its legal birth, Hamilton presented his long overdue Report on Manufactures. More than a few were afflicted with postpartum blues.

II

Jacob Cooke argues persuasively that "the SEUM was a practical demonstration of the arguments that would be included in the Report on Manufactures."[8] Long ago Arthur H. Cole observed that "the state of domestic industry should not be looked upon as the occasion for Hamilton's advocacy of protection." His mind, as Cole further points out, was on new enterprise.[9] Letters that Hamilton received from existing manufacturers pertaining to the report, as Cooke notes, "did not significantly influence" the final document.[10] These are important points in assessing the report. These observations are consistent with the report itself, which revealed misapprehension of and an insensitivity toward the serious problems confronting American manufacturers. Hamilton directed the report toward the kind of men who would own and control the SEUM.

The time element in the presentation of the report has not received the attention it warrants. Generally, its origins are traced to January 15, 1790, when a message from President Washington extolling the utility of domestic manufacturing induced the House to order a manufacturing report from Hamilton. As the previous analysis demonstrates, it was not so much this House directive as the security market's troubles and the SEUM which were the ultimate catalysts of the report. Within two weeks of the directive the Treasury Department dispatched a circular requesting information on manufactures to Benjamin Lincoln, to the directors of the Manufacturing Society of Philadelphia, and possibly to other societies. Lincoln never received it, and Hamilton made no attempt to ascertain why he had not responded, though he regularly corresponded with Lincoln on Treasury business. The Philadelphia society did receive the circular, however, and in February 1790 Tench Coxe responded on its behalf with an extensive discussion of domestic manufactures. Subsequently, Coxe's political mentors in Pennsylvania's congressional delegation, who were crucial to the passage of the assumption bill, induced Hamilton to hire him as assistant secretary of the Treasury in May 1790. Hamilton charged Coxe with the responsibility of collecting information on manufactures for the Treasury. After these two acts, Hamilton did not take up the matter of the report again until, at the earliest, February 1791— thirteen months after the House directive.[11]

Apparently, at the time of the directive and for a year or more thereafter, Hamilton gave it a low priority in the context of his efforts to establish government fiscal arrangements. The importance of priorities is strengthened by a comparison of the hiatus between House directives to Hamilton for reports and their completion. He presented the funding and bank reports approximately four months after the directives' issue. This speed is not surprising, since he had been planning the fiscal program and bank for a decade. In the 1780s, however, he planned no manufacturing program. The Report on Manufactures arrived some twenty-four months after the directive—a period six times as long as that required for the other reports. What is more striking about this delay is that the House ordered the bank report eight months *after* it ordered a manufacturing report. Nevertheless,

Hamilton presented the bank report one year before the one on manufacturing.[12]

While Hamilton attended to his fiscal program, Assistant Secretary Coxe, an avid proponent of domestic industry, twice requested information on manufacturing, in May 1790 and March 1791. Around January 1791, he drafted a report for Hamilton's perusal. Sometime thereafter Hamilton revised Coxe's draft, making some minor additions, and put it aside until the late spring or early summer of 1791. Meanwhile, he formulated the plans for the SEUM, a project, as was noted, directed in large part toward stabilizing the security market. In June 1791, Hamilton dispatched a department-wide circular requesting information on manufactures, but his language suggests that this information still held a low priority. The circular concluded "that there is nothing so urgent in the Object of this request as to require that you should, in the least, interfere, with your other Engagements." This circular stimulated a response from Treasury agents in September 1791; they began sending a large number of reports written by manufacturers.[13]

Why after one and a half years of little or no action on the report did Hamilton suddenly begin a concerted effort to complete it? His general unresponsiveness to domestic manufacturers discussed below, his lack of interest in existing enterprises, and his prolonged delay in obeying the House directive support the idea that the catalyst of the report had to be some particular event in spring 1791. To identify the SEUM as the catalyst of the report accords with Jacob Cooke's conclusion about its orientation toward the SEUM. It would appear that the SEUM largely prompted the report, and the security market problems largely prompted the SEUM. Hamilton's stabilization program remained the ultimate arbiter of his activities as Treasury secretary.

To aid in an evaluation of the report, it is useful to compare it to an earlier draft prepared by Coxe. Significantly, Coxe's draft differed with Hamilton's final report in several major ways. In general, Hamilton expanded Coxe's defense of the utility of manufacturing while he tailored Coxe's concrete proposals to conform to the parameters of his stabilization program. Coxe's draft concentrated on developing a market in which domestic manufacturing could flourish. Unlike Hamilton, who depended to a great extent on existing financial intermediaries to provide capital for manufactures, Coxe mentioned the funding program and United States Bank only as stabilizers of an expanded circulating medium. Instead, he sought to stimulate investment in manufactures through the creation of a profitable market for domestically manufactured products. To create such a market, raw material costs would have to be reduced, an internal transportation system built, incentives offered to potential investors, and a tariff enacted for protection from foreign imports. Within such an environment manufacturers would expand their resources and profits and possibly attract capital from commerce and land speculation.[14]

In a fundamental sense, a secure profitable market is an integral part of industrial development. Without access to such a market manufacturing could retain no substantial capital. No one would invest in nor long sustain ventures that promised no return. Thus, Coxe presented six proposals for securing that market for domestic manufacturers: a protective tariff on manufactured imports, outright prohibitions of some such imports, abolition of all duties on coastal trade, government construction of roads and canals, direct federal loans, and federal land grants to manufacturing entrepreneurs from a reserve of one-half million acres.[15]

These were substantial proposals which, if implemented, would have provided a solid ground for American manufacturing. Coxe stressed the development of an internal market system to wean the domestic economy from foreign manufactures. The land grant proposal anticipated the chief method by which the government subsidized railroad construction in the latter half of the nineteenth century. During the 1790s, it was land that attracted foreign, especially Dutch, capital to the United States. Thus, if used as a premium, a land reserve promised to be a strong inducement for investment in manufactures. Yet, not only did Hamilton reject the land bounty; he also rejected or emasculated all of Coxe's proposals for stimulating manufacturing and attached himself instead to proposals that Coxe had rejected. A careful analysis of the report demonstrates Hamilton's selective revision of Coxe's draft.

In his report, Hamilton began with his renowned defense of manufacturing development and a systematic discussion of contemporary political economic theories. Although he attempted to demonstrate the interrelationship of agriculture and manufacturing, he neglected to deal at all with the problem that enlarged domestic manufactures would present to the political base of his stabilization program, merchants importing British manufactures, nor to the revenues those imports provided for his fiscal program. Unlike Coxe and other manufacturing advocates, who always strove to demonstrate the benefits manufacturing would bestow on most merchants, Hamilton did not confront this central issue. His neglect is comprehensive if one assumes that he planned no measures that would interfere with those merchants and the revenues their imports yielded. Indeed, the enterprise he had in mind was to be owned and directed by those merchant-creditors to the exclusion of existing manufacturers.[16]

After the introductory remarks Hamilton began an analysis of domestic manufacturing. He discounted the complaints of the manufacturers—who had written of labor shortages, high wage rates, and capital deficiencies—on the grounds that they "are not sufficient to prevent the advantageous prosecution of many very useful and extensive manufactories."[17] Historians have often interpreted Hamilton's optimism about manufactures, which permeates the report, as the great advocate of industrialization rallying his forces. But to American manufacturers, who were swamped by British imports, debts, and high labor costs, such optimism tended to undermine the urgency of their demands for aid. Another way of interpreting Hamilton's optimistic tone is that he was thinking not of the manufacturers, but of promoting the SEUM, whose backers possessed the capital and the political power to overcome, at least ephemerally, many of these difficulties.

In many respects, capital was the crucial issue. Adequate capital would allow manufacturers to purchase machines which would assuage labor shortages and generally expand their enterprises. But Hamilton's proposals for capital aid to manufacturers were dubious at best. Indeed, he seemed to have assumed that those interested in manufacturing had access to or already possessed the necessary capital. Such assumptions would be consistent with the report's orientation toward the SEUM.

Hamilton described three major capital resources for manufacturing: domestic banks, the funded debt, and foreign investment. The first resource promised to be of little use to manufacturers. The banks of the last quarter of the eighteenth century were basically a "clubbing together" of merchant capital to discount short-term notes during intravoyage periods. Bray Hammond observes that these banks "specialized in short term, self-extinguishing credit and exercised a function that was almost purely monetary." The average loan period was thirty to forty-five days.[18] A manufacturer required long-term loans to acquire land, plant equipment, and skilled labor. To erect a factory, install machines, purchase materials, hire laborers, make products, and market them were not sixty-day operations. Manufacturers found it difficult, if not impossible, to obtain money from banks.[19] Banks could not serve as a source of manufacturing capital, although, as Hamilton noted, they did facilitate commercial transactions and provide credit and, in effect, capital to merchants. Hamilton's orientation again appears to be toward the merchants, who invested in the SEUM and had access to bank loans, not the manufacturers.

He designated the funded debt as the second major source of capital. "Usually held by monied men," government securities provided a capital asset to the holder that was easily liquidated for investment purposes. He argued that taxes supporting the debt had served to increase the "active capital" in the nation and had fueled an economic recovery in "Industry" and commerce. The problem was that the bulk of this capital went into speculation and commerce with the British, including imported manufactured goods. Manufacturers perceived this and complained of it bitterly. Although Hamilton thought that some of this capital might flow into manufacturing, the creditor, who was "possessed of a sum . . . ready to be applied to any purpose, to be embarked in any enterprise which appear to him eligible," invested the bulk of his "active capital" in commerce, land, and securities.[20]

An investor's criteria of "eligibility" are the profitability and security of his investment. If an enterprise portended a profitable and secure return, then a portion of the "active capital" might well flow into it. Although commerce and speculation in land or stock met these criteria, profits in manufacturing were marginal and uncertain. Thus Hamilton's proposal offered no real capital to manufacturers. As long as the rate of return in manufacturing was below other enterprises, then it was not "eligible" for serious investment. The capital generated by his economic program would flow into manufactures only if Hamilton managed to enact a strong protective tariff or general embargo. Under those circumstances the importation of foreign manufactures in particular and commerce in general would become difficult and domestic manufacturing very profitable. This action, however, would strike a debilitating economic blow to the same merchants whom he held to be the foundation of economic stability. Moreover, it would slash tariff revenues and cripple his financial system. Hamilton simply could not condone such an action.

The third source of manufacturing capital that Hamilton discussed was foreign investment. Stating as "a well-known fact" that a glut of capital existed in parts of Europe, he argued that this "deficiency of employment" and "a very material difference in profit . . . operate to produce a transfer of foreign capital to the United States." Although this transfer was "introduced merely with views to speculation in the funds, it may afterwards be rendered subservient to the interests of agriculture, commerce, and manufactures."[21] Foreign capital was found largely in security speculation, commerce, and land purchases because they were the most profitable outlets for investment in America. The capital from Britain served chiefly to finance merchant importations of British manufactured goods and the exportation of American raw materials. In this respect, foreign capital was actually an impediment to domestic manufacturing. In any event, why would British investors, the greatest potential source of foreign capital, finance the development of competitors to their own industry? Moreover, American manufactures were nowhere near as profitable as British industry. Certainly, the English government worked through its agents to retain its near monopoly in world manufacturing.[22]

Despite Hamilton's expressed desire for government "incitement and patronage" of manufacturing through intervention in the marketplace, he made not one proposal to insure capital for manufacturers. Once he established the general availability of investment funds in the nation, he left it entirely to the workings of the market to redirect its flow into domestic industry. Unlike Coxe or, later, Albert Gallatin, Hamilton did not suggest direct government loans to the manufacturers.[23] His fiscal priorities proscribed any such aid. He could rely only on the "invisible hand" to put capital into the manufacturers' purses.

Throughout the remainder of the report Hamilton discussed the manufacturing market itself. As in analyzing the labor and capital problems, he began by playing down any pressing need for the protective tariffs and prohibitions sought by manufacturers. Explaining that transportation costs, cheaper raw materials, and existing revenue tariffs tended to "wear a beneficial aspect toward the manufactures of the country," he advocated "pecuniary bounties" as "one of the most efficacious means of encouraging manufacturers and . . . in some views, the best."[24] He argued that bounties were a "more positive and direct" encouragement. Yet on the grounds of preventing fraud, he excluded "every private family in which manufacture was incidentally carried on" and those manufacturers for whom the making of the article was not "a regular trade."[25] This exclusion could easily have been used to prevent the payment of bounties to many people whose nascent attempts at manufacturing had a great potential for the industrial development of America. A protective tariff or prohibition would have had a universal effect in stimulating the smallest artisan or entrepreneur to expand production and meet a growing demand. Hamilton's method would have aided only those enterprises, such as the SEUM, large enough to qualify. In his draft report Coxe rejected bounties because he believed that they would do little to aid manufacturers. Twenty years later Gallatin in his Report on Manufactures also rejected bounties as "more applicable to articles exported than to those manufactured for home consumption."[26] Yet Hamilton made them the centerpiece of his report's recommendations.

In his final argument for bounties, Hamilton noted that "the duty upon the importation of an imported article can no otherwise aid the domestic production of it, than by giving the latter greater advantages in the home market." However, "it can have no influence upon the advantageous sale of the article produced in foreign markets—no tendency, therefore, *to promote its exportation*."[27] In other words, by acting on the domestic market alone protective tariffs did not benefit and might well injure many merchants. Bounties had no comparable effect. They could, in fact, help promote the exportation of goods and serve as the link between merchants and a manufacturing company like the SEUM. Their capital could build the manufactory and their ships export its products—subsidized by government bounties. Hamilton emphasized bounties not without good reason.

In proposing tariff changes he dissembled; the tariff directly involved both government revenues and merchants importing manufactures. In reference to iron manufactures, he followed Coxe's suggestions about raising the duties on steel, nails, and iron products. However, with the exceptions of firearms and starch, he proposed to increase duties only to 10 percent or less, in no sense a protective level.[28] He modified Coxe's suggestion about eliminating all duties "where the material is itself an object of general or extensive consumption, and a fit and productive source of revenue."[29] Thus, any raw material used in manufacturing, regardless of its importance, would continue to be taxed. His concern for any possible loss of tariff revenues, if a domestic manufacture replaced a foreign import, led him to state that an "indemnification can easily be found . . . out of the manufacture itself."[30] Bound by his fiscal program Hamilton thus would have had to tax any manufacturer who did succeed in "lessening" an imported article's consumption by increasing sales.

In discussing Coxe's plan for government construction of canals and roads, Hamilton hedged in making a commitment. "It were to be wished," he wrote, "that there was no doubt of the power of the National Government to lend its aid on a comprehensive plan." He described the "Jealousies" and "local or partial spirit" which would interfere with any comprehensive plan.[31] He then dropped the matter as a plan dashed on the rocks of partisan politics. His reticence about aiding transportation stemmed from the priorities he had set for government revenues. To expend large sums of money on internal improvements would have enervated his fiscal program. Thus, Hamilton allowed the proposal to pass without further discussion or future efforts to promote it.

He made no mention of Coxe's proposals to abolish duties on coastal trade and to grant land to investors in manufacturing. His failure to take up the former was doubtless a product of Hamilton's concern for government revenues derived from coastal duties. He did employ Coxe's suggestion of establishing a board "for promoting arts, agriculture, manufactures, and commerce." The commissioners of the board would encourage invention, immigration of skilled workmen, and importation of machinery. Since he planned to commit revenue from land sales to the sinking fund, he could not propose a land reserve to support the board's activities. He instead suggested financing it out of any surplus revenues from his newly proposed tariff structure. Those revenues, however, would become available only after "a competent substitute" for any loss of duties now "pledged for the public debt" had been subtracted from the surplus.[32] Before one dollar from any source could go toward the manufacturing board, the public debt would have to be fully serviced.

In summary, Hamilton rejected Coxe's proposals for the abolition of duties of coastal trade, government loans to manufacturers, and land grants to manufacturing entrepreneurs. He advocated bounties, which Coxe had rejected as inappropriate. He declined to eliminate duties on raw materials if such duties contributed significantly to government revenues. He demurred from any efforts toward fostering government construction of an internal transportation system. He proposed tariff changes which, by his later admission, were of little protective value and primarily revenue measures. While he endorsed Coxe's plan for a board to promote manufactures, he offered to finance it out of "surplus" revenues. Since the government debt commanded nearly half of the revenues and Hamilton had to borrow $2.6 million in 1792 just to meet expenses, any board would have been without funds even if one had been created. Hamilton's fiscal program established the parameters of all the government aid he proposed, and those parameters precluded significant aid to manufacturing.

When the House received and tabled the report, they provoked no protest from its author. Hamilton, who spared no effort to enact his other major proposals, did nothing to promote those in the Report on Manufactures as a comprehensive program. What energies he invested in manufactures went to the SEUM. Several of the recommended tariff revisions in the report were incorporated into his subsequent proposal to increase revenues in the face of government deficits. In it he pointed out that "our Merchants . . . procure the supplies, which they import from abroad, upon much more cheap, and advantageous terms than heretofore; a circumstance which must always alleviate to them the pressure of somewhat higher rates of duties."[33] In other words, because the prices of foreign manufactures had declined, an increase in duties on them would not affect the general price level. Sales would continue at the present volume, government revenues would be unimpaired, and domestic manufacturers would reap little benefit from the higher duties. The report's only exemplification, the SEUM, died in infancy.

Examined within its historical context the Report on Manufactures loses much of the superhistorical aura accorded to it in retrospective analyses. Like Hamilton's other reports, it was a polemic, however eloquent and portentous, and served a specific end: advancing the SEUM. He no more conceived of it as a grand plan for an industrial America than an advertising writer would consider his jingle a purely aesthetic endeavor. He hoped only to convince investors of the SEUM's viability and possibly induce some congressional legislation amenable to its prosperity. Indeed, Hamilton was so involved in the daily chore of running the Treasury and the fiscal program that it is virtually impossible to conceive of his putting aside the Bank of the United States, the security market problems, the SEUM, and the complex affairs of the sinking fund to pen a theoretical piece on manufactures without an intimate link to these overwhelming concerns. Only by yanking the report from its context can one impose on it the sorts of anachronistic visions so prevalent in historiography.

III

Owing to the SEUM and attendant publicity, stock prices continued to climb until March 1792. Meanwhile, Hamilton sought to block an attempt to open another bank in New York, assuming that more speculation would be the only result. "These extravagant sallies of speculation," he warned Seton, "do injury to the Government and to the whole system of public Credit, by disgusting all sober Citizens and giving a wild air to everything." No new bank would destroy the relatively stable market he had so patiently built.[34] Hamilton was optimistic and rightly so. The beginning of 1792 was in many respects a high point for his fiscal program. The stock market was rising steadily, foreign loan rates were low, and the SEUM promised a productive outlet for otherwise volatile speculative capital. There was, however, reason for doubt.

A few of Hamilton's correspondents had warned him of possible trouble, particularly with the SEUM. Fisher Ames noted that "some object that . . . domestic manufactures will be injured by the company."[35] One pensive businessman declined to invest in the society. He believed "that there is a great risk in pursuing it in the manner in which it is proposed, and its advantageous execution must depend on fortune, more than reason." The encouragement of manufactures, he added, would be better accomplished "by becoming partners . . . with undertakers of known abilities and character" through loans directly to manufacturers. He concluded that only heavenly intervention could bring success to the society.[36] One of the SEUM's chief mechanics, Thomas Marshall, advised Hamilton of the inadequacies of the society's site and offered an alternative.[37] Marshall's choice was overruled. Speculators and merchants, not manufacturers, held executive power in the society and several stood to profit from the land purchased as a site. Finally, there was Hamilton's choice of the SEUM's managing director, William Duer, described to Hamilton by a fellow financier as "unfit as a Leader, & unpopular as a man."[38] Even by eighteenth-century standards, Duer was a rogue. Ignorant of manufacturing, he had little regard for anything beside his own pelf.[39] In retrospect the fate of the SEUM is not surprising.

The stock market crashed in March 1792. Duer and two other directors, Alexander McComb and John Dewhurst, had used $80,000 of the society's capital to support their stock speculations. All the funds were lost.[40] His worst fears about Duer confirmed, Hamilton must have felt some relief when Duer's creditors ensconced him in debtors' prison.[41] Outraged at the market's collapse and pessimistic about the society's future, he attacked stock speculation in a tone even Jefferson would laud. "This time," he wrote Phillip Livingston, "there should be a line of separation between honest Men & Knaves; between respectable stockholders and dealers in the funds, and mere unprincipled Gamblers." He then expressed the angry frustration that grew with mounting attacks on speculation resulting from his fiscal program. "Public infamy must restrain what the laws cannot."[42] It was a revealing admission. Government, he was in effect conceding, was powerless to proscribe the speculation endemic to his program. Though he lamented "the partial ills of all over-driven speculation," he knew "at the same time that they are inseparable from the spirit & freedom of commerce & that the cure must result from the disease."[43] To attack speculation was to assail the whole fiscal program and challenge the rights of contract and property. Hamilton was compelled to defend the speculation he abhorred because it was "inseparable" from the economic system.

In the absence of a bull market, with its directors overwhelmed by their own financial problems and lacking skilled guidance, the SEUM slowly stumbled into oblivion. In what were his final attempts to salvage his plan, Hamilton wrote to William Seton of the Bank of New York and requested a $5,000 loan for the SEUM. He guaranteed "*in confidence* that the Bank of New York shall suffer no dimunition of its *pecuniary faculties* from any accommodations it may afford to the Society in Question." He felt his "reputation must concerned in its welfare," and pledged the "public Stock" as perfect security.[44] Although he succeeded in obtaining the loan, it is important to note that it was an extraordinary exception to the general rule of short-term,

commercial credit usually extended by banks. The loan was made at
Hamilton's specific request, secured by the Treasury Department, and
thus represented no new source of capital for manufacturers. Seton's
reply to Hamilton reflected its special character. "Be assured My Dear
Sir," he wrote, "[the bank's directors] have so much confidence in any
measure pointed out by you, & take so much pleasure in promoting
your views . . . that by complying with your wishes, they have not
even an opportunity of retaliating the obligations this institution is
under to you."[45] Hamilton's influence on the New York commercial
banking community was such that an alchemist could have obtained a
loan with his support.

The society's declining fortunes brought much advice from Hamilton, but to no avail. He appointed the French architect, Pierre L'Enfant, to design the SEUM's plant. The latter's grandiose plans led the
society's new manager, Peter Colt, to complain strongly of the disruption caused by L'Enfant's presence. "*An English Manufacturer*," he
insisted, "cannot bring himself to believe that a *French Gentleman* can
possibly know anything respecting manufactures."[46] Hamilton's ap-
pointments to the society continued to be poor; manufacturing was
simply not his forte. When it peacefully passed into oblivion in 1796,
there remained only $19,542 of the society's original subscriptions of
$600,000.

Although Hamilton's funding program endured and his central
banking system survived a decade of Republican rule, the society died
before the conclusion of Washington's second term of office. The
SEUM's failure was a result of incompetence in both conception and
management. Manufactures were not the directors' field of business
expertise. Even if successful, the SEUM would probably have produced the kind of industrial development broached in the southern
Confederacy's wartime desperation or czarist Russia's equally unbal-
anced and government-franchised manufacturing enterprises.[47] The
SEUM so alienated public opinion that no manufacturing society was
chartered for two years after its demise. Promotion of manufactures
thus suffered. The society served as another rallying point used by the
Republicans to organize the opposition of American manufacturers to
Hamilton's policies. It became the symbol on which the frustration of
those whom Joseph Davis labels the "class of small-scale producers"
focused their wrath.[48] The SEUM definitely alienated the small-scale
manufacturers and their spokesmen. No doubt the interests of larger
entrepreneurs were little helped by the repercussions of its ignomini-
ous collapse.

Throughout 1792 attacks on Hamilton's fiscal program escalated,
speculation persisted, and the SEUM declined. Government revenues

covered only 60 percent of expenditures. The remaining $2.6 million were financed with loans. Jefferson's severe attacks on Hamilton's policies led the president to request a written response. Hamilton sent a detailed letter explaining his system and refuting the charges against it. He wrapped the cloak of property rights around his program and warned Washington of licentiousness and demagoguery. Partisan polemics, however, had not yet replaced reason. He concluded his letter by noting that the charges bandied about were fraught with exaggerations by both parties.[49] Nonetheless, in his draft of the annual presidential message to Congress, Hamilton felt obliged to reassure friend and foe of his determination "to enter upon systematic and effectual arrangements for regular redemption and discharge of the public debt" under congressional guidance.[50] Questions about his fiscal program and speculation persisted but were soon overshadowed by a more serious conflict over the program and its implications for foreign relations. Over this issue—the very independence of the United States— was waged the most significant political conflict of the period.

CHAPTER FOUR

Hamilton's Stabilization Program
The Question of Neocolonialism

It will no doubt have occurred to you that the fund has been mortgaged for the public Debt . . . [and] it would be essential that the same act which should destroy this source of revenue should provide an equivalent. This I consider as a rule which ought to be sacred, as it affects public Credit.
—Hamilton to Jefferson, commenting on the latter's efforts to exempt France from tonnage duties under the most-favored-nation clause in the Franco-American Treaty, January 11, 1791

Charles A. Beard, Samuel F. Bemis, Paul Varg, and other scholars have propounded the link between Hamilton's fiscal system and the revenues from British imports.[1] This link was real and did have great impact on his foreign policy. There were, however, complications. First of all, revenue was not the only British connection. Hamilton's stabilization program attached large, established merchants to the new government. They traded in whole or in substantial part with the British empire. Any Anglo-American conflict would have not only reduced tariff revenues by one-half but also alienated these merchants, the bulwark of the Federalist party. Whether the funding system could survive the revenue loss became academic in light of the political ramifications of disaffecting this group of merchants. Secondly, Hamilton's system is generally assumed to have included manufacturing within its "capitalist edifice." In stressing the revenue–British trade connection, scholars have overlooked the enormous significance that an uninterrupted flow of English manufactures had for American manufacturers. It is difficult to maintain an argument that holds Hamilton's concern for import revenues to be a primary policy determinant without recognizing that this concern entailed abandoning domestic manufacturers to their British competitors.

Genuine support for manufacturing involved more than stirring affirmations of government "incitement and patronage." It required the enactment of policies that advanced the development of manufactures. Whatever his rhetorical flourishes, Hamilton was throughout the 1790s an opponent of commercial discrimination and protective tariffs, and an advocate of an unrestricted flow of imports. Indeed, his stabilization program raises the whole issue of what relationship importing merchants have to manufacturing development. Manufacturers believed them to be harmful and voiced that belief repeatedly to Hamilton and the Congress.

In the context of commercial expansion, the link among American merchants' trading with Britain, British imports' providing revenues, and those same merchants' receiving interest payments and capital gains from debt service opens the question of Hamilton's concern for general economic development. Acquiescence in British restrictions on American commerce and markets injured not only manufacturers but that growing group of merchants trading outside the British empire. That trade was the engine of prosperity and economic advancement for the nation in this era. Independence rested no less on economic development than on political support of the federal government. In this respect, Hamilton's foreign policy transcends its obvious function of protecting his fiscal program and raises the more serious question of his commitment to the economic development of the United States.

I

The security of public credit and the ability of the government to govern depended ultimately on tax revenues. Throughout the 1780s Hamilton turned repeatedly to the need of providing an independent revenue source for the Confederation. In the Constitutional Convention, jurisdiction over revenues and debts was the chief, practically the sole, object of his proposed judiciary system. He devoted at least one-quarter of his Report on Public Credit to a detailed plan for revenues. The problem of revenues haunted him throughout his tenure at the Treasury. Deficits averaged 7 percent annually and had to be financed out of loans, which added to the $70 million Revolutionary debt. A new tax, such as the excise, would improve America's creditworthiness abroad while igniting political opposition at home.[2] The most productive of all taxes, however, was the import tariff.

The tariff accounted for 90 percent of government revenues. Hamilton believed that it had to be "moderate," for "moderate duties are more productive than high ones." Low tariffs did not obstruct trade and "arising on a greater quantity of commodities, will yield more in the aggregate, than when they are so high as to operate either as a prohibition, or as an inducement" to smuggling.[3] Congress enacted a tariff levying on average 7.5 percent ad valorem. The chief imports taxed were finished manufactured goods, staples, and wines. Imports from the British empire constituted over 60 percent of the tariff revenue, and seven-eights of British imports were manufactured goods such as iron products, woolens, linens, cotton cloths, sailcloth, and the like.

If all British manufactured goods were prevented by protective tariffs, war, or any other means from entering the United States, then nearly two-thirds of government revenue would disappear. In a new nation, struggling to pay its bills and debts, such an eventuality could be catastrophic. To Hamilton's mind any reduction in revenue, especially in the tariff, threatened his stabilization program, and he reacted accordingly. This dependence on British imports for revenue possessed a certain symmetry with Hamilton's overall program. Generally, the chief importers of British goods were the wealthy, established merchants—the same group of men he had sought so vigorously to attach to the new government through the public debt. These merchants had established their trade relationships in the antebellum period and had renewed them at war's end. They had a double motive for good Anglo-American relations: their trade *and* their stocks. This connection became the crux of Hamilton's foreign policy.

The first instance in which fiscal exigencies translated into foreign policy occurred when Madison proposed protective tariffs and discriminatory tonnage duties against nations without a commercial treaty with the United States.[4] Protection for manufacturers and commercial discrimination would operate almost exclusively against Great Britain. Moreover, a protective tariff is of a very different sort from a revenue tariff. The former seeks to retard the flow of imports regardless of revenue, while the latter seeks to increase trade and revenues. Hamilton found protective tariffs and commercial discrimination repugnant to his fiscal program. Through his chief spokesman in the House, William Smith of South Carolina, he fought Madison's proposals and with the aid of the Senate eliminated the protective tariffs and commercial discrimination. Instead Congress enacted a revenue tariff and a simple tonnage duty to favor American vessels. He explained to George Beckwith, England's clandestine agent in America, that he "was decidedly opposed to those discriminatory Clauses."[5]

Over the first two years of the new government, Hamilton explained his strong pro-British sentiments to Beckwith. "I have always preferred," he repeated time and again, "a Connexion with you, to that of any other Country. . . . We wish to form a Commercial treaty with you to Every Extent, to which you may think it for Your interest to go." He assured Beckwith that any problems Jefferson, as secretary of state, might raise for England could be "readily explained." Continued Anglo-American rapport was "the essential interest of this country."[6] The bond between England and America was commercial. Americans "shall be great consumers, [and] have a preference for Your manufacturers . . . I cannot forsee any solid grounds of national difference, between us."[7] He constantly assured Beckwith of American's solicitude for British trade and his opposition to any legislative interference with it.[8] An unfettered commerce with Britain, affirmed by commercial treaty, was Hamilton's object. The role of that commerce in his stabilization program made it in "the best interests of this Country." To achieve it he would willingly repudiate America's treaty with France.[9]

Hamilton had placed himself in a dilemma. He wanted a commercial accord with Britain to expand America's trade opportunities within the empire and to defuse any commercial conflict. Yet, he could cajole the British ministry only into treating with America. The coercive moves advanced by Madison and Jefferson would, he believed, lead to commercial warfare. Any violent interdiction of trade would reduce government revenues, destabilize the stock market, disrupt American credit, and alienate his chief political supporters. Thus, Hamilton resisted any legislative or administrative attempts to coerce Britain or reward her enemies regardless of their respective willingness to enter into trade agreements with the United States.

The policy course he advocated prior to the European War of 1793 was free trade. "My commercial system," he explained to Jefferson, "turns very much on giving a free course to Trade. . . . And I feel a particular reluctance to hazard any thing which may lead to commercial warfare with any power." He went on to reject Jefferson's proposals for a foreign policy which stressed reciprocity through commercial agreements and discrimination against nations, specifically Great Britain, which declined any treaty.[10] It is absolutely imperative to recognize that in the context of the prewar 1790s "free trade" meant acquiescence in British restrictions on an open commerce with all countries and colonies. To abjure retaliation against foreign discrimination was to forsake the only method America possessed to insure a genuinely free trade. Hamilton's commercial laissez faire did not mean "let trade alone," but "let trade alone be dominated by Britain."

He persisted in his efforts to tie America to England. In May 1791, he suggested that William Short turn to British leaders for American loans. "I think a train of good consequences involved in the idea of opening the purses of monied men in that Country to the Government of this." Though even he realized that once the news of such transactions spread "it would not be long tolerated,"[11] nevertheless, loans would secure a more interdependent relation between the two countries. For Anglo-American rapport, Hamilton tried to keep tariffs low. He proposed increases very judiciously and with great regard to the costs and profits of merchants importing taxable goods.[12] To close the budget deficit he proposed a more comprehensive tax on liquor and snuff manufacturers.[13] Though an excise was galling to all manufacturers, he saw little alternative. The government needed more revenue, and further tariff increases would either retard imports or encourage smuggling and surely incur the wrath of merchants importing British goods. Thus, the burden fell on manufacturers.

Hamilton's stabilization program was slowly establishing parameters for his foreign policies. Britain had to be courted for her trade. Commercial ties with the empire were integral to revenues, public credit, and political support of the government. Tariffs could not be used as tools for protection of manufactures because revenues would fall, merchants would complain, and Britain would be offended. The federal government could not finance internal improvements or manufacturing because debt service drained all available revenues and then some. Still, no crisis compelled Hamilton to choose between national economic development and his stabilization program. Many could whisper of his "attachment to the British Interest," but he could point to the tariff, to the SEUM, and to the Report on Manufactures as evidence of his desire to promote manufacturers.[14] He could continue to argue that America's national interest lay in a bond with England. Indeed, with the single exception of ships built in America, he did assert that Britain's commercial regulations were more favorable than France's.[15] The exception, like the excise, was all-important to American manufacturers, many of whose livelihoods depended on the construction, outfitting, and maintenance of ships.

If support of domestic manufacturing were the sole criterion of a policy of national independence, Hamilton's program would be found wanting. Support of manufacturing, however, was not the only criterion of national independence. There were others: expanding foreign trade, opening new markets for farm products, settling the West, resisting foreign domination. Hamilton's program had yet to be measured against these criteria. Then in January 1793 the Jacobins beheaded Louis XVI and pledged the destruction of European monarchies. The war that followed became the crucible of an independent United States.

II

The advent of war precipitated a consensus, both in and out of government, for American neutrality. The administration accorded France's revolutionary government recognition, received its minister Genêt, but no more. Despite the Franco-American alliance, dating from the Revolution, Washington proclaimed neutrality in April 1793 with good reason. Militarily, America could do little or nothing against the Royal Navy, and war would cripple the economy by sweeping American commerce from the oceans. Neutrality meant not only freedom from war, but freedom to trade and carry goods throughout the great European empires. When Britain's navy eliminated the enemy's merchant marine and reduced its own to man its warships, America became a principal carrier of the world's trade. Shipbuilding, exports, reexports, investment, and employment mushroomed between 1793 and 1795. American tonnage increased by 150 percent, domestic exports by 208 percent, and reexports by nearly 500 percent.[16] Remarkably, stock prices fell not because of any lack of confidence or speculative manipulation, but because merchants found a more profitable and productive outlet in this commercial boom.[17] Despite popular sympathies, mostly for France but some for England, a desire for neutrality fixed itself on the politically powerful in each state.[18] James McHenry spoke for all when he wrote Hamilton: "Our people wish to be able to carry our produce freely to all the parties at war who may want it, without having any thing further to do with the war."[19] Though he hated the French revolutionaries, Hamilton, too, wanted neutrality, which he interpreted as no aid to France.[20]

During the ensuing two decades of war, neutral rights were the central issue of American foreign relations.[21] This issue centered above all on two conflicting doctrines of international law: "free ships, free goods" and "unfree goods, unfree ships." Despite their many nuances, the doctrines dealt primarily with the right of belligerents to seize neutral ships. The "free ships, free goods" doctrine argued that the status of goods traveling to a belligerent port depended on the status of the country in whose vessel they traveled. A ship of a neutral power was free from the conflict; hence, its goods were also free from seizure, regardless of their point of origin. In practice the doctrine asserted that American ships were immune from seizure when they carried goods of domestic or foreign origin to a belligerent power, provided they included no contraband military supplies. The counterdoctrine, to which Britain adhered, held that the goods themselves were the chief determinate of neutral rights. If a neutral ship carried the goods of a neutral country, provided they were not contraband articles, then it was free from seizure and confiscation. However, if the carrier transported the goods of a belligerent power, it was liable to seizure. Also a neutral nation, if its goods were seized while on a belligerent's ship, was entitled to compensation by the confiscating nation. Blockades, reexports, and impressment complicated these basic issues substantially.

Militarily, the British navy could interdict French merchant traffic, but could not stop French privateers. It used convoys to protect its own merchantmen from privateers. On their part the French could harass British trade, but they needed the goods and revenues from their international and intra-imperial trade. To block this trade the British required an expanded navy and drew on its merchant fleet for seamen to staff that expansion through a rather brutal form of a draft, impressment. Military service amounted to seaborne slavery and was no less brutal than the onshore variety. Civilian sailors understandably absconded rather than face military service. Thus, with one empire in need of a carrier for its commerce and another whose seamen were prepared to flee en masse, the situation ripened for an enterprising neutral nation to expand into this commercial vacuum. America did, with vigor.

International, particularly English, recognition of the "free ships, free goods" doctrine was manifestly in America's interest. Freedom from seizure and condemnation would allow the United States to become the merchant carrier of the French empire and assume any slack in the carriage of British trade due to their need for naval manpower. The great commercial depot of the West Indies would become an American market by default. More exports, more ships, and more carriage would accrue to America. Farmers exporting their products, merchants carrying exports, manufacturers building and servicing ships, and manufactures exporting their wares would all reap enormous benefits from an unrestricted neutral commerce.

After some vacillation, the French acquiesced in the "free ships, free goods" doctrine. They needed the trade to sustain their empire and augment their war effort. Besides, they could not interdict America's commerce with Britain. Their privateers could serve only to drive American ships into British convoys for transatlantic voyages. Within the Caribbean even a small American navy could control their privateers. Thus, France accepted America's position on neutral shipping. Not altruism but a coincidence of national interests determined Franco-American support of "free ships, free goods."

Great Britain refused any similar acquiescence. Her navy could interdict severely American trade with France and within the French empire. No American navy could possibly contest British superiority anywhere. A blockade of France and its possessions would destroy its empire and undercut its war effort. Just as unrestricted neutral trade would make America a de facto ally of France, so a suppression of it could coerce America into a de facto alliance with Britain. Effecting through diplomacy and naked aggression American acquiescence in a proscription of its trade within the French empire would force France to retaliate with privateering attacks on American shipping. America would then be forced to join British convoys for protection and trade only where those convoys would permit. Control of the labor force of commerce would regain commercial dominance for Britain's merchant marine at America's expense. If Britain could compel American acquiescence in her denial of "free ships, free goods," it would effect an economic reintegration of the United States into the British Empire. The doctrine involved was not a mere dispute in international law; it was the very essence of an economically independent America.

In spring 1793, at the onset of war, the issue of "free ships, free goods" arose in a private conversation between George Hammond, the British minister, and Hamilton. Hammond asked the Treasury secretary what the administration position was on Britain's refusal to accept this doctrine. Hamilton replied that he believed Britain's position to be just and added that he could guarantee the government's acquiescence in the position and any British blockade to enforce it.[22] It was both a stunning and damning admission — stunning, because Hamilton informed the British government through its minister that America would not resist attempts to control her international trade, and damning because in it, there was an implicit recognition that Hamilton's stabilization program made an independent commercial policy and national independence itself impossible in the face of a serious confrontation with Great Britain.

Hamilton's statement to Hammond made its way into government policy in 1794. After the British Orders in Council of November 1793 translated into wholesale seizures of American ships bound for France, a crisis developed which revealed the incompatibility of his program with defiance of England. The most cogent example of this came in January 1794, when James Madison proposed a series of "commercial propositions" to coerce Britain into repealing her orders.[23] Their central thrust was the interdiction of English manufactures and the development of domestic industries. He endeavored to do exactly what Hamilton's biographer, Broadus Mitchell, conceives as the central purpose of Hamilton's political economy: to "bring America, as rapidly as possible, into the new industrial age which had become the condition of national advance."[24] Yet, it was Hamilton who, above all others, led the fight against Madison's proposals and others of similar bent.

Writing as "Americanus" he explained why industrial development through protective tariffs was impossible. "Nine tenths of our present revenues are derived from commercial duties." War or measures tending to provoke war would "annihilate" foreign trade and the revenues it yielded. Government credit would be destroyed, causing a "sacrifice of the public Creditors and the disgrace of a National bankruptcy."[25] Any prohibitions on British goods or private debt service, he told Washington, would inflate the prices of imported goods, deflate the prices of exports, derange "our revenue and credit," and deprive America of needed commodities. "These circumstances united may occasion the most dangerous dissatisfaction & disorders in the community." More prosaically, Hamilton's stabilization program would be destroyed.[26]

Statistics provide a perspective on why the expansion of American trade had precipitated a crisis for Hamilton's stabilization program. When Hamilton designed and implemented his stabilization program, resting his fiscal system on the British trade connection was sound politics (see Graph 3). Two-thirds of American trade during Washington's first term was with the British empire. American trade seemed destined to flow in this channel in the future. The symmetry was perfect: two-thirds of the trade was with Britain, and that trade produced two-thirds of government revenue. Then the war came. By 1794 Britain accounted for less than one-half of the total American trade; a year later it was under one-quarter. Nevertheless, British imports *still* constituted two-thirds of the revenue. A chasm yawned in Hamilton's stabilization program. In 1795, for the first time in history, American merchants found more markets outside the British empire than within it.

Madison's efforts to legislate retaliation against British seizures commanded wide support from patriots and profiteers. Fifty to eighty percent of American trade was at stake. All Hamilton could perceive was the interruption of British imports—an act which three years earlier would have devastated most merchants. Now, however, a failure to retaliate would alienate a great many merchants. In effect his stabilization program rested only on that part of the mercantile community still trading principally with Britain. If he acted to save that part, he would be serving only a political faction. The economic tentacles of the commercial expansion reached into the hubs of the major states and involved mechanics and farmers was as well. To rescue the rentiers and his fiscal system Hamilton would have to rupture his stabilization program. The two were no longer compatible. He had built his program on a political economy wedded to the British empire. Since that reality had changed radically, Hamilton acted to preserve what had been. Madison acted to protect what was coming to be. Of the two, Hamilton became in 1794 the "idealist." In Madison's commercial sanctions he would have no part.

Even if Madison's resolutions did not provoke war, their execution would disrupt his fiscal program. He also believed, with good cause, that the Dutch bankers would cease extending loans to America.[27] His outrage at British seizures was more than mollified by his fear of the effects of American retaliation. No promise of domestic manufacturing could outweigh to any degree the harm to the merchant-creditors, who, in one stroke, would lose their trade in English manufactures and their stock portfolio. On the basis of earlier statements Hamilton might have reasoned that a suspension of debt service like the decade-long one of the 1780s would be tolerable in a national emergency; that domestic manufactures would compensate for essential British imports as they had during the Revolution; that price declines in agricultural goods, additional labor freed from shipping industries, and unused merchant capital would mitigate capital deficiencies, labor shortages, and the inflation resulting from an abrupt demand for domestic manufactures; that foreign loans, particularly from France, would ease national financial stringencies until excise revenues could be raised on new manufactures; and finally, that the economic pressure on Britain might indeed wrest commercial concessions from her ministry. Such reasoning would have led him to forsake the merchants dealing primarily with England, forsake the political stability the debt service purchased, in short, forsake all those means that his political economy revered as essential to the protection of property and the maintenance of national government. He would have to forsake his political economy, his world view, and in effect himself. This, no man of honor could do.

Circumstances compelled him to make a choice, which Madison had once said no man should have to make. This decision, as Madison wrote, was "the melancholy duty of chusing between the loss of the Union, and the loss of what the Union was meant to secure."[28] For Hamilton the union was absolutely dependent on his fiscal program. To risk that program against the possibility of economic independence wrought from rapid commercial and industrial development was unacceptable. Acquiescence in British commercial strictures would save his program but sacrifice the only other possible American road to independence as a nation: an unrestricted commerce with the world. He chose to preserve the union by preserving the only means he believed capable of securing it, his fiscal program. In doing so he sacrificed the purpose of that union: an independent nation. Having made his

choice, he fought successfully to make it government policy and to
have that policy ratified by the people's representatives.

Hamilton's refusal to protect American merchant property from
British attacks was a violation of what he called "the chief object of
government." It was still an acceptable violation because of the single
"limitation" on it. "The united strength of the community ought to be
exerted for the protection of individuals so far as there is a rational
prospect of success; so far as is consistent with the safety and well
being of the whole." In 1794 success was in his mind dubious and the
risk to the community's safety and well-being too great. Economic
sanctions against Britain would be "enterprises of a manifest rashness"
and, "in event of success, would be productive of more mischief than
good."[29] Though these statements were made at a different time and in
a different situation, there is little doubt that he rationalized his refusal
to oppose action against Britain on these principles.

Hamilton's efforts to undercut Madison's congressional sanctions
against Britain concentrated on the appointment of a special envoy,
John Jay, to negotiate the issues.[30] These efforts bore fruit in the form
of a sixty-day embargo—in effect a move to forestall harsher retaliatory measures against England that further seizures might provoke.
Having stymied Congress, he acquired time for Jay to treat with Lord
Grenville in London. He then outlined the terms that a treaty might
stipulate. These terms amounted to a complete capitulation of America's sovereign rights to trade throughout the world, to protect domestic industry, to control alien property, and to make commercial treaties. Long ago he had surrendered the principle of "free ships, free
goods" to British regulation. He further offered to forswear any "extra
Tonnage and duties on British Vessels and goods imported in British
vessels . . . [so] that the commodities and manufactures of Great Britain & Ireland may be imported into the Ustates upon terms equally
good with the like commodities & manufactures of any other nation."
In one sentence he had undermined America's ability to make commercial treaties, since no nation could ever gain an advantage over
Britain from such a treaty, and its ability to discriminate selectively for
the benefit of American ships and shipbuilders.[31]

After abandoning an independent merchant marine and foreign
trade, Hamilton next sacrificed domestic manufacturing. "The duties
upon such of [British manufactures] as now pay ten per Cent ad valorem & upwards shall not be increased and that the duties upon such
of them as now pay under 10 per Cent ad valorem shall not be increased beyond 10 per Cent." Without a doubt, this proposal banished
any ambiguity concerning his commitment to domestic manufacturing; he had none. He then abandoned another attribute of national

sovereignty: the right to sequester the debts of a foreign nation, England. In return he asked for British evacuation of the northwest forts, indemnification for seized vessels, some trade concessions for *small* ships in the British West Indies, and most-favored-nation status for American exports to the British empire.[32]

The first proposal was merely a request that Britain fulfill its 1783 treaty commitments. Indemnification for seizures was the sine qua non of merchant acquiescence in any agreement. Trade with the West Indies for ships of prescribed tonnage was an attempt to open intra-American trade while leaving transatlantic commerce to British bottoms. Since emergency power grants had allowed West Indies governors to open their islands to all American ships at the outset of war, this limited proviso would have curbed American commerce to the islands. When it was incorporated in the treaty, the Senate rejected it on precisely these grounds. Finally, Hamilton asked for lower tariffs on American exports to the empire. Though of some minor benefit, it was not a plea unique to Hamilton. For years British manufacturers had been petitioning for the reduction of duties on American-produced raw materials. His proposal found much support among English industrialists. Four minor British concessions and Hamilton's fiscal program in return for American economic independence: more than one citizen believed the bargain poor.

Perhaps the one advantage Jay possessed in his negotiations, since economic coercion had been effectively waylaid by Hamilton's congressional allies, was armed neutrality. Led by the Scandinavian countries, neutrals whose shipping Britain had victimized sought protection in mutual alliance. At a time when France retained its navy, a coalition of neutrals acting in consonance with it might challenge British dominance of the seas. As a large maritime power, America's participation would be a vital and potent addition to neutral demands for security from seizures. Although the cabinet had decided secretly to abjure any alliance, the mere threat could provide effective leverage for Jay in his negotiations with Grenville. Hamilton, however, elected to reveal the secret decision of the administration against any alliance to Hammond, the British minister, before Jay arrived in England.[33] The secretary, in an act approaching treason, tipped Jay's hand. Regardless of the efficacy of this bargaining chip, Hamilton's indiscretion leaves him badly tainted.

III

Jay's departure meant a summer hiatus in the foreign policy debate. Fall's onset brought the harvest and annual distillation of western grain for easy transportation to market. Also to the whiskey market came Hamilton's excisemen to enforce the tough new taxes on spirits. The farmers in western Pennsylvania reacted violently to the levy. At Hamilton's prodding the administration marched an army of out-of-state militia into Pennsylvania to restore order. Although expensive and politically damaging to Hamilton's standing among farmers, distillers, and other manufacturers, the exhibition of massive federal force did improve government credit abroad.[34] While Hamilton worked to increase excise revenues, he knew that enforcement of these laws would generate resistance. Still he pursued them rather than raise import duties to meet revenue requirements. His fears of antagonizing importers and straining Anglo-American relations dictated that decision.[35] In this respect Hamilton was the first American statesman, before Lincoln, to choose a domestic conflict over a foreign one.

Turning from this crisis, Hamilton received word of the treaty Jay had negotiated. He pondered it that winter with great discontent. It contained the provisions he had suggested, but now confronted with them in their final form, he was severely chagrined.[36] Digging through its humiliating terms, he seized on its two positive provisions: possession of the northwest forts and peace.[37] In secret session the Senate ratified it, and after much anguish, Washington signed it into law on August 14, 1795. Prior to his signing the document was made public. Against the groundswell of indignation and opposition, Hamilton became the anchor of support.

Writing as "Camillus" he explained candidly that a rupture with Britain would destroy the government's fiscal program and derail the national economy. Commercial freedom had been the price of peace.[38] He rejected cries for protection from British impressment as impractical in light of the multinational composition of America's seamen.[39] He rejected calls for sequestering British debts as violations of property rights and useless measures of retaliation.[40] Finally, he defended Britain's denial of "free ships, free goods" as a legitimate interpretation of international law.[41] Despite the cogency of Hamilton's polemics, which led Jefferson to label him a "colossus" and "an host within himself,"[42] the majority of the ruling elite acquiesced in the treaty for reasons beyond the persuasiveness of "Camillus."

The power of grassroots opposition to the treaty had frightened the ruling groups in the commercial cities. Generally, they abhorred the treaty, but they realized that Hamilton's fiscal system, the mainstay of the federal government, was inextricably tied to peaceful relations with England. For all its faults the treaty promised peace. To join with the small property holders against the treaty would destabilize the government, perhaps irretrievably. Already the burden of war preparations and national diffidence had weakened American credit, exacerbated budget deficits, and enervated trade. Less than a year had elapsed since the Whiskey Rebellion. Hamilton had said, in effect, the treaty or chaos. They chose the treaty.[43]

A favorable agreement with Spain on American rights to navigate the Mississippi River coupled with the political muscle of merchant support to secure implementation of the treaty. Some members of the House sought to withhold funds for the treaty pending examination of Jay's instructions. On Hamilton's advice the president claimed executive privilege and refused to submit any diplomatic documents. Hamilton feared that publication of these instructions would "have a very ill effect." Parts of Jay's instructions, he believed, could be construed "as an intentional sacrifice of the interests of this Country to G.B."[44] The House initiative failed, and funds were allocated for the treaty's execution.

On February 29, 1796, Washington proclaimed Jay's Treaty without the clause on West Indian trade. In the Constitution treaties possess a legal authority superior to legislative enactments. They stand only a notch below constitutional amendments. Thus, the president and the Senate, the two least representative parts of the government, acted on consonance without consent of the House, the states, or the people to levy what amounted to constitutional restrictions on American sovereignty. Congress could make no law sequestering British debts, prohibiting British goods, discriminating against British ships, or aiding British enemies. Through the treaty, Hamilton had legally bound the government and the nation itself to the foreign policy dictated by his fiscal program and its political constituency. An inchoate opposition was thereby transformed into a national political party. In 1795 the cosmopolitan groups that had ratified the Constitution divided politically.

CHAPTER FIVE

Jefferson, Madison, and Hamilton
A Parting of Ways

Our best interest would be to employ our principal labour in agriculture because to the profits of labour which is dear this adds the profits of our lands which are cheap. But the risk of hanging our prosperity on the fluctuating counsels & caprices of others renders it wise in us to turn seriously to manufactures, and if Europe will not let us carry provisions to their manufactures we must endeavor to bring their manufactures to our Provisions.
— Thomas Jefferson to David Humphreys, June 29, 1791

Not those, in a word, who would force on the people the melancholy duty of chusing between the loss of the Union, and the loss of what the Union was meant to secure.
— James Madison discussing the "Friends of the Union" in the *National Gazette,* April 2, 1791

The antagonism between Hamilton and Madison and Jefferson was the focal point of so much of this period that it is easy to forget their close political alliance during the creation of the new government. Madison and Hamilton were sufficiently akin in world view to collaborate on the premier polemic in support of the Constitution. Whatever nuances discriminate their *Federalist* essays, they are far outweighed by a similarity in outlook. In many respects the ideological origins of political division in the 1790s lay in the growing alienation of Madison and Jefferson from Hamilton. Understanding precisely where they disagreed and why is critical to reconstructing the Republican leaders' political economy. A precise reconstruction is also necessary to evaluate the historiographic conception that the "idealism" of the Republican leaders in the 1790s gave way to a "realism" once they assumed power.[1]

I

Returning from France in 1789 to the seat of government at New York City, Jefferson immediately confronted the problems of organizing the State Department, formulating foreign policy, and pondering the funding.[2] Not surprisingly, he believed the debt had to be funded "for the sake of the union, and to save us from the greatest of calamities, the total extinction of our credit in Europe."[3] He was also instrumental in the passage of the assumption bill through the now famous bargain between Madison and Hamilton over the capital's location. Jefferson arranged the compromise because he perceived that "a rejection of the [assumption] measure . . . will prevent [Congress from] funding any part of the public debt, and will be something very like a dissolution of the government."[4] The striking aspect of Jefferson's profound concern over the funding is that it could well have been expressed by Hamilton.

Madison, too, believed the funding and prompt redemption of the debt an unavoidable exigency. In Congress he advocated a 15 percent tariff for revenue to service the debt. Writing to Hamilton he suggested a liquor excise, a levy on land, and a stamp tax. These burdens, he explained, were less harmful to the nation than prolonged indebtedness and large foreign acquisitions.[5] He penned a long response to Jefferson's argument, "the earth belongs to the living," which was essentially a theoretical attack on enduring public debts. Madison reminded his friend that "improvements" made by past generations are charges on the living. The accumulation of property and the security of contract depended on permanency. He concluded that Jefferson's idea was a nice theory (conceived, no doubt, in France) but wholly impractical. Congress should strengthen, not weaken, the laws governing contract and debt.[6] If Hamilton had had a copy of this letter, he might have appended it to his Report on Public Credit to disarm critics.

Madison did oppose indiscriminate assumption, at least publicly. Some effort, he asserted, should be made to compensate debt holders who had earlier sold their debentures at great discount to speculators. His position was rooted very much in his efforts to rebuild his Virginia political base, severely shaken by his support of the Constitution and of a funding plan favorable to mercantile interests. Discrimination among debt holders pleased his constituency. Moreover, it reflected Madison's sincere concern that the new government at least make a gesture toward the many small property holders largely forsaken in Hamilton's fiscal program. Despite this hesitation, which the relocation of the capital on the Potomac assuaged, Madison, like Jefferson, supported the funding and its attendant fiscal policy.[7]

Over the following two years their support waned for Hamilton's program and the foreign and domestic policies it entailed. They parted ways with Hamilton initially over what Madison called the "public plunder" by the speculators. There were also deeper strains centering on the proper policy the government should pursue to achieve economic independence. In foreign affairs Jefferson confronted Hamilton's policy of accommodation with England as early as fall 1790. The controversy involved Louisiana, the Floridas, especially West Florida, and the commercial water routes to the Gulf of Mexico their possession accorded. Jefferson could tolerate Spanish obstruction of these routes if "our Western citizens have had vent at home for their productions." However, a "surplus of production begins now to demand foreign markets."[8] Spain could be dealt with militarily, but a more serious threat was an impending Anglo-Spanish War. If this conflict resulted in British occupation of Louisiana and the Floridas, he feared that the western United States would be drawn into the market system of Great Britain. Economic integration foreshadowed political assimilation. Jefferson told Washington that "we ought to make ourselves parties in the *general war* . . . should this be the only means of preventing the calamity."[9]

While Jefferson would fight to prevent England's invasion of the West, Hamilton would join England in attacking Spain. Hamilton's proposal was very much in line with his general position on Anglo-American relations. In addition, he believed Anglo-American occupation of the West would free the water routes from Spanish interference. Jefferson thought any military alliance that advanced Britain's influence in North America would place the United States on the tiger's back. Better to suffer some ephemeral interference and negotiate with a declining Spanish empire than replace it with the most formidable power on earth. For Hamilton the stability of the present union rested on close relations with Britain even to the extent of allowing it to expand its power in North America. For Jefferson potential control of the continent assured the expansion of the union and creation of an American empire. To acquiesce in British continental expansion would sacrifice the future to present exigencies—an unacceptable compromise.[10]

In a sense the conflict between Hamilton and Jefferson was a struggle between the preservation of what was and the vision of what might be. Was the union, as it existed, capable of sustaining economic independence through commercial and territorial expansion without undermining the foundations of the union? This question was not susceptible to an academic answer—that is, no judgment could be made about which answer was "realistic" or which "idealistic." Only in practice and over time could any theory be proven valid or invalid. Jefferson worked to answer the question affirmatively, Hamilton to answer no. Success, not judgment, was the proof of this pudding.

As discussed in previous chapters, Hamilton supported "giving a free course to Trade" to preserve his "commercial" (i.e., fiscal) system.[11] Operationally, this support meant acquiescence in existing foreign, chiefly British, restrictions on American trade. Jefferson, on the other hand, believed the government had "the obligation of effectuating free *markets*" for American goods. The distinction is crucial: "free trade" was not the same as "free markets." The sole means of "effectuating free markets" were commercial discrimination and reciprocity treaties. A nation that placed duties on American ships or goods had to be confronted by similar duties on its ships and goods in American ports. Agreements could then be reached between the parties to reduce duties and open their respective markets on reciprocal terms. Simply giving a "free course to Trade" was tantamount to relinquishing the nation's sovereign power to promote its economic well-being.[12]

Jefferson's foreign economic policy was twofold: commercial discrimination to "free" markets from restrictions on American trade and development of domestic industry to attain independence from closed markets. Ostensibly a universal foreign policy, in practice Jefferson's discrimination and domestic strategy was directed at Great Britain. England alone steadfastly refused to agree to reciprocal treaties with America. His strategy, then, demanded two countermoves: discriminate against English ships and products, and foster the development of an indigenous manufacturing base in America. The second move would serve to wean the United States from British manufactures *and* substitute a home market for those goods restricted in British and other European markets. He phrased it as an axiom: "If Europe will not let us carry our provisions to their manufactures we must endeavor to bring their manufactures to our provisions." It is of monumental importance to recognize that Jefferson's foreign policy mandated the development of domestic manufactures and that Hamilton's did not. Indeed, Hamilton's mandated the precise opposite: increased Anglo-American trade of raw materials for manufactured goods. As Merrill Peterson observes, "Ironically, the factories and workshops [Jefferson] had preferred to keep in Europe would the more likely result from his commercial system than from Hamilton's fiscal system."[13]

Jefferson's fundamental disagreement with Hamilton over foreign policy predated his alienation from Hamilton's fiscal policy. Indeed, it was in large measure the *cause* of his alienation. Granted, the rampant speculation of stockjobbers was repugnant to Jefferson, but it was distasteful and disruptive in Hamilton's opinion as well. When Jefferson first wrote friends of his dismay at the speculative binges, he stressed *not* "whether these measures be right or wrong, abstractedly," but that "more attention should be paid to the general opinion." Government "being founded on opinion, the opinion of the public, *even when it is wrong*, ought to be respected to a certain degree."[14] Apparently, it was not the funding nor even the unavoidable speculation that upset Jefferson, but the callous disregard of the small property-holders, "the public," and their almost total exclusion from what had been effectively the sole function of the new government until that time—funding the debt.

Jefferson realized that many citizens believed the government was employing its fiscal power to transfer wealth from the public to a handful of speculators. He recognized that some transfer of this sort was inevitable, perhaps even desirable for capital accumulation, but the burgeoning speculation and Hamilton's actions strained his belief that this transfer was merely an unavoidable consequence of the funding. Over the first half of 1791 he came to believe that the speculative transfer of wealth was not merely a side effect of funding but an essential goal of Hamilton's fiscal program. With good reason, he believed that the funding had ceased to be a necessary affirmation of the conditions of political society—property and contract. On the contrary, it had become a calculated effort to build a politically dominant mercantile faction in a few northern cities and, through the federal largesse and patronage, to employ that faction to subvert popular rule. Madison summed up Jefferson's and his own conclusions about Hamilton's fiscal program in a letter to his friend that July. "It pretty clearly appears also in what proportions the public debt lies in the Country. What sort of hands hold it, and by whom the people of the U.S. are to be governed. Of all the shameful circumstances of this business, it is among the greatest to see the members of the legislature who were active in pushing this Job openly grasping its emoluments."[15]

Not only was the fiscal program undermining the integrity of the political processes; it was enervating the economy and making an independent foreign policy impossible. "Our treasury," Jefferson angrily informed Monroe, "still thinks that these new encroachments of G. Brit. on our carrying trade must be met by passive obedience and non-resistance lest any misunderstanding with them should *affect our credit, or the prices of our public paper*."[16] Above all, he lamented the destructive effects of the "spirit of gambling in the public paper" on "Commerce, Manufactures, the Arts & agriculture. Every thing *useful* must be neglected, when the *useless* employment of money is so much more lucrative."[17] He could neither combat British efforts to control American commerce, nor advance domestic economic development: Hamilton blocked the former action for fear of his fiscal program, while speculation sapped the capital necessary for development of manufactures, shipping, and agriculture.

No single issue alienated Jefferson. Rather, the cumulative impact of Hamilton's fiscal program on the nation's economy and political stability created a major obstacle to the independence Jefferson had envisaged. All those attributes he believed essential to a republic — economic independence, political integrity, opportunity for small property holders and productive enterprise — were being sacrificed on a cross of paper. Again it was Madison who best articulated the nature of this crisis. "The true difference" between the Confederation and the Constitution, he wrote Jefferson, "seems to be that by the former the few were the victims of the many; by the latter the many to the few." Under Hamilton's system the "stock-jobbers will become the pretorian band of the Government, at once its tool & its tyrant; bribed by its largesses, & overawing it by clamours & combinations."[18]

Beginning in 1792 Madison and Jefferson moved in tandem against Hamilton's stabilization program. Their onslaught began with Jefferson's detailed indictment of Hamilton's fiscal program to Washington. He accused the "system" of "withdrawing our citizens from the pursuits of commerce, manufactures, buildings, and other branches of useful industry" to promote an immoral, corrupt, and destructive "species of gamblings." By corrupting legislators and ignoring constitutional constraints on federal power, Hamilton was subverting republican government.[19] What Jefferson expressed privately to Washington, Madison trumpeted publicly through a series of polemics in the *National Gazette*. There were, he explained, three types of government: military dictatorship, corrupt oligarchy, and republic. America was fast developing a government of the second sort. Because of the systemic bribery, avarice, and "corrupt influence," the federal government no longer worked for "the benefit of the whole" and now merely accommodated "its measures to the avidity of a part of the nation," fostering "a real domination of the few." The engine of domination was the "unnecessary accumulations of the debt of the Union" and the consequent aggregation of power and taxes to support it. Repeatedly, Madison hammered on the *unnecessary* accumulation of the debt for political purposes as the central failing of Hamilton's stabilization program. Not the obligations of contract, nor the accumulation of wealth, not the promotion of commercial or industrial enterprise, not federal taxes, but the corrupt enrichment of the few and the arrogant disregard for the many incensed Madison and Jefferson.[20]

The distinction between opposition to political uses of the debt and opposition to commercial development is best illustrated in their response to the SEUM and the Report on Manufactures. Jefferson first heard of the SEUM in April 1791 when Tench Coxe sent him a copy of the plan and an explanatory letter. Informing him about a new manufactory accorded with Jefferson's known advocacy of domestic manufacturing. But a moment's perusal of the letter and plan immediately shifted Jefferson's attention from manufacturing to the debt, corruption, and speculation. The "mode of raising *the fund*," Coxe wrote, "was obtained from the Secretary of the Treasury."[21] Given the manufactory's location in New Jersey near the center of speculation, New York City, and the fact that it was subscribable only in federal stock, Jefferson discerned in it only a "new scheme . . . for bringing more paper to market by encouraging great manufacturing companies to form." Hamilton, he believed, was incubating another plot to satisfy "the appetite for gambling" and weaken further the capital resources available to "commerce, manufactures, buildings, & agriculture."[22] Clearly, the basic issue for Jefferson was not large-scale factories versus household manufactures or industrialization versus independent yeomanry, but wasteful speculation versus productive uses of capital — uses that included manufacturing.

In response to Hamilton's Report on Manufactures, Jefferson and Madison focused their criticisms not on his advocacy of manufacturing but on his expansion of the general welfare provision of the Constitution. In the context of Hamilton's often expressed desire to increase federal powers beyond republican bounds and his informal aggrandizement of government support through the debt, they perceived in the report the subversion of the Constitution under the guise of aiding manufacturing.[23] To meet this challenge publicly, Madison chose to confront federal support of manufactures per se as well as to oppose expansion of federal powers beyond those clearly prescribed in the Constitution.[24]

From their perspective Hamilton's three main artifacts — the funding, the bank, and the SEUM — had become agents not of economic development but of political manipulation that enervated productive enterprise. Jefferson regretted his part in the assumption deal between Hamilton and Madison that fueled the speculation. The "gamblers" had won two successive victories in the bank and the SEUM. With the Report on Manufactures, there was no way of ascertaining the additional damage that direct federal bounties to these speculators might inflict on the republic. Burned by their acquiescence in his fiscal program, they were shy of all Hamilton's plans. The promise of the Report on Public Credit had not been kept, as speculation waxed and production waned. Despite Hamilton's grandiose claims of commercial and industrial prosperity, the bank and the SEUM had merely incited the speculation further. Not ideological repugnance at industry and commerce, but the politicization of the debt, rampant speculation, and economic stagnation had led Madison and Jefferson to oppose Hamilton's plans for manufacturing and banking.

Nonetheless, if the acid test of support for America's economic independence was support for domestic manufacturing, Madison and Jefferson stood firm for protective tariffs and nonimportation; Hamilton vacillated according to the needs of his fiscal system.[25] He acted sometimes with and sometimes against manufacturing, depending on the exigencies of the funding system, while Jefferson and Madison acted similarly, depending on the exigencies of economic independence. In the end it was not he but they who affirmed manufacturing because it came to be an essential condition of independence. It served no similar function in Hamilton's fiscal system; indeed, if anything, domestic manufacturing was a threat to importers and tariff revenues.

II

Jefferson and Madison had split with Hamilton over reconciling stability with republicanism, the weakening of the economy by speculation, and the aggrandizement of federal powers by loose construction of the Constitution. In a broad sense all these issues involved the question of an independent nation, economically and politically stable. Although most of this debate centered on the political aspects of stability, the bad commercial effects of speculation had weakened the economy. The war in Europe and Hamilton's successful campaign to negotiate and ratify the Jay Treaty made the issue of economic independence overshadow the rest.

For Jefferson, foreign policy involved a basic presupposition: "We have a right to judge what market best suits us, and they [the British] have none to forbid [it]."[26] To enforce this right Jefferson and Madison borrowed from the Revolutionary tactic of nonimportation in the more comprehensive form of commercial discrimination. Lacking the military power to compel concessions from European empires, Madison had proposed in the First Congress that America employ selective trade and tariff barriers to induce these concessions. "Nations," Jefferson explained, "may be brought to do justice by appeals to their interests as well as by appeals to arms." The value of the American market, its export of raw materials and import of finished goods, could restrain British aggressions on American commerce. Beyond this re-

straint, interruptions in the flow of manufactures would stimulate
America's own industry and lessen its dependence on England.
Whether through unrestricted international markets or industrial de-
velopment America would become economically independent.[27]

On December 16, 1793, Jefferson presented his Report on Commerce to the House. In it he provided a comprehensive statement of
the Republican political economy and policy proposals for the American economy. He and Madison hoped to employ it as a lever against
Hamilton's laissez-faire commercial policy. They sought to break England's economic hold on American trade through a reciprocity agreement (wrought by discriminatory tariffs and tonnage duties) or
through the development of domestic markets to replace English imports and exports. As Jefferson had observed earlier, either England
would open its markets to American products or America would bring
English manufacturing to the United States. His Report on Commerce
was a systematic plan for achieving one of these two goals.

Jefferson began by recounting the restrictions under which American commerce labored. He offered two methods of redress: "friendly
arrangements with the several nations" and "the separate acts of our
own legislatures of countervailing their effects." Although he praised
the ideal solution of commercial reciprocity—open markets in every
country—he recognized that "free commerce and navigation are not to
be given in exchange for restrictions and vexations; nor . . . to produce a relaxation of them." America's navigation had to be protected
from the economic hegemony of a foreign power. Without a strong
merchant marine, America's "productions will lie at the mercy of the
nation which has . . . the means of carrying them, and [American]
politics may be influenced by those who command its commerce."
Economic subordination begot political control and neocolonial status.[28]

Against high duties and prohibitions on American products, Jefferson proposed retaliation: "first burdening or excluding those productions which they bring here, in competition with our own of the same
kind; selecting next, such manufactures as we take from them in greatest quantity[,] . . . imposing on them duties lighter at first, but
heavier and heavier afterwards, as other channels of supply open." In
his proposal to foster manufacturing, protective tariffs were to be supplemented by "the State governments . . . opening the resources of
encouragement which are under their control [and] extending them
liberally." At the time, states aided manufacturers through loans, lot-
teries, and legal charters. Two aspects of Jefferson's proposal are salient. It involved, first of all, massive federal *and* state government aid to
large manufacturers capable of producing the goods imported from

Britain. In this respect his proposal is very similar to the one which Tench Coxe articulated, and Hamilton deleted, in an early draft of the Report on Manufacturers. Indeed, Hamilton did not even suggest state aid to manufacturers. Secondly, Jefferson explicitly differentiated "household" manufactures from the larger manufactories. The former would be fostered "by some patronage suited to the nature of its objects." His purpose was clearly not to elevate the self-sufficient farmer's handicrafts, but to loosen through domestic industry the hegemonic grip of Great Britain on America's market system.[29]

Throughout the remainder of the report Jefferson proposed a commercial lex talionis against all nations refusing reciprocity with the United States. Though "we must expect some inconvenience in practice from the establishment of discriminating duties," he explained, these "are nothing when weighed against the loss of wealth and loss of force, which will follow our perseverance in the plan of indiscrimination." This "plan of indiscrimination" was Hamilton's brainchild. Again, the issue for Jefferson was not free trade or laissez-faire but "fair and equal access to market with our productions," wrought by "our own means of independence and the firm will to use them."[30]

In Congress Madison used the report to promote legislation for commercial discrimination and the development of manufactures. Aided by the British seizures of late 1793 and early 1794 he managed to pass some measures of retaliation against England, but Hamilton's peace policy undercut his success. Madison's failure to effect a policy change resulted in passage of the Jay Treaty. Jefferson wrote Madison that the merchants were "open mouthed at first against the treaty . . . but the general spirit of indignation has alarmed them for the strength of the government."[31] Both abhorred the treaty. Madison listed four principal sacrifices of American interests. The treaty allowed Britain to counter the American tonnage duty discount to domestically manufactured ships, weakened the rights of neutrals, insured continued British control of the fur trade and consequent influence over the Indians, and barred the United States from granting commercial favors to other nations in exchange for reciprocal favors without extending such favors to Britain. This last sacrifice "would monopolize us to G.B. by precluding any material improvement of our existing Treaties, or the hope of any new ones that would be of much advantage to us." Madison concluded that the "whole Treaty . . . assassinates the interest" of American merchants.[32]

Jefferson and Madison's failure to block the treaty or alter its terms led them to conclude that a profound political crisis was at hand. Jefferson articulated the crisis to Madison. "Where the rights, the interest, the honor & faith of our nation are so grossly sacrificed;

where a faction has entered into a conspiracy with the enemies of their country to chain down the legislature at the feet of both; where the whole mass of your constituents have condemned this in the most unequivocal manner, and are looking to you as their last hope to save them from the effect of the avarice & corruption of the first agent, the revolutionary machinations of others, and the incomprehensible acquiescence of the only honest man who assented to it."[33] Hamilton and his phalanx of partisans were in control; Washington was subdued; and Madison, leading a small group in the House, alone resisted the apocalypse. The crisis demanded extraordinary action.

To prevent what they believed to be the destruction of the republic, Jefferson and Madison began to organize the dissident groups within each state into a national party. Their decision to factionalize American politics was not made lightly. The organization of a national party was difficult. It involved building on the extensive networks of state political groupings that had arisen from a complex interaction of local and national issues. In most of the states outside the South, political leaders sympathetic to them were not in power. They needed to broach new organizational and campaign techniques to unseat incumbents. Within the South the planter elite was easily converted with little grassroots political activity. Elsewhere, necessity, not choice, mandated the Republican inauguration of popular politics; there was no other means of unseating Federalist officials. Republican leaders justified it as a legitimate popular groundswell to dislodge a faction from power. Once victorious, the leadership tried to retreat as much as possible from majoritarian party politics and return to the informal, consensual rule of elites that characterized the pre-Revolutionary era.[34]

At the national level the last years of the 1790s were a time for Republicans to wait and obstruct. In Congress, Madison found a new and very effective ally, Albert Gallatin. Together they sought to block funding of the Jay Treaty commissioners. Gallatin managed to pass several resolutions requiring extensive reports on Treasury Department activities. They fought Federalists effort to make war on France—an action they believed would be tantamount to formal alliance with England. The French were a disease of the skin; the English, of the blood. Finally, they struggled against domestic political repression authorized by the Alien and Sedition Acts. Compelled to defend Republican editors, they expanded the definition of freedom of the press beyond exemption from prior constraint. As in the case of grassroots politics, once in power the Republican leadership retreated somewhat from the First Amendment vanguard to jail an opposition editor or two themselves.[35] Despite growing Federalist political repression, Jefferson still found dissent repugnant. "Political dissension," he wrote to Thomas Pinckney, "is a great evil, and it would be as worthy the efforts of the patriot as of the philosopher, to exclude it's [sic] influence, if possible, from social life."[36] Factionalizing American politics was something Jefferson and Madison were compelled to do; they perceived no intrinsic benefit from a permanent party system.

III

The words and actions of Jefferson and Madison before and during the period of their leadership of a national political movement reveal consistently pragmatic economic and political policies. Their strong criticisms of Hamilton's programs and centralization of power were rooted not in vague philosophical notions but in a hardheaded analysis of the destructive effects his actions had on the economy and the political cohesion of the union. Rather than opposing federal power or commercial enterprise per se, they opposed Hamilton's use of them to create a government of a faction, by a faction, for a faction. What ideological assumptions the Republican leaders made were common to members of America's ruling elites. Individual preferences for noble yeomen, manufacturers, or free trade cannot be identified as policy determinants because policymaking involved too many different actors with diverse views. Only comprehensive assumptions wedded to specific problems can explain Republican policies.

The limited-government, yeoman-farmer rhetoric of Republican leaders might best be interpreted as a polemical device to attack those activities conducted under Hamilton's aegis, which ran against their concept of a liberal political system, and to attract support from small farmers in a transitional phase between family-centered agriculture and market-oriented production. The breakup of the constitutional coalition's leadership, then, was not a product of Jefferson's and Madison's philosophical distaste for finance or economic development. On the contrary, when the causes of the slow dissolution of consensus among America's ruling elites after ratification of the Constitution are detailed, the evidence points to *specific* disagreements over programmatic issues and not fundamental schisms over the essential role of government. In other words, it was to what ends the federal government exercised its power, rather than philosophical objections to the exercise of federal power per se, that the Republican leadership called into question.

The disagreement was not over federal action to repay the debt but over Hamilton's methods, which encouraged speculation and enriched a few financiers. It was not over the prospect of federal legislation regulating trade and compelling foreign nations to open their markets or face reprisals, including the development of domestic manufacturing, but over Hamilton's efforts to prevent commercial sanctions against England and his overall *unwillingness* to exercise federal power in this manner. It was not over Hamilton's alleged support of manufacturing but over his use of manufacturing to sanction speculative windfalls and expand federal subsidies to a faction. It was not about American resistance to all foreign domination but about the use of France's relatively minor aggressions to place the United States further under the economic hegemony of England. It was not about federal suppression of factions through imprisonment and fines but about a faction's tyranny over advocates of the "true" public interest through repressive laws. In short, it was not the exercise of federal power that alienated Republican leaders but the exercise of that power to realize ends they perceived as inimical to the interests of the nation as a whole.

There are two distinct elements of this interpretation, one involving ends and another involving means. After the Revolution a consensus existed among American leaders concerning the nature and purpose of political society. They shared a common grounding in liberal thought. Through this world view they analyzed the America of the 1780s and identified certain significant problems. Then, still operating on liberal premises, they created a new political structure to correct these problems and bring society's workings more in line with their world view. Hamilton's practical methods of correcting these problems—his political economy—grew out of this shared world view. Yet his methods, though employing structurally legitimate (constitutional) means, were such that in themselves they threatened to undermine certain essential elements of the liberal world view. This threat was articulated in the critique of his methods offered by the two most significant opposition leaders, Madison and Jefferson. Despite their violent disagreement, no one on either side questioned private property, contract, the continued leadership of large property holders, or the need to retain a central government. Indeed, no one seriously attacked the Constitution itself. Their disagreement was over the extent to which Hamilton was unnecessarily sacrificing some essential principles to secure others.

Jefferson and Madison believed Hamilton was compromising elements of the liberal world view unnecessarily, under the penumbra of securing other elements. Simply stated, the security of the political structure was in Hamilton's mind dependent on enlisting a major section of the mercantile elite, dependent on British trade, in support of that structure. For Jefferson and Madison, the public spectacle, the injury to the economy, the threat to national independence, the politicization of the debt, and the flagrant disregard of small property holders damaged the federal government and its ability to insure a stable society far beyond any support afforded by these few merchants. Indeed, the damage was so extensive that they began to question whether Hamilton shared their world view at all, whence the charge of monarchist. Hamilton viewed their criticisms as reckless and anarchical. Above all, Madison and Jefferson came to believe that Hamilton's methods inevitably subordinated American to English hegemony — a charge Hamilton implicitly accepted. The fundamental conflict of the 1790s was neither over the ultimate purposes of political society nor over the exercise of federal power to realize those purposes, but over the effects of particular policies and programs and a general distortion of the purposes toward which power could be legitimately exercised.

The issues of corruption and faction illustrate the methods-and-proximate-ends explanation of political conflict in this period. Hamilton employed the debt payments to reinforce his congressional support and secure a Federalist constituency. Jefferson and Madison objected not to promoting a strong government or repaying the accumulated debt but to sacrificing national unity and economic independence in an effort to protect a *rentier* faction and its congressional cabal. In essence they argued: if judicious use of the debt enhances national independence and political stability, then use the debt judiciously. Soon, however, it became obvious to them that manipulations of the debt were undermining independence and inciting dissent. When they pleaded to no avail with Hamilton to adjust his methods, Jefferson and Madison concluded that he had ceased to be a statesman concerned with the whole nation and had become the leader of a pro-British faction. The only solution was to throw the rascal and his "fellow-travelers" within the Federalist Party (including John Adams) out of government and rebuild the original constitutional coalition, avoiding some of the more egregious political errors Hamilton had committed. They began this process in 1796, when Jefferson opposed Adams in the presidential election. Though Jefferson was defeated, the two Virginians with Gallatin at their side continued to build their party and bide their time until 1800.

CHAPTER SIX

Economic Origins of the Republican Political Coalition

We are daily making improvements in the manufacture of Cloths and are in hopes of procuring Machines . . . so as to enable us to meet the British on equal terms: and that as soon as the rage for Speculation in the funds of the United States shall have ceased, part of the Money of the country, which now circulates only in paper traffic, may be directed into this channel for the aid of our infant Manufactures.
—Elisha Colt, a Connecticut manufacturer, to John Chester, a Treasury agent, August 20, 1791

What[,] are they going to Tax our Cloath too[?]
—Anselm Bailey, a Virginia clothmaker, to Thomas Newton, Jr., a Treasury agent, responding to the latter's request for information on Virginia manufactures, August 23, 1791

The line is now drawing so clearly as to shew on one side 1. the fashionable circles of Phil, N. York, Boston & Charleston (natural aristocrats), 2. merchants trading on British capitals, 3. paper men (all the old tories are found in some one of these three descriptions). On the other side are 1. merchants trading on their own capitals, 2. Irish merchants, 3. tradesmen, mechanics, farmers & every other possible description of our citizens.
—Jefferson to Madison, May 12, 1793

Within a liberal political system the demands and reactions of propertied citizens are the crucible through which government policies must pass. What economic interest groups supported the Republican party and why are basic questions in the analysis of the party leadership's political economy in this period. In a republican political system political leaders must be responsive to their constituencies. The grassroots composition of a party reveals much about the leadership's programs and their impact on the society. The interaction between the world view of the leadership and the interests of its political constituency must be taken into account in any analysis of policymaking.

I

The great issue in late-eighteenth-century America was national independence, both political and economic. Political independence came with the success of the Revolution, but the completion of independence was in substance an economic issue. Liberal thought held that a nation, like an individual, must be self-sufficient to be free and independent. Self-sufficiency meant autarky, but not in the sense of a commercially isolated entity, as early liberals conceived of China. Rather, it meant a national economy capable of sustaining political actions to maintain conditions for economic growth and prosperity. Foreign markets or territorial expansion might be integral to an expanding economy. In this respect, independence depended on external conditions. Such dependence, however, was only admissible insofar as the basic strength of the economy could secure through diplomacy or military coercion the external circumstances needed for domestic prosperity.

Great Britain was the classic counterexample to China. Though her prosperity depended on world-wide commercial intercourse, England's military power secured its commerce and independence. Although its navy was the agency of independence, it was not the cause. "It is [Britain's] internal industry," Albert Gallatin explained in Congress, "and the protection afforded to manufacturers and commerce which have produced its wealth, that wealth has produced its immense commerce and has enabled them to support a powerful navy."[1] In other words, political independence rested on comprehensive economic development. A strong economy provided the means to sustain growth, resist imperialism, and realize national independence.

America in the early 1790s had a strong agricultural base and a growing merchant marine. Britain's continuing effort to control American trade and markets threatened the expansion of agriculture and shipping. Both to provide an alternative home market and the means of defense, America required an industrial base. Manufacturing was a necessary ingredient to an independent economy capable of assuring the political power to enforce commercial interests in territory and trade. In this respect manufacturing was synonymous with national independence. The greatest threat to independence was the economic hegemony of Great Britain's manufactures and navy. A syllogism of sorts developed out of this situation: national independence required breaking Britain's hold on the American economy; Britain's hold could be broken only by domestic manufacturing; thus, national independence required the development of manufacturing. And conversely, rapprochement with Britain meant neocolonial status for the United States. For these reasons, American manufacturers were a vital component in the political and economic struggles of the 1790s. Though relatively few, they were in symbol and fact the vanguard of an economically independent nation.

The manufacturing interest was heterogeneous in the late eighteenth century. Before the Revolution wage labor was relatively rare in domestic manufacturing, but population growth in the urban areas steadily eroded guildlike labor relations and made wage employment more common. The demographic changes and rapid economic expansion of the 1790s swelled the number of mechanics and workers and provided a labor pool for the new enterprises stimulated by the commercial expansion. The mechanic-manufacturer ranks became a critical urban political constituency whose support of the Constitution insured ratification and whose support of the Republicans would in 1800 put Jefferson in the White House.

Nomenclature is important, since it reveals an aspect of consciousness which indicates individual identification with larger socioeconomic groups. A mechanic or "manu-facturer" was one who worked with his hands in a nonagricultural endeavor. An entrepreneur could be subsumed under the terms "master mechanic" or "master manufacturer." In a very large enterprise the master mechanic might be only a foreman and the entrepreneur a manager in the more modern sense. Contemporaries also used "tradesman" to denote a manufacturer of a particular craft or trade. These broad categories subsumed the numerous crafts—coopers, cordwainers, ironmongers, ropemakers, sailmakers, shipwrights, and so forth. Nonetheless, when they organized or petitioned, these various crafts called themselves mechanics, tradesmen, and manufacturers. It is therefore not invalid to identify their shared consciousness as a manufacturing interest group.[2]

By no means was there perfect correspondence among manufacturers. At least three major divisions existed among them: those involved in shipbuilding and outfitting, those in consumer goods, and those in household manufactures. Among these groups the consumer-goods producers were probably the largest. Most were protected from import competition by natural barriers: they produced customer-specific items or items unsuited to mass production, they were in the construction trades, or they were quasi-service-providers such as tailors, blacksmiths, and cobblers. These artisans were concerned largely with the general economic prosperity of their locale and were indirectly affected by commercial changes that affected their area's economy. Among those very directly affected by commerce, the largest were the maritime trades of shipbuilding and related support industries that congregated in and around shipping centers. These manufacturers called themselves shipwrights, tradesmen, and manufacturers. The central thrust of their political demand in the 1790s was a strong federal navigation law. They sought to encourage the use of American-made ships in commerce and to counter the discrimination of foreign nations, particularly Great Britain, against American bottoms.

Most of these manufacturers were very specific about the kind of navigation laws they wanted and the direction they wanted American foreign commercial policy to take. Charleston's shipwrights wanted discrimination used against foreign nations without commercial treaties with the United States.[3] Philadelphia's shipwrights sought to establish "principles of reciprocity" with Britain and Spain similar to those then existing with France. They proposed the same duties on all foreign-built ships regardless of ownership, no duty on American-made ships, and diplomatic efforts to secure commercial reciprocity abroad.[4] These sentiments were echoed among shipbuilders in other cities.[5]

For shipbuilders, navigation laws were tantamount to protective tariffs. Ancillary industries such as sailcloth and cordage manufacturing sought more specific tariff protection against foreign imports. In Boston, Norfolk, and New Hampshire, cordage and sailcloth manufacturers worried about competition from British and Russian producers. Capital shortages and inadequate local supplies of hemp (for rope) and flax (for sails) inhibited the expansion of these manufactures.[6] A ropery owner in Virginia thought "the Duty laid on imported Cordage . . . not sufficient to encourage him as most of the Ships are British & give a preference to English Cordage." This preference persisted despite the higher price and inferior quality of the English product.[7] General postwar declines in all shipbuilding industries were also attributed to English ships and imperial restrictions. Not surprisingly, these manufacturers supported Madison's proposals for discrimination against British commerce.[8]

Manufacturers of consumption goods that had to compete with imports pointed out two salient problems: British imports and capital shortages. As noted earlier, these manufacturers looked toward federal tariffs to alleviate "the misfortune of a foreign intercourse" and unfetter America from the "commercial shackles which have so long bound her."[9] They produced glass, iron, linen, cotton cloth, woolens, hats, buttons, leathers, and other products in direct competition with English imports. Though concentrated in the northern coastal states, they extended as far south as Carolina and as far west as the Allegheny

Mountains. Competition from imports harassed all these manufacturers in several ways. The "price of all kinds of Manufactures," William Williams of Connecticut observed, "are very much governed by that of imports." Connecticut "Hatters Complain that Foreign Importations Yet, very Much Injure the business here." Tanners and saddle-makers "suppose that the duty on imported Saddles is not sufficiently high . . . [and] that the duty on tanned leather is too low." Rhode Island's tanners, too, were harmed, "owing to the large Quantities of Leather imported from the West Indies, the Duty on which is small."[10] Across the Union, cloth, paper, button, and glass manufacturers all repeated these demands for tariff protection from imports. And whenever they specified a foreign competitor, that competitor was Great Britain.[11]

British competition assumed a more invidious form in its use of credit and agents in the American market. Moses Brown of Providence, a prominent merchant-entrepreneur, explained: "British Agents have been Out in this and Other Manufacturing Towns with Large Quantities of Cotton Goods for Sale and strongly Solisiting [sic] correspondence of people in the Mercantile Line to Receive their Goods at very long Cre[dit] . . . doubtless for the Discouragement of the Manufactory here. The bate [sic] has been too Eagerly taken by Our Merchants." Brown conceived of this practice in conspiratorial terms. The "Abilities of the Manufacturing Interests of Great Britain to intercept the sale of Our Own Goods, at a price as low as theirs has been heretofore sold by Our Importing Merchants, the Actual Combination of them . . . forms a very great Discouragement of Men of Abilities to lay Out their Property in Extending Manufactures."[12]

The technique of these British agents was simple. American manufacturers were plagued by cash shortages. They required prompt payment from retail merchants and shopkeepers to finance raw materials, labor, capital replacement, and expansion. British exporters, on the other hand, had huge credit reserves. They could discount their commercial paper at any bank, as could their American counterparts. They gave manufactures to retailers on consignment for extended periods and employed their large cash reserves to carry on the trade while awaiting sales. Domestic manufacturers lacked the resources to compete with this sort of credit extension. Thus, even if the transportation costs and tariffs raised British goods to a price American producers could match, the produce credit limitations often caused them to lose market outlets.[13]

American manufacturers were strapped for capital. Banks of this era discounted only commercial paper and never lent on real property. Indeed, part of the reason importing merchants could offer good credit terms to retailers was precisely the support rendered by state banks and the Bank of the United States. The merchant-directors of these institutions would hardly consider lending money to domestic manufacturers in competition with their fellow importers and their own businesses.[14] Finally, most venture capital, which might have been invested in manufactures, was absorbed by the omnipresent sponge of stock and land speculation. This situation led Peter Colt, a Connecticut arms manufacturer, to hope that "when the Active Stock of the Citizens shall no longer be embarked in paper Speculations, then we may expect to see part of it turned to the promoting & extending our manufactures & then those which languish and dwindle for want of being supported by proper Capitals may be expected to prosper & this Country freed from a disgraceful dependence on Europe for their ordinary cloathing."[15]

Speculation in federal stock was a serious problem not only to manufacturers. The demand it placed on funds available for loans drove up interest rates. High interest rates raised discount rates for commercial paper and increased the cost of trade to merchants. Prices on imports rose while demand for exports declined in a sluggish commerce. Investment in land fell off, lowering the value of farms. Capital for farmers, merchants, and manufacturers became very expensive. Hamilton was well aware of these effects, since he had warned of them in his Report on Public Credit. In that context he had used them to advance the cause of federal funding and assumption.[16] Funding and assumption, however, had not eliminated speculation in government securities.

Most manufactories of consumption goods were smaller than shipbuilding industries. A few, however, employed over forty people in cotton textile production. One Massachusetts concern boasted sixteen hundred women and children in their "putting-out" workforce.[17] Women and immigrants were the mainstay of the labor force in these and other industries. Surprisingly, one manufacturer reported skilled labor to be cheaper than in Britain, but he added that unskilled labor was much dearer. There was hope that child labor could compensate for unskilled adults. Another manufacturer noted that "poor children, who, while they are earning Something toward their subsistence, are prevented from contracting bad habits, and are introduced thereby to a Habit of Industry, by which we may hope to see them useful Members of Society."[18] In addition to protective tariffs, these manufacturers requested government loans, contracts, and inspection of products to control quality. Significantly, northern manufacturers exported their goods to southern states and the West Indies. These exports included woolens, cotton cloth, iron, leather, furnishings, and several other items. This trade was substantial enough to induce Tench Coxe to attack the Jay Treaty publicly for its restrictions on manufactured exports to the West Indies.[19]

Among the more vexing problems of political analysis in this era is the political affiliation of large manufacturers. Insofar as Coxe reflected the politics of these manufacturers, one can infer that at least some became Republicans. Jefferson had a close personal relationship with the munitions maker Pierre DuPont as well as a nascent political following among manufacturers in Brandywine Valley. Though apolitical, Eli Whitney also established an early rapport with Jefferson. Matthew Lyon, an iron manufacturer, became a Republican. There were others. Undoubtedly, the rising entrepreneurial character of the northern Republicans accorded with the interests of these manufacturers. Moreover, Republican banks often arose to provide credit and capital to groups excluded by Federalist institutions. "Farmers and Mechanics" banks, founded at the end of the 1790s, reflected in their nomenclature their economic orientation. During this period, however, state aid far outweighed federal support. Whatever the impact of national policies, a Federalist state legislature might find it politic to make loans available to manufacturers and assure, if not their political allegiance, at least their acquiescence. This road could be traveled both ways; Republicans might sway Federalist manufacturers with similar aid. (This important question of state versus Federal aid is taken up in greater detail in Chapter 10.) During the 1790s the evidence of large manufacturer support for Republicans is scattered and ambiguous.[20]

The most common manufactures in this period were household. Homespun clothing and household goods were the products of farm women providing necessities for themselves and their families. They produced their own because they lacked either the money or the access to commercial manufactures. Protective tariffs, therefore, would have little impact on their output. Still, many household producers mixed purchases of goods with homespun and could turn more toward one source than the other depending on price fluctuations. The principal interaction of farmers and manufacturers occurred in the crude processing of farm products into more marketable forms: tobacco into snuff, wheat into flour, grain into whiskey. These manufactures—and they were considered manufactures by all concerned—were widespread and important to the farm community, especially in the western areas of the nation.[21]

Although farmers and manufacturers were connected materially in their exchange of consumption goods for farm produce, their strongest link was in this crude processing of farm produce for markets. Farmers often doubled as distillers. Regardless of its narrow application, the federal excise on liquor was seen by all as a tax on manufactures. Hamilton defended it as such; distillers and farmers attacked it as such. And all who identified themselves with manufacturers felt threatened by it as bad precedent. When Treasury agents made inquiries among Virginia household manufacturers concerning their output, products, and problems, some refused information for fear of subsequent taxation. When the excise passed Congress and Hamilton dispatched a swarm of tax collectors into western Pennsylvania, the urban Democratic Societies condemned the law as an affront to all manufacturers. The societies were also bastions of manufacturers. Though the excise was a tax on manufactures, it was farmers who rose to combat it and against whom Hamilton marched his federal militia.[22]

One perceives a small-producer consciousness in all these groups of manufacturers, a consciousness created during the Revolution and shared by many small farmers. While the manufacturers found government excise tax levies repugnant, they sought aid, protection, and recognition from the great men of Philadelphia. They were democratic, for in democracy lay their hopes for an impact on government policies. They were nationalistic, for their prosperity depended on a strong and independent economy. They were the progeny of the "Spirit of '76" born in the General Societies of Mechanics and Tradesmen. Their small-producer consciousness ultimately found a home in the Republican party as the events of the 1790s again transformed collective thought into political action.

II

The breakdown of the manufacturers' alliance with Hamilton and the Federalists began with a tension implicit in the constitutional coalition. Hamilton oriented his program to large merchants and speculators, the centerpiece of his support. His tariff proposals were deemed inadequate by the goods producers in shipbuilding and nonshipbuilding industries. Shipbuilders thought federal navigation laws an insufficient counterbalance to British regulations. Rampant speculation in securities pressed all manufacturers for capital at reasonable interest rates. Hamilton's program engendered this speculation and proved incapable of controlling it. Above all loomed the British, their imports, their ships, their credit, their American correspondents. More than the excise, antipathy to Great Britain brought together the disparate manufacturers. Such antipathy boded ill for a man who believed a connection with Britain to be in best interests of America.

After the conflict over the issue of tariff and navigation laws, a major rupture occurred between Hamilton and manufacturers as a result of the SEUM. Most of the other societies for promoting manufacturers disseminated technical information and offered prizes for new machinery or loans to manufactures. The SEUM did not. On the contrary, it was a quasi-public corporation engendered by wealthy speculators and aided by the New Jersey legislature. The SEUM offered nothing but competition to existing producers. Although a few manufacturers expressed interest in the project, speculation and mismanagement soon disenchanted them. Other manufacturers raised a hue and cry over this "political monster" as a creature of speculation sapping the foundation of industry.[23]

George Logan, who ran the gamut from president of the Germantown Society for Promoting Domestic Manufacturing through Democratic Society organizer to Republican senator, attacked the SEUM as a monopoly constructed for the speculators. "Should this scheme take place," he warned, "a valuable class of citizens, *personally engaged* in useful manufactures, will be sacrificed to the wealthy few." Logan held up the society as symbolic of the government's orientation toward wealth and privilege in its laws and programs. Finally, he made the inevitable connection to British efforts to suppress American manufactures. "Had the Court of Britain," he harangued, "pensioned a number of men in America, to effect the ruin of the infant manufactures of our country, they could not have adopted a scheme better calculated to answer that purpose, than the scheme of DUER and HAMILTON."[24] Had Logan been privy to Beckwith's reports and codes, he might have believed this charge to be more than hyperbole.

The "panic" of March 1792, which wounded the SEUM mortally, further strained Hamilton's relations with urban manufacturers. In New York the manufacturers were already angered by the Federalist-controlled assembly's rejection of their petition for incorporation of their General Society. The collapse of the market destroyed Duer and ruined many tradesmen who had lent him money. Hamilton's efforts through his urban allies to control the stock speculation and commercial expansion only exacerbated tensions between the manufacturer-mechanic interest and the Federalist leadership. The subsequent recession and tight money weakened Federalist support among manufacturers.[25] The scene was repeated in Maryland and other areas affected by the market's collapse.[26] As yet, however, no event had crystallized manufacturers into organized opposition against Hamilton's program. Then England and France went to war.

In part the excise, in part sympathy with France and opposition to England, but principally the sense among manufacturers, mechanics, small farmers, merchants trading outside the British empire, and oth-

ers that those administering the government were abrogating their interests led to the formation of the Democratic Societies in 1793.
Though specific in their economic demands, the societies recaptured
part of the Revolutionary spirit and a strong sense that the government
had grown away from many of its citizens. They became a lobby for a
more democratic republic. This ideological stance flowed naturally
from the members' perception that their economic interests were not
adequately considered in policy decisions. Economic growth, the
profits from stock speculation, and heavy immigration increased both
the wealth and the poverty in the seaport cities. Federalists sought to
impose their policies and politics on manufacturers and mechanics.
The manufacturers and mechanics concluded that the government was
unrepresentative and, owing to its solicitude of large merchant-
creditors and Great Britain, aristocratic as well. The Democratic Societies, as Eugene Link observes, "rolled up mass opposition to the
antidemocratic tendencies of the period."[27]

From Charleston to Boston, in the cities and the hinterlands, societies were organized. A typical society was led by merchants and master manufacturers. Its rank and file consisted chiefly of mechanics and
manufacturers, with significant elements of the farm community and a
sprinkling of seamen, lawyers, and physicians. Proportions varied
with location. Many Irish, Scotch, and German immigrants entered
the societies. Opposition to British economic hegemony and ideological kinship with France's revolutionaries welded the members together.
The corollary to anglophobic sentiments was strong advocacy of domestic manufactures. Organizations of manufacturers and mechanics
shared membership and goals with the Democratic Societies. In virtual concert they demanded an end to the liquor excise, resistance to
Britain, protection for manufactures and American-made ships, and
an end to the Treasury Department's alliance with the rentiers. In
essence, they sought to restructure radically Hamilton's stabilization
program.[28]

The societies' leadership was perhaps the most significant and striking political alliance of the 1790s: merchants trading outside the British empire and manufacturers. In New York City's society the presidents included David Gelston and James Nicholson. Both were very
wealthy merchants; Nicholson was Gallatin's father-in-law. Among
the leaders of Philadelphia's society was John Swanwick, another prosperous merchant. The majority of established merchants shunned the
societies, yet, in numbers too large to be ignored and with wealth
equal to the Federalist grandees, merchants assumed key positions in
the Democratic Societies of the nation's cities.[29]

The political activities of the societies peaked between 1794 and

1795, with the Whiskey Rebellion and British commercial depredations serving as rallying points for this activism. The societies, however, did not survive concerted Federalist efforts to destroy them. Washington's condemnation and the links to armed rebellion imputed to the societies by their critics were blows from which they could not recover. Despite an ephemeral existence, they demonstrated that manufacturers and mechanics were not alone in their dissension and foreshadowed the coalition of merchants, farmers, and manufacturers that would constitute the Republican party after 1795. Finally, the societies revealed that the economic concerns of significant groups of citizens could translate into an activist commercial program opposed to Hamilton's. The key elements of this program were opposition to British economic hegemony in any form, support of domestic manufactures, and advocacy of world trade restricted only by choice. With the passing of the Democratic Societies, many merchants, mechanics, and manufacturers throughout America looked toward the nascent Republican party to continue the battle for these goals.[30]

III

Because the merchant connection of Hamilton's stabilization program has been much touted, recognition must be accorded to the significant group of wealthy merchants who came to oppose his program in the mid-1790s: the Crowinshields of Salem, James Nicholson of New York, Stephen Girard and John Swanwick of Philadelphia, and Samuel Smith of Baltimore.[31] They were all merchants of substantial wealth and all leaders of Hamilton's opponents. In common they conducted a significant and very lucrative trade with non-British markets in the French West Indies, continental Europe, South America, and to a much lesser extent, the Orient. Since they traded largely outside the British empire, they carried fewer of the English manufactures than their Federalist brethren. Breadstuffs, salted fish, some American manufactures, and reexports filled their holds for the West Indies and Europe. Since their ships went largely to Britain's enemies, they suffered when the Royal Navy seized six hundred American ships in a five-month period after November 1793.

It is instructive to examine briefly the political and economic characteristics of these significant Republican merchants. In Salem the Crowinshield family experienced a serious decline in their business during the 1780s.[32] They attributed this bad fortune to British restrictions on their trade. Faced with the closed markets of European empires they broached a new trade with the Orient. When war began in 1793, they entered the burgeoning trade with the French West Indies and Europe. By 1795 their newest ship, the *America,* had the distinction of being the largest merchant vessel in the country. It symbolized their growing prosperity. The family was hurt by British seizures in 1794 and vehemently opposed America's acquiescence in the terms of the Jay Treaty. About this time Jacob became the family's political spokesman and a prominent Republican leader in Massachusetts. Subsequent to the treaty, Jacob led forces opposing a Franco-American conflict which threatened their French West Indian and Mediterranean trade.

The Crowinshields continued to support Jefferson and the Republicans in the nineteenth century. They upheld the embargo of 1807 and advocated nonimportation from Britain. Jacob pressed for U.S. seizure of the Floridas in 1804. From 1803, he served as a Republican spokesman in Congress and would have, if he had lived, become Jefferson's secretary of the navy. During these years he established a state bank in Salem despite Federalist opposition in the state legislature. His desire to break the hold of the pro-English, Federalist establishment on finance led not only to the Salem bank, but to his opposition to rechartering the symbol of old-line wealth, the Bank of the United States. He and his family were advocates of entrepreneurial opportunity, economic growth, and access to new markets and capital. The Crowinshields were the preeminent link between the Republican leadership and their New England constituency. They led and symbolized the "powerful Republican commercial interest" which Paul Goodman identifies in Massachusetts.

New York's James Nicholson supported the Constitution and captained the barge carrying President-elect Washington to his inauguration. A wealthy merchant with broad trading interests, Nicholson became president of New York's Society for the Encouragement of Manufactures in 1792. With the opening of the French West Indies he expanded his commercial dealing with France and became a supply agent of its fleet. For Genêt and his successor, Nicholson arranged loans and government purchases in New York. Outraged by British restrictions on Franco-American trade, he helped to found New York's Democratic Society and served as president. Nicholson was in the forefront of the mechanic-merchant protest against Jay's Treaty, and his conflicts with Hamilton nearly resulted in a duel between them. Throughout the 1790s and until his death he maintained close ties with his son-in-law, Albert Gallatin, and championed the Republican party in New York. He epitomized the small but growing group of Republican merchants in the state.[33]

John Swanwick and Stephen Girard reveal the pattern and leadership of Republican merchants in Philadelphia. They pioneered the commercial expansion into the French West Indies and France. Girard, soon to be among the richest men in America, was particularly injured by British seizures throughout these two decades. As a French immigrant, he was often treated as a French national by Admiralty courts. Girard expanded his Latin American trade in the early 1800s and ran guns to revolutionaries in the region with President Madison's tacit approval. Throughout his life the British navy harassed his trade to foster its own merchants. Girard's Republicanism was intensely anti-English.[34]

Swanwick joined the Democratic Society in Philadelphia to protest British economic hegemony. He opposed the liquor excise. In Congress, he became chairman of the House Committee on Commerce and Manufactures. There, he worked to bar British goods as punishment for England and an aid to American manufactures. Indeed, his 1794 election to Congress as the first Philadelphia Republican came about through strong manufacturer-mechanic support. Philadelphia in general had a very large group of merchants trading outside the British empire; their investments and political ties also encompassed manufacturing. Swanwick expressed their credo in a campaign speech advocating a "balanced economy given to commerce, manufactures, shipping, and agriculture."[35]

Among the leading Republican merchants none attained the national prominence of Samuel Smith of Baltimore.[36] Like the Crowinshields, Smith saw his trade decline in the closed West Indian markets of the 1780s. A Federalist in 1788, he anticipated the central government's aid in breaking these commercial fetters. The 1793 war boom made him one of the wealthiest merchants in Baltimore. Although injured by the 1794 seizures, he still prospered from his West Indian trade, which included both the French and British islands. A champion of new business he founded a state bank and ran successfully for Congress in 1792 with the help of the mechanic-manufacturer vote. Because of the conflict with Britain, Smith joined the Republicans in Congress and opposed Jay's Treaty. He opposed Federalist military preparations against France and the government's continued acquiescence in English assaults on trade. Smith's strong nationalism, his refusal to truckle to either major power, and his opposition to the excise tax consolidated his support among mechanics and merchants. Angered in particular over the harm the Alien Laws inflicted on foreign commercial agents and trade in Baltimore, he assumed the leadership of Maryland's Republicans by the end of the 1790s.

Elected to the Senate in 1800, Smith consistently resisted British restrictions on commerce. He and other Baltimore merchants led

America's economic penetration into Latin America. Where his constituents benefited, he supported high tariffs; otherwise, moderate duties were adequate. His dislike of the Bank of the United States' competition with his Bank of Maryland and political squabbles with Gallatin induced him to oppose recharter in 1811. If anything, Smith's early conversion to the Republican party was more measured than that of his Baltimore constituents of merchants and manufacturers.

The differences among these five merchants demonstrate that there was no monolithic mold for a Republican merchant. Like the hundreds they represented and led, their interests and motivations varied. Nonetheless, they had in common an entrepreneurial orientation in their business pursuits and a lack of strong establishment ties. Mechanics and manufactures figured in their politics and, at times, their economics. One should also note that Smith and Crowinshield opposed rechartering the Bank of the United States.

Although these Republican leaders rapidly approached the pinnacle of American society, the rank-and-file merchants were most likely aspiring entrepreneurs. Excluded from trade within the British empire by the established merchants, they seized the opportunity afforded by war to expand their trade throughout the world. As demand for American products increased through their efforts, an economic affinity developed between these merchants and the farmers meeting this new demand. The steady expansion of American ships into the world's commerce increased their businesses and induced them to purchase more ships. This commercial expansion fueled the growth not only of new merchants, but of farmers and shipbuilders as well. In effect, a new commercial interest arose whose fortune rested on continued expansion of commerce in a world of empires now opened by war.

The war had enormous impact on American commerce and markets. Although American trade with British possessions increased between 1792 and 1795, its trade outside the empire exploded (see Graph 4). Only 23 percent of America's 1795 trade was still with the British empire—one-third of the prewar level. Fantastic opportunities appeared for every merchant, however large or small his enterprise, to enrich himself in trade with the French, Spanish, Germans, and Dutch. As Graph 5, which plots American exports and reexports, illustrates, many seized this opportunity. The war's impact was not limited to merchants. Shipbuilding trades were overwhelmed with new orders, and American tonnage rose precipitously (see Graph 6). Prosperity in the urban areas enhanced artisan businesses, increased construction of houses and buildings, and raised consumption levels for personal goods and services. People from American farms and from

Europe swarmed into the cities seeking opportunity and finding opportunity and poverty. Wholesale prices rose 172 percent between 1791 and 1796 (Graph 7). The prices of farm products doubled over those years. A prosperity unknown since the onset of the Revolution returned to the nation.

Detailed wholesale price indices for Philadelphia (graph 8) reflect the war boom. For manufacturers, the prices of imports rose and industrial prices followed — aid no tariff had yet provided. Labor costs fell as wages failed to keep pace with prices. For farmers the demand pull of the cities and foreign markets on the prices of their commodities created an inducement to expand their output and cultivate more land. Farmers not yet integrated into the market economy were slowly drawn in by these prices. Marginal producers saw profits as demand curves shifted upward. "The multiplier and accelerator effect from this growth in income in the export sector," Douglass North explains, "was pulling people out of self-sufficiency and into the market economy."[37] Much of the demand for farm products was for flour, liquor, and snuff. Excise levies on the last two items were not well received, particularly in light of the proliferation of small producers to meet demand. Any interruption in trade threatened the new prosperity.

When Britain began to constrict commerce and reimpose the hegemony of the antebellum era, these manufacturers, merchants, and farmers were the first victims. Their markets and trade threatened, they demanded government protection. When they received instead the Jay Treaty, they turned against Hamilton and the Federalists. Paul Goodman captures this response succinctly: "Traders, capitalists, and mechanics whose welfare Federalists rule threatened forged a new political instrument seeking to reshape the young Republic."[38] What was true in Massachusetts was true throughout the nation. Upon the bitter disappointment and frustration at Hamilton's foreign policy was built the Republican party.

The economic issue here is not simply how many tons of grain the British imported vis-à-vis the French. America's commercial market in the metropolitan areas was fairly well developed. If the demand for grain declined because of British seizures of French-bound ships, all grain exporters were hurt. Grain prices were a function of aggregate demand. To eliminate one-fifth of the total demand lowered all prices. Even to interrupt a carrying trade involving no grain exports lowered prices because shipbuilding and maintenance would suffer. Thus, the demand for food in local markets would decline. Any farmer or planter, regardless of whether one ounce of his product went abroad, could be injured if foreign nations prevented exports from finding markets. Whatever increased domestic grain supplies lowered all grain prices. The same was true for all commodities, provided they were linked to exports in some manner. And potentially all were— something of which producers were fully cognizant.[39]

These bad effects were not limited to producers. Merchants whose trade was interdicted were outraged. Others less directly involved were also affected by lower-priced cargoes, more competition for open markets, and higher insurance rates. One did not have to have one's ship seized or one's market obstructed to feel the effects. Shipbuilders suffered when trade slowed. Theoretically, non-shipbuilding manufacturers could benefit from trade interruptions provided the victims included imported manufactures. The British, however, did not seize ships hauling British industrial goods to America. British assaults on commerce also threatened the livelihoods of seamen and laborers in the urban areas.

Despite the fact that French markets accounted for only half as much of American exports as Britain and only one-seventh the imports, the French imperial market was very significant for the American economy. Its importance increased as American ships replaced the French merchant marine driven from the seas. In addition, the antebellum French trade was principally carried in American ships. Twice as much American tonnage was involved in French trade as in British trade. Although the Jacobin leaders vacillated, they finally agreed to America's insistence that free ships made free goods. They seized few ships prior to 1796. It was the English that seized American ships, obstructed America's foreign markets, and condemned American cargoes and then resold them a premium prices to their American owners. Self-interest and a strong sense of nationalism led the Republicans to assail Great Britain and those in America who would appease her.

Although Republican strength grew in the four major ports during the Anglo-American conflict, Republicans' greatest gains among merchants occurred in Philadelphia and Baltimore. A compelling reason for this differential growth can be found if one examines state-by-state participation in the carrying trade through the distribution of drawbacks (see Graph 9). To evade the British Orders in Council of November 1793 and January 1794, which prohibited Americans from carrying on a trade between France and its colonies, American merchants began landing their goods in U.S. ports, paying duties, and reexporting them to non-British markets, usually in France. They then drew back all but a small fraction of the duties. Thus, the higher the percentage of drawbacks to gross import duties, the greater the port's participation in the carrying trade—a trade almost entirely outside of British markets. Despite the higher percentages for Maryland and Pennsylvania all four port cities participated in the trade, and in all four some merchants became Republican during the crisis of 1794–95.

The Jay Treaty acted as the catalyst that precipitated the Republican coalition. Hamilton's stabilization program had generated discontent, but only the wholesale sacrifice of the interests of so many merchants, farmers, and manufacturers could have created the dissension and disunity necessary for a nationwide political party. Manufacturers, who had sought federal protection and aid, were trapped by a treaty giving the highest legal sanction to an unobstructed flow of English manufactures and British-made ships. Merchants, who had sought federal discrimination against foreign ships and protection of their world markets, were fettered to an agreement compelling acquiescence in British restrictions on their commerce. Farmers and planters, who had sought federal guarantees of new markets for their grain, meat, and produce, were forced to trade through British markets or at British discretion in foreign markets. The breakup of the constitutional coalition was unmistakable.

IV

"This history of the agricultural population of pre-industrial America," James A. Henretta observes, "remains to be written."[40] Still, some things are known about these small farmers, particularly those outside the South. Two are salient: the tension between the developing market economy and the traditional family-centered community, and the pressure for new land exerted by population growth. The family was the basic economic unit providing the labor, a scarce commodity, for agricultural production. For obvious reasons its subsistence was the primary purpose of production. Within the community there was a local market, through which goods were exchanged frequently by barter; in many cases the local market involved the rudimentary manufacture of flour, snuff, lumber, and leather. Beyond this local market the early national period witnessed the extension of the national and international market into local communities. This extension provided farmers with extra income for their surplus and, as it increased the value of products, raised land values. The demand-pull effects of the war boom on crop and land values served, as noted above, to shift production toward national markets.[41]

Rather than disrupting family relations, these changes often provoked adaptation in a family's allocation of its labor. More effort might be concentrated on marketable staples, less on family needs which an enlarged market system could provide. Where manufacturing developed, female family members might enter factories or, more commonly, become part of a putting-out system of production. The question, then, is not so much whether farmers were or were not producing for a market, but how they integrated both activities into their lives. What emerges in this period from the available evidence is an agricultural sector in the process of change. It was here that the Republican proposals locked in to the political concerns of small farmers. For those moving into the market economy these proposals offered new outlets abroad and, subsequently, a federally funded transportation network. Yet, to assuage the fear of change among farmers, Republican rhetoric lauded the self-sufficient yeoman as nature's nobleman. Small farmers found great appeal in the pronouncement of their calling as noble and in the condemnation of the "monied men." The Republicans offered an attractive combination of policy and poetry.

The other salient characteristic of the agricultural sector was population growth. Knowing that their parents' holdings were inadequate for more than one child's inheritance, sons sought out new land for their homesteads.[42] They were receptive to promises and policies of continental expansion. The displacement of Indians and the acquisition of another nation's territory were actions favored by small farmers and their dependents. Over the decade, the sons and daughters of these farmers settled the frontier and helped add to the union four states: Vermont, Kentucky, Tennessee, and Ohio. They also swelled the ranks of the seaport cities. Republicans policies toward continental expansion and Indian removal were politically appealing to these small farmers. Large farmers and planters were concerned more directly with foreign markets than were their smaller brethren. Both groups, however, were staunch supporters of acquiring new land and securing the frontier.

Despite the ultimate congruence between the concerns of agricultural interests and Republican policy and rhetoric, the exact relationship of agriculture to politics remains unresolved. Hamilton's fear of antagonizing importers cost him support among farmers. His imposition of the excise tax on liquor and snuff enraged farmers in Pennsylvania. The Whiskey Rebellion and, later, Fries Rebellion were manifestations of the political hostility generated by internal taxes. On the other hand, frontier farmers appreciated Federalist successes in clearing the British out of the northwest forts, opening the fur trade, and defeating the Indians. Pinckney's Treaty enabled America to settle and develop lands to the edge of the Mississippi River. In vivid contrast to the traditional characterization of the Republicans as agrarian, several state studies suggest that the Federalist political strength persisted

among farmers even while it deteriorated in commercial centers. Mark
Renzulli concludes that Maryland's Federalist support was "always
strongest in the state's agrarian areas." John A. Munroe labels Delaware's Federalists "the party of the landed gentry." He describes the
political transformation of this era: "As the Democratic party became
the party of manufacturers in Delaware, the Federalists became the
agrarian party."[43] Such a transformation is all the more significant,
since the area of greatest Republican strength was the Brandywine
Valley, a major manufacturing center. In New York, Alfred Young
finds the Republicans in 1797 "still primarily dependent upon mechanics," though he notes the farmers' allegiance changed several times. In
agricultural areas of New York dominated by manors, resentment of
the landlords fueled Republican support among the independent yeomanry, while dependence and deference maintained Federalist support
among subsistence farmers and tenants—a pattern doubtless repeated
in other states.[44] Indeed, one might speculate that the agrarian tilt in
some areas of Republican party propaganda was a product of their
lack of a strong agricultural constituency in many areas outside the
South.

Frontier farmers in the northwest might be pleased by the removal
of Indians, the opening of the Mississippi River, and British evacuation of the northwest forts. On the other hand, the enforcement of an
excise tax by government troops might undermine Federalist political
support among those same farmers. A Federalist land speculator who
offered welcome credit to a new settler might soon become a burden-
some mortgagee employing his financial power to coerce votes. In
Pennsylvania the western farmers were Republican under Gallatin's
leadership. They were twice invaded by excisemen and soldiers—
preelection reminders of what the current administration thought of
them.[45]

The established elite constituted the bulwark of the Federalist party
in the North, but not in the South. Already anti-British because of
their indebtedness and anti-Hamilton because of his fiscal program's
bestowal of a federal largesse on northern speculators, the planter elite
joined Republican ranks. Their allegiance became almost total when
the Jay Treaty incorporated a clause for recovery of prerevolutionary
British debts, owed largely by southern planters.[46] This Republican
alliance with the planter elite pushed small southern farmers into the
Federalist camp. There they sought help in weakening tidewater control of state governments.[47] The Federalist, however, failed to organize
this yeoman discontent in the South as effectively as Republicans did
in the North.

Jay's Treaty intensified opposition to Federalist rule, but this opposition was rooted in a complex of economic interests, local politics, the specific effects of treaty provisions, skills in political organization, personalities, and ideology. Throughout the nation the Republicans broached partisan politics and trumpeted the theme of popular rule. To many small property holders, this rhetoric heralded their march toward the Republican party. It remained, nonetheless, a long walk to the election of 1800. In the mid-1790s perhaps the most accurate summary of political parties and their constituencies is that the Republican opposition to Federalist policies included merchants, mechanics, manufacturers, planters, and farmers, and that Federalist support included persons from each group, more merchants than planters. Unquestionably, though, both parties, particularly the Republican party, were working to politicize the populace on national and state issues.

In his analysis of members of Congress during 1797 to 1804, Paul Goodman presents results that reveal the broad economic basis of each party. Among the Federalists whose occupations could be identified, he finds that 59 percent were involved in the professions, 16 percent in commerce, 4 percent in manufacturing, and 20 percent in agriculture; among Republicans, 42 percent were in the professions, 17 percent in commerce, 5 percent in manufacturing, and 35 in agriculture. In the South, Republican congressmen were of a higher social stratum than in the North. Unlike the rising group of Republican challengers to a Federalist establishment in the North, the southern Republicans were the establishment.[48] The rank and file of the parties represent a division within the constitutional coalition as well as outside of it. There could be no stronger symbol of this breakup than the emergence of the two principal founders, Hamilton and Madison, as leaders of opposing political factions.

CHAPTER SEVEN

Gallatin as Critic
The Transition to Power, 1796–1801

It may have been supposed by some that the debt by rendering the creditors dependent on government, gave it an additional stability. But it should be recollected that although an artificial interest in thereby created, which may at times give an useful support, it may at some future period lend its assistance to bad measures and to a bad administration. So far as that interest is artificial, so far as it is distinct from the general interest, it may perhaps act against that general interest and become as pernicious as it is supposed to have been useful.
—Gallatin, *A Sketch of the Finances of the United States* (1796)

There [is] no object of so great importance to the United States as the extinction of the curse of the country, the Public Debt.
—Gallatin speaking in Congress, February 18, 1796

The management of the Treasury becomes more & more difficult. The Legislature will not pass in gross. Their appropriations are minute. Gallatin to whom they all yield, is evidently intending to break down this Department by charging it with an impractical detail. The duties are high, the merchants are embarassed.
—Secretary of the Treasury Oliver Wolcott to Hamilton, April 4, 1798

Although the Republican party did not become an organized national opposition until 1796, its local and state roots developed years earlier. Undoubtedly, local issues were significant to party divisions at the state level. Equally significant, however, was the role of national issues and leaders in drawing disparate geographic groups together. The party's leaders had to respond to their constituent groups with concrete proposals. More importantly, the leaders had to integrate these responses into coherent programs to subsume the aims of each group while advancing an overall political policy. They needed to formulate a political economy that incorporated the fundamental interests of their constituents into their conception of the capacities, requirements, and purposes of the society as a whole.

Three men rose to lead the Republican party in the 1790s and through the ensuing decade: Jefferson, Madison, and Gallatin. Jefferson was the senior statesman, standing among those national figures slightly below Washington. Author of the Declaration of Independence, governor of Virginia, minister to France, secretary of state, planter, slaveholder, agronomist, musician, inventor—the list is endless. Madison, the Founder, became congressional leader and chief party organizer. Neither planter nor native, Gallatin emigrated from Geneva, Switzerland. As a tutor and land speculator he dreamed of a "New Geneva" in western Pennsylvania but settled for a small manufactory of munitions and glass. Politics soon supplanted plantations and business.

Elected to the statewide conventions on amending the federal Constitution and rewriting the Pennsylvania constitution, Gallatin became a powerful legislator in the Pennsylvania Assembly. At heart an advocate of new enterprise, he championed road construction, public education, and a state bank. Public aid to develop a modern market system was the goal of his legislation. As had Hamilton, he married into the highest circles of New York City's merchants. His father-in-law, however, was no Federalist: James Nicholson was the city's most prosperous Republican. In 1793 Gallatin graduated from state politics and small business into the U.S. Senate. Through a questionable application of residency requirements, Federalist senators unseated him only a few months into his term. The voters of western Pennsylvania then returned him to Philadelphia as their congressman. Consummating his political ascent, he became Madison's lieutenant and, when Madison retired in 1797, succeeded him as Republican congressional leader.[1]

In symbol and in fact these three men were the economic and intellectual synthesis that created the Republican party. Jefferson, the revolutionary, espoused the ideals of political equality, republican virtue, and private property; the great democrat owned two hundred slaves. Madison, the intellectual, wrote the Constitution creating the central government. A planter educated at Princeton, he thought in terms of socioeconomic systems and political stability. Gallatin was the modernizer. Bound to entrepreneurial groups and the northern commercial elite, he promoted government aid to new enterprise, development of capital resources, and investment in education and transportation. He was the sole national leader of either party to own and manage a

manufactory as his principal business. Gallatin bridged the gap between planter and merchant, farmer and manufacturer. If the Beardian
(and neo-Beardian) mold for the Republican party is to be broken,
Gallatin is the hammer.

I

Despite some reservations about the exact provisions of the Constitution, Gallatin believed the "federal government is the one that can
preserve the liberties and serve the happiness of the inhabitants of such
an extensive empire as the United States." The Confederation was
simply too "weak" to provide "some of the greatest advantages we had
a right to expect" from a national government.[2] His measured support
of the Constitution, his popularity in western Pennsylvania, and his
advocacy of a state bank, internal improvements, and public education
made him an attractive candidate to both the conservative and radical
parties in Pennsylvania. A small businessman who championed government aid to industry and commerce, Gallatin received political
support from farmers, manufacturers, and merchants. This broad
support led to his election in 1793 to the Senate.

Among his first legislative initiatives was to demand a comprehensive report from Hamilton on Hamilton's conduct of Treasury Department business. Such effrontery in a body as Hamiltonian as the Senate
led in large part to Gallatin's ouster. His challenge to Hamilton's heretofore unassailed domain placed him within the opposition ranks in
Congress. His standing among Republicans was enhanced further by
his link through marriage to New York's mercantile elite. Returning to
Congress in 1795, Gallatin had impressive credentials for party leadership: strong connections with Pennsylvania's and New York's Republicans and an excellent background in fiscal policy from his time in the
Pennsylvania legislature and the federal Senate. It is easy to understand
why he assumed the role of party leader when Madison left Congress
in 1797.

While Madison organized a national party and prepared for the
election of 1800, Gallatin continued the political battle in Congress.
This battle had two major fronts: Hamilton's fiscal policies and Federalist foreign policies. Gallatin's critique of Hamilton's fiscal policies
culminated in the most comprehensive and informed analysis of
American finances since the Report on Public Credit itself, *A Sketch of
the Finances of the United States*. Published in November 1796, the
Sketch was read by all major political leaders, including Oliver
Wolcott and Hamilton.[3] Overall, it established the Republicans as
competent to confront Hamilton and his party on the same plane of

economic sophistication. Specifically, Gallatin used it to refute Hamilton's contention that the debt had brought political stability to the nation. On the contrary, he argued that Federalist fiscal policies had disrupted the union and rendered it subservient to domestic factions and foreign powers. In Gallatin's mind, Hamilton's fiscal program was more than an economic issue. Since the exigencies of debt service had compelled American acquiescence in British commercial restraints, his fiscal policy involved issues of foreign policy, international trade, and national independence. The *Sketch,* then, was no mere statement of federal accounts. [4]

Unlike the usual partisan polemic of this era, the *Sketch* lacked vituperative excess. The prose was reasoned, almost scholarly. Even in writing of an issue as controversial as the Bank of the United States, Gallatin measured and qualified his criticisms with words like "perhaps," "in some degrees," and "in some instances" when detailing abuses. [5] He did this both to avoid blanket condemnations of institutions and activities that were integral to economic development, and to reassure potential political allies that the Republicans were not ranting levelers bent on overturning the fiscal system. In effect he was telling the "monied men" of America that the system, properly used, was the solution, that it was Hamilton who had politicized the government's efforts to bolster the economy, and that the Republicans planned only to set things right again. With his northern political base and his ties to the New York mercantile community, Gallatin alone could make the Republican party credible at the national level among the commercial elite. He designed the *Sketch* to achieve that credibility.

Gallatin began with a strong affirmation that the Revolutionary debt should be funded. Government debts were obligations of "common honesty" whose repudiation would be "the most flagrant and pernicious breach of public faith and national morality." He acknowledged federal responsibility for the assumption of state debts. Hamilton's *method* of assumption, however, had failed to distinguish states that had exceeded their share of the Revolutionary debt from those that had not fulfilled it. The former alone should have been assumed. The other states should have been obligated to pay their share—particularly since the states were by and large in much better financial shape than the federal government. The failure to distinguish among the states added by Gallatin's calculations $11 million to the federal debt and led to "suspicions that private interest and speculation were amongst the most powerful causes of the measures." He concluded that "so far from strengthening government, [assumption] had created more discontent and more uneasiness than any other measure." [6]

Burdened with a $75 million debt in 1789 the government not only had failed to reduce it, but had added $3.2 million in the seven subsequent years. Gallatin pointed out that government deficits, like all government expenditures, drew labor from private pursuits, where it best increased "the capital of the community," into government service, where all "labor, however useful and necessary it may be, [was] totally unproductive."[7] Unlike other nations, whose borrowing resulted from the exigencies of war, America under Federalist rule was so "improvident" as to suffer a debt enlargement during peace—a malady whose etiology he traced to improper assumption, extravagant military spending, and the expensive overreaction to the Whiskey Rebellion.[8] He then assessed the effects of this huge debt on the nation.

Government borrowing and other "abuses" had turned the Bank of the United States from an institution "beneficial" to government financial needs and of "great commercial utility" in supplementing monetary circulation into one evoking fear and apprehension. Its use as a "political engine," particularly the selective employment of its loan facilities to buoy the stock market, had "left many enemies to the institution." In response to Hamilton's claim that the debt had "created a large productive capital," Gallatin pointed out that it had only transferred wealth through the tax system from the productive segment of the society to rentiers and speculators. In this manner the debt prevented "an accumulation of capital" by the "industrious part of the community." Even that part of national income taxed without harm to production the debt holders merely consumed. "A public debt," he maintained, "does not increase the existing amount of cultivated lands, of houses, of consumable commodities; it makes not the smallest addition either to the wealth or to the annual labor of a nation." Nor did the debt increase the money supply because the bonds themselves were objects of speculation and barter. They required a large amount of specie to support their market price. Gallatin concluded that without a stable value the bonds could neither replace specie nor secure bank notes. Fluctuations in bond markets "have caused some of the greatest distresses which the mercantile world has experienced."[9]

He acknowledged that funding was in principle one "means of drawing to American foreign capital to a large amount," but in this instance it "has been an acquisition of wealth to the speculator in stock alone, and not the nation." To be of value foreign capital should have "a low rate of interest and a proper application." Although the rate of interest approached 8 percent, the foreign capital still could have been profitable if productively applied. Yet, only a "small proportion" had been so applied. The rest had enabled speculators "to consume, to spend more, and they have consumed and spent extravagantly." Gallatin concluded the "elegant houses" of the large cities stood as monuments to the massive waste of capital borrowed from abroad.[10]

Finally, he struck at Hamilton's argument that "by rendering the creditor dependent on government," the debt "gave it an additional stability." The creditor attached in this manner was "an artificial interest" liable, Gallatin argued, to "lend its assistance to bad measures and to bad administration." If the artificial interest differed from the general interest, "it may perhaps act against the general interest and become as pernicious as it is supposed to have been useful." Undoubtedly, he asserted, "the jealousies, the apprehensions, the discontents excited by the public debt have been more injurious to our domestic peace, have gone farther to weaken our real union, than any other internal cause." Politically "every nation is enfeebled by a public debt." Eventually, such a debt could overwhelm the government itself, as it had in France.[11]

Gallatin hammered very heavily on the debt as a means of political stabilization because it was the central assumption of all Hamilton's fiscal policies. He argued that it had disrupted national unity and only its extinction could "strengthen the bonds of our Union and give additional vigor and respectability to the nation." Elimination of the debt would give America "respectability and independence in relation to other nations." America's "unprovided and enfeebled" state rendered the nation susceptible to foreign pressure. Here was a thinly veiled reference to the dependence on the revenue tariff and English imports that had circumscribed American resistance to British manipulation. Extinguishing the debt would not insure victory in future clashes, but it would provide a stronger basis for resistance.[12]

Gallatin next considered various ways to raise revenue and repay the debt. He advocated continuation of the import tariff as the "cheapest to collect, the least vexatious, and in general the least oppressive." In addition a land tax of some type would supplement revenue and equalize the tax burden between North and South. Since the import tariff fell chiefly on the southern consumers, a flat per-acre land tax would fall more heavily on the North because less labor was employed in its agriculture. Less labor meant a lower yield per acre in the North than in the South, thus a higher proportional tax.[13] He opposed most taxes on manufactures as low-yielding and difficult to collect, but he did suggest an excise tax designed to consolidate liquor production into larger, more productive units and reduce to some extent drinking that interfered with productive labor.[14]

Gallatin concluded with the proposal that western lands be sold to settlers to lessen the debt. "Lands," he explained, "are so much more valuable to us than the Indians, that whenever they are actually wanted we may afford to pay for them a much higher price than they ever do ask." He assumed that four dollars per acre paid in installments would attract settlers and raise revenues.[15] This proposal, which he elaborated in congressional speeches, contained the embryo of many future Republican policies. The government would sell large tracts of western lands to private companies. These land companies would agree to parcel their holdings into large and small lots and extend credit to settlers purchasing the small lots. In this manner the federal debt could be reduced and small property holdings encouraged. Land sales would provide the government with revenue from speculators incorporating land companies. The credit and parceling requirements would control to some extent speculative manipulations of sales.[16] Ultimately, federal control over the sale of western lands would promote "the happiness of this country" by insuring "an obligation to settlement." This obligation "was not only a sure mark of prosperity; but afforded comfort to the poor man."[17]

Gallatin's plans for the American West contained several ideas central to Republican policies after Jefferson's inauguration—chiefly the acquisition and development of western lands. Acquisition and then settlement would enlarge the nation and provide property for a growing population. Settlement was "valuable" and "a mark of prosperity" because it expanded the market system, cultivated the soil, and eventually yielded a surplus of goods. Marketing those goods required internal transportation and consumers at home and abroad. In this respect, Gallatin was building a program on the economic proposals of Adam Smith, whom he often cited as an authority in the Sketch's arguments. The political-economic program, which Gallatin sought to implement as Treasury secretary, and its relationship to Smith's political economy are discussed in Chapter 8. Suffice it to say that the Sketch was much more than a critical analysis of Hamilton's fiscal program; it did in fact broach several programmatic elements of the Republican political economy.

II

In Congress Gallatin spent most of his time on questions of foreign policy. Simply stated, he tried to maintain America's commercial integrity by avoiding war with France and resisting British impositions on American trade. His first efforts to prevent British hegemony centered on the funding of Jay's Treaty. Since treaty provisions required a joint commission to settle private disputes over seizures and debts, an appropriations bill for the commission had to pass the House. The appropriations measure became a vehicle to attack the treaty. In doing so, Gallatin presented what became and remained the basic tenets of Republican relations with Britain.

"The intercourse," he told the House, "although useful perhaps to both parties, was more immediately necessary to England." America traded food and raw materials for English luxuries and manufactures. It could do without English goods or build its own factories, but a loss of American commodities would close England's factories and starve her people. "We had no fleet to oppose or punish Great Britain; but, from our relative commercial situation, we had it in our power to restrain her aggressions by restrictions on her trade, by a total prohibition of her manufactures, or by a sequestration of the debts due to her." An acceptable agreement with Britain had to affirm that free ships make free goods, "the only provision which could give us security . . . for our navigation." In other words, only unrestricted international markets would insure prosperity to a basically agrarian nation. Confined to British markets, America was no more than her colony. Jay's Treaty had forsaken "liberty of commerce." It was, he concluded, "a dereliction of national interest, of national honor, of national independence."[18] Jefferson thought Gallatin's charges against the treaty and his insistence on the House's right to judge its merits "worthy of being printed at the end of the Federalist, as the only rational commentary on the part of the constitution to which it related."[19]

However worthy, Gallatin's efforts failed, and the treaty's implementation placed enormous pressure on Franco-American relations. In French eyes American acquiescence in British commercial restrictions made the United States a de facto ally of England. The Paris Directorate recalled their minister, Adet, to express their displeasure at this turn in American policy and at John Adams's recall of U.S. minister to France James Monroe. Without Monroe's steadying presence, relations deteriorated. French privateers escalated their assaults on American merchantmen trading in the British West Indies. By spring 1797 President Adams proposed defense measures to Congress and nominated Elbridge Gerry, C. C. Pinckney, and John Marshall to sail to France on a peace mission.

Adams wanted Franco-American differences resolved peacefully. To accomplish this he intended to negotiate while preparing for a defensive war. If negotiations failed, a small naval force could control Caribbean privateers. At home he used the Alien and Sedition Acts to enforce a domestic consensus against France. A settlement would be likely if America demonstrated its determination to resist French depredations. His strategy succeeded, but the domestic repression it entailed alienated Republican leaders from his policies. Moreover, they were never convinced that he (and his cabinet) wanted peace with France and not alliance with England. His strategy also split the Federalists when the pro-British faction in the party realized that he did indeed want peace. Adams's foreign policy triumph meant domestic political disaster.[20]

Gallatin's role in Congress is not significant for its impact on Federalist policies: he and the Republicans lost practically every major contest involving implementation of those policies during the Adams administration. His definition of America's international interest, however, did portend much of Republican foreign policy after Jefferson's election. In April 1798, when the bribery scandal (the XYZ Affair) became known to Congress and military measures against France approached their peak, he gave perhaps his most succinct explanation of the national interest in foreign relations.

He began with the basic issue: "whether we think it in our interest to declare war against [France], or not. . . . For if war or war measures were necessary, it was not because there were corrupt individuals in the French Government. . . . But the true ground, if we thought it in our interest to make war, consisted in reiterated depredations upon our trade, and the refusal of receiving or treating with our Envoys on that subject." American commerce with the Continent still prospered with little interference from France. If the French had obstructed that trade, then he asserted that he would be the first to call for war measures. But under present circumstance war would only deepen national indebtedness, destroy commerce, and impoverish the prospering nation. All France had done was slow America's importation of British goods. Gallatin concluded that he "would rather see a total want of British manufacturers, and abandon that part of our trade, than take measures that not only will be war, but worse than war."[21]

Beyond pride and pique, honor and jingoism, there were in Gallatin's mind hard commercial issues which should determine war or peace. In his speech he synthesized the economic interests of groups within the Republican party and an overall sense of the national interest. His concern for American trade with the European continent reflected Republican support among merchants and farmers whose markets lay outside Britain. Their commerce largely escaped French seizures. Interference with the importation of British manufactures aided domestic manufacturers—many of whom constituted the Republican party's urban base. War with France would expand its seizure of American ships and force the United States into a de facto alliance with England. Convoyed by English warships British manufactures would flow unmolested into American ports. Above all, federal expenditures would mushroom to cover military costs, and a basic cause of America's problems, the debt, would be exacerbated.

Gallatin's opposition to construction of a navy and mobilization of an army was rooted in his determination to reduce national indebtedness. the protection of commerce and national defense were laudable goals, but "our monied resources are limited, and the only source of danger to us is in our consuming those resources for useless objects and exhausting ourselves for fear of imaginary dangers."[22] Foreign hegemony threatened national independence, but a debt-ridden government and an overtaxed people also threatened national unity and a republic's viability. "We must preserve self-dignity," he wrote his wife, "not suffer our Country to be debased, and yet preserve our Constitution and our fellow citizens from the fatal effects of war."[23]

Gallatin's concerns were unfounded; Adams intended no war with France. His navy successfully resisted French seizures in the Caribbean. Insurance rates on U.S. shipping fell by 50 percent after a five-fold increase when France began its attacks. Talleyrand agreed to a settlement guaranteeing free ships for free goods, commercial reciprocity, a narrow list of contraband goods, a blockade restricted to the actual presence of warships, and a commission to settle merchant claims.[24] Despite Adams's political courage and statesmanship the French Convention led to his downfall and Jefferson's victory in 1800.

The agreement with France alienated Hamilton's wing of the Federalist party. Other war-related measures, particularly mobilization of the army and the Alien and Sedition Acts, created great political resentment among moderate Federalists. Hamilton's repression of Fries Rebellion in Pennsylvania did much to weaken Federalist support among farmers in that state. Enforcement of the Sedition Act struck mechanics and many small farmers as inimical to republican principles. The Alien Act compelled many foreign commercial agents to leave American ports, complicating trade to non-British areas. These laws were also employed in attempts to suppress growing Republican support among immigrants in urban areas. Thus, the domestic element of Adams's foreign policy resulted in Republican political gains.[25]

Republican political organizations, established in 1796, grew in the ensuing four years into a formidable party force. Condemning the Alien and Sedition Acts, military expenditures, and taxation, Republicans recaptured support lost over the XYZ Affair and continued to build their political coalition. Britain's repeated attacks on American commerce reinforced the sense that France was not America's real enemy.[26] Spain's involvement in the European conflict weakened its already loose hold on Latin America. U.S. trade with its southern neighbors grew rapidly after 1796. England alone competed for these new markets. A source of irritation in 1800, this competition became a major cause of conflict in the next decade. The American merchants most involved in this trade were Republican.[27]

III

Previous interpretations of the presidential election of 1800 are unsatisfactory in light of this essay's analysis of the political divisions in the 1790s. The still dominant Beard-Dauer view stresses the rising opposition of agrarian interests to Federalist commercial and fiscal policies. This analysis is untenable in light of Republican strength among commercial interests in the cities. Indeed, the evidence of party distribution, as reflected in congressional voting patterns, reveals persistent Federalist support in the predominantly agricultural areas of New England, New York, central Pennsylvania, southern Maryland, Delaware, and the frontier areas of the Deep South. Strong Republican support came from the areas in and around Baltimore, Philadelphia, New York City, and Salem, Massachusetts, as well as from the rural South, western Pennsylvania, and various agricultural sections of Massachusetts, Vermont, and New York. This distribution and state studies reveal a slow growth of the Republican coalition, interrupted by a brief surge of Federalist support in the aftermath of the XYZ Affair, during the years between the Anglo-American crisis of the mid-nineties and the election of 1800. In the end Jefferson won because he carried the cities (except Charleston), and he carried the cities because the manufacturer-mechanic vote went Republican.[28]

Jefferson garnered significant political support in Philadelphia, Baltimore, New York, and Salem, where the opportunities of commercial expansion had fostered rising groups of merchants, mechanics, and large farmers. Most of the South remained Republican owing to the resentment of large planters toward Britain and the speculative machinations involving the debt. Adams drew his support from the areas, noted above, less affected by economic change where British trade relations and deferential behavior determined political allegiance. For example, in an analysis of electoral patterns within Maryland during this presidential election, David A. Bohmer discovered a pattern of continuity in the electorate between 1796 and 1800. Bohmer found that Republican support slipped slightly in the XYZ election year of 1798 but recovered and increased by 1800. Changes were incremental; totals grew marginally without any massive swings or realignments. Although Bohmer did not analyze his data in economic terms, it does reveal the Republicans' greatest strength in the upper Chesapeake region, the most commercial area of the state. Baltimore gave Jefferson the second highest winning percentage in Maryland; nearly 80 percent of the county voted Republican. Only adjacent Harford County gave Jefferson a greater margin of victory. The most heavily agrarian counties in southern Maryland favored the Federalist party.[29]

Similar patterns appear in New York City, where Republican strength among merchants, manufacturers, and mechanics carried the state assembly and, consequently, the electoral delegates for Jefferson. Federalist strength in New York State came from agrarian areas as well as from elements of the commercial groups in the city. Alfred F. Young concludes that competition with British imports and the entrepreneurial character of the party accounted for Republican strength in commercial areas of the state. In 1800 Republican political support throughout the nation, reflected by congressional elections, followed the pattern of New York and Maryland. The agricultural areas split between Republicans and Federalists, while in the urban areas the Republicans dominated by sometimes slim margins. In New York City, for example, the Republicans garnered 54 percent of the vote — a substantially narrower margin of victory than the 80 percent Baltimore County gave them. More significantly, it was New York's twelve electoral votes which the narrowly-elected Republican assembly gave Jefferson that proved to be the margin of victory in 1800.[30] Seeking an agrarian backlash to explain Jefferson's victory seems pointless, given the evidence from state studies.

Recalling James A. Henretta's comments concerning the pressures on the *mentalité* of small farmers, one discovers a basis for a reconsideration of the rhetoric of the Republican party and the reality of its political constituency.[31] The twin motifs of its rhetoric were praise for the noble yeoman and affirmation of equal opportunity for all.[32] The latter theme spoke directly to the rising entrepreneurial character of its constituency in the commercial centers. Combatting Federalist control of Anglo-American trade, banking, and not infrequently, local government, Republican supporters in the commercial centers found great appeal in the promise of equal opportunity in trade, finance, and government. This rhetoric, backed by the policy proposals of Republican leaders, was less attractive to small farmers, most of whom participated only marginally in the new opportunities of this commercial expansion. These same farmers constituted a significant Federalist voting bloc in areas such as upstate New York, central Pennsylvania, southern Maryland, Delaware, the frontier of the Deep South, and much of New England. Conservative and mimetic in political orientation, many of these small farmers regarded family-centered agricul-

ture, in Henretta's words, as "an abiding core of symbolic and emotive
meaning . . . and reliable guide to behavior amid the uncertainties of
the world."[33] The commercial expansion and economic change that
were central to a large part of the Republican constituency were in
large measure the essence of the uncertainty threatening these farmers.
The Federalists, on the other hand, promised social continuity and
order. The efficacy of this Federalist appeal is aptly demonstrated by
the Federalist strength in agrarian areas.

It would have been eminently sensible for Republican political strat-
egists to couch their electoral appeal to these farmers in the rhetoric of
agrarianism: the noble, independent yeoman. As grist, they had Jefferson's *Notes on Virginia* as well as the speculative excesses of Hamilton's fiscal policy. The Federalists, they argued, were the money
changers in America's yeoman temple. Noble E. Cunningham sub-
stantiates this interpretation: "Agrarianism was but one element in the
Republican appeal, and it was stressed only in those regions which
were predominantly agricultural." He concludes that "agrarianism was
not the common denominator of Republican campaign appeals."[34] It
would not have been the first time that a political movement clothed a
program of radical change in the rhetoric of preserving an idealized
past.

The Republican victory was not sweeping. Broadly based it was,
but so was Federalist support. Stephen Kurtz speculates that Adams
was more popular in 1800 than in 1796.[35] The very fact that voting
patterns resist easy political or economic analysis suggests multiple
causes. Although it is undeniable that political divisions of the mid-
nineties had an economic basis, the fact that these divisions were not
between commercial and agrarian interests, but within each, renders
the specific economic bases very subtle. Indeed, the divorce of agrarian from commercial interests is altogether artificial. A farmer selling
flour to the French West Indies was no less injured by an English
blockade than the merchant carrying the flour, the manufacturer
building the ship, or the artisan vending his wares to any one of them.

The political economy of the election of 1800 involved more than
the fundamental economic divisions rooted in the mid-nineties. These
divisions explain the economic origins of the party. Then, Hamilton
dominated the government and the Federalist party. American foreign
policies were acquiescent in English neocolonialism. Nationalism and
self-interest wrought the Republican party and its policies. When the
French began to assault American commerce while England rested on
the structural constraints of Jay's Treaty, circumstances changed. The
politics became more complex. Talleyrand's heavy-handed attempt at
extortion allowed pro-British Federalists to cloak their anti-French

posture with nationalism. John Adams's successful resistance of France, unlike Hamilton's failure to resist England, molded a new Federalist image and recouped some party losses. The Republicans were opened to charges of foreign influence.

Adams, one might speculate, should have won reelection easily on a peace and prosperity platform. The French had been forced to settle, and the economy had experienced significant growth. But fate, in the guise of the Hamiltonian Federalists, intervened. Unwilling to settle for less than war with France and a de facto English alliance, Hamilton broke with Adams and split the party. Moreover, the Republicans, despite some mid-term losses in the 1798 election, were too well organized and their political coalition too strong simply to wither. Their ideological touchstone—liberty in the forms of economic opportunity and political freedom—linked the rising entrepreneurs, the democratic yeomen, and the mechanics. The agrarian rhetoric weakened Federalist support among small farmers in the North. The Alien and Sedition Acts as well the insufferable arrogance of many Federalist politicians, who disdained popular politics almost as much as they disliked the general populace, limited Federalists' ability to retain their agrarian constituency and translate their new nationalist image into an election victory in 1800.

Success with France and the general prosperity made a challenge on bread-and-butter issues less effective than a more abstract assault on Federalist ideology. The Republicans could point to Federalist-sponsored legislation to silence political dissent and levy heavy internal taxes as manifestations of Adams's disregard for the rights and liberties of the people. The speculative binge in government securities tarnished the Federalist image as the party of social conservativism. Hamilton's break with Adams and his military histrionics were merely welcome aids to the Republicans' campaign. Hamilton's political economy had given Jefferson a party; his personality gave Jefferson the presidency. Had Burr shot his nemesis six years sooner, Jefferson might have had to wait until 1805 to have entered the White House. Jefferson ran against the Hamiltonian Federalists, their aristocratic mien and their neocolonial political economy. While the Republicans hung the antidemocratic noose around Adams, particularly through his *Defense of Constitutions,* Hamilton pulled the gibbet's lever. John Adams, being John Adams, went down kicking. Despite their rhetorical differences, Adams and Jefferson believed in the same independent nation, free of foreign, especially British, dominance. They shared a common political economy. Hamilton was different. Adams lost because he shared a party with the wrong man.

The same years that witnessed the Republican rise to power also marked Hamilton's fall from political influence. After the XYZ Affair, Hamilton abandoned his intention to use French depredations to revoke the Franco-American Treaty of 1777. His hatred of the French Revolution, his desire to cement Anglo-American commerce, and his dreams of military glory had combined to infect him with an itch for war and conquest. He seriously entertained the fanciful schemes of the Spanish renegade Francisco de Miranda for conquering Louisiana and Latin America. "The plan in my opinion ought to be, a fleet of Great Britain, an armmy [sic] of the ustates, a Government for the liberated territorey [sic] agreable to both the Cooperators."[36] Although the Republican leaders and Adams might have sympathized with Hamilton's designs on Louisiana and Latin America, they would brook no alliance with England in the conquest nor any war with France.

Adams's dispatch of a moderate commission to negotiate with France and his angry dismissal of Hamilton's allies in his cabinet disrupted all the former secretary's plans for the election of 1800. His dreams of conquest punctured, an outraged Hamilton publicly attacked the president, split the Federalist party, and guaranteed Jefferson's election. In the process he destroyed his political career and his party. Desperation drove him to suggest that Governor John Jay recall the New York State Legislature and overturn the Republican victory at the polls.[37] Failing in this and lamenting an American world no longer meant for him, he resigned himself to practicing law and editing a newspaper.[38] For a man like Hamilton, death was merely an epilogue—written long after the true denouement. He did, however, live to see his most persistent critic, Albert Gallatin, become secretary of Treasury. Gallatin's "importance to the new administration," Merrill Peterson writes, "rivaled Hamilton's to the first."[39] The political world had been turned upside down.

CHAPTER EIGHT

The Republicans in Power
The Political Economy of Albert Gallatin

It is so important for the permanent establishment of those republican
principles of limitation of power and public economy . . . that they
should rest on the broad basis of the people, and not on a fluctuating
party majority.
—Gallatin to Jefferson, August 10, 1801

The republicans are the *nation*.
—Jefferson to William Duane, March 28, 1811

The great object of the political economy of every country, is to increase
the riches and power of that country.
—Adam Smith, *The Wealth of Nations* (1776)

Jefferson's triumph in 1800 was less than overwhelming. Better political organization and the position of moderate, which had eluded him
four years earlier, brought victory. Although Republicans counted voters from all economic interests within their ranks, his inaugural pronouncement of Federalist and Republican reunion indicated the tenuous nature of his victory. He wanted to rebuild the constitutional
coalition without Hamilton. In power, Republican leaders sought to
dampen partisanship, end polemics, and make the practitioners of
these arts political pariahs. To restore national unity they planned to
employ not force but heuristics. They proposed to forge a new consensus and provide equal federal support for each economic interest
within the social order. In instances where market forces provided
adequately for an interest, government intervention would be minimal.
Where the market forces were inadequate or where national security
was involved, the government would intervene with appropriate vigor.
The exact mix of laissez-faire and regulation depended on circumstances.

Republican political economy rested on the principles of liberal thought. The primary principle was that government should serve the interest of its propertied citizens (the words were redundant). Secondly, government should integrate these interests into an aggregate, the national interest, which it then advanced in some coherent, mutually satisfying manner. These principles are synthetic; they transform each other over time in interaction within the nation and with other nations. As secretary of the Treasury, Gallatin had to be particularly conscious of domestic economic interests and the impact of international affairs on the economy. He proved during his cabinet tenure to be master of integrating interests, ideology, and circumstances into a political economy that rivaled Hamilton's in its subtlety and surpassed Hamilton's in its vision. From opposition leader to policymaker Gallatin proved himself a master of both trades.

His political economy was of two parts: a world view rooted in liberal thought and government programs designed to promote economic development. Although the timing of his programs was often dictated by circumstances, the content and the character of his responses to those circumstances developed out of his own vision of the future. His tactic was that of a statesman, not an ideologue. Patiently he confronted national problems and conceived of solutions sensitive to present limitations and overall national goals. His affinity for finance, commerce, and manufactures eased his party's transition from a political-economic program chiefly based on development of agricultural resources and unrestricted international markets to one promoting federal aid for internal improvements, manufactures, and banking. In all his policies and programs two purposes are salient. First, to be a republic America had to be free of foreign hegemony and have a government representative of the whole nation. Secondly, the fundamental bond of union was economic, and the government's chief purpose was to facilitate commercial interaction among its citizens. Political unity was inseparable from a national market system.

I

Gallatin affirmed what liberal thinkers conceived to be the foundations of civil society in a letter to Jefferson. He concluded the "moral causes" preventing Indian "improvement" were the lack of "the social institutions which establish and secure *property* and *marriage*."[1] Subsuming property under morality was perfectly consistent with the liberal world view. His inclusion of marriage involved in one sense another affirmation of property, in this instance the wife and children. In a broader sense marriage and the family secured the temporal continuity of a social order by according property a tenure through inheritance. The chief "social institution" insuring civil society was a government "founded on law, that might insure liberty, preserve order, and protect persons and property."[2] Ideally, such a government was republican in principle. Republican governments, he explained, practiced "limitation of power and public economy." By their nature they promoted economic development. National wealth was "always eminently increased under governments which, abstaining from the exercise of every species of arbitrary power, govern by equal laws and, without favoring or oppressing any particular class of people or species of occupation, afford complete security to persons, industry, and property."[3]

As a nationalist, Gallatin sought to build an independent and "extensive empire" through efficient government.[4] National wealth was a product of "internal industry" and "laws for the protection of property."[5] He came to realize that the development of American industry required government aid in the form of transportation improvements, protective tariffs, federal loans, and a sound credit system. Gallatin justified government intervention in the market system out of the necessity of preserving independence and insuring the property rights of all economic interests. Indeed, the protection of property and its exchange sometimes mandated massive intervention by the government in individual activities. Commenting on the Embargo of 1807 he expressed both the danger of and the authority for this intervention. "Government prohibitions do always more mischief than had been calculated, and it is not without much hesitation that a statesman should hazard to regulate the concerns of individuals as if he could do it better than themselves."[6] Nonetheless, his liberal economic nationalism did sanction the greatest invasion of property rights before the Civil War, the embargo.

To understand the political economy of Republican leaders, especially Gallatin, it is useful to reexamine economic liberalism and the economic theory of the preeminent liberal of the era, Adam Smith. In a seminal study of economic liberalism William D. Grampp argues convincingly that classical liberals were not constrained ideologically in their efforts to promote economic development through government activity. In place of the commonplace laissez-faire label for the school, Grampp crafts a more sophisticated interpretation of economic liberalism. He takes seriously the assertion by liberal thinkers of the right of property holders to determine government activities. The issue of government intervention or nonintervention thus loses its ideologically a priori character and becomes a function of the political process. Grampp concludes that "in a liberal economy the state may do whatever the people want it to do and that it is able to do." The "people" were property holders, "those persons who are represented in government, whose opinion the government must take for its guide, and who in the end control the government."[7] Though he fails to mention it, the government would not act in any manner that intentionally undermined the property system, if for no other reason than because the propertied citizenry would never allow it.

Grampp's interpretation is consistent with the overall presentation of liberal thought in this essay. Indeed, it is fatuous to assume that after a century of liberal thinkers' asserting government's responsibility to property holders, a major liberal such as Adam Smith would have replaced this responsibility with a set of eternal proscriptions on government behavior. Such proscriptions would have stripped property holders of their power to determine government action. Government intervention or nonintervention in the economy was a tactical question, open to debate and conditioned by circumstances. In the most famous passage of the *Wealth of Nations,* Smith made it very clear that unrestrained self-interest is only one tactic, and limited, at that, towards increasing national wealth. The pursuer of self-interest, he wrote, "neither intends to promote the public interest, nor knows . . . he is promoting it . . . he intends only his own gain, and he is in this, as in many other cases, led by an invisible hand to promote an end which was not part of his intention." Smith added, cautiously: "Nor is it always the worst for the society that it was no part of it. By pursuing his own interests he frequently promotes that of the society more effectually than when he really intends to promote it."[8]

Such qualifying phrases as "in many other cases," "[not] always the worst," and "frequently," indicate that Smith was proposing a new approach to political economy and not asserting maxims that precluded government intervention in the economy. Where government regulation abetted the accumulation of national wealth, he affirmed it; where it interfered with that accumulation, he proscribed it. Regulations, which in an earlier period were successful tactics in amassing wealth, now retarded national development. Smith labeled those regulations the "mercantile system," and he condemned them. The *Wealth of Nations* was an imaginative summary of existing economic wisdom, an analysis of present economic conditions, and a bold series of policy suggestions derived from a synthesis of the two.[9]

Smith's policy suggestions are relevant to understanding the economic mind set of the Republican leaders, particularly Gallatin.[10] Among Smith's primary suggestions was reduction of the national debt and government expenditure. "The sovereign . . . with all the offices both of justice and war who serve under him, the whole army

and navy, are unproductive labourers." Their "service, how honoura-
ble, how useful, or how necessary soever, produces nothing." The
"great fleets and armies, who in time of peace produce nothing, and in
time of war acquire nothing which can compensate the expense of
maintaining them, . . . are all maintained by the produce of other
men's labour." Governments were "themselves always, and without any
exception, the greatest spendthrifts in the society." They accumulated
"enormous debts which at present oppress, and will in the long-run
probably ruin, all the great nations of Europe." Government debts,
even if repaid, a moral imperative, risked "transporting a great part of
the nation's capital from the hands which were likely to increase and
improve it, to those which are likely to dissipate and destroy it."[11] In
addition to the political problems engendered by the national debt,
Gallatin could find in Smith's writings hard economic reasons to extin-
guish the debt.

Although Smith opposed needless government expenditures on military establishments and bureaucracy, he did recognize the necessity of
national defense and the administration of justice. It was also necessary for the government to erect and maintain "those public institutions and those public works, which, though they may be in the highest degree advantageous to a great society, are, however, of such a
nature, that the profit could never repay the expense to any individual
or small number of individuals." The "works and institutions of this
kind are chiefly those for facilitating the commerce of the society, and
those for promoting the instruction of the people." He elaborated:
"Good roads, canals, and navigable rivers, by diminishing the expense
of carriage, put remote parts of the country more nearly upon a level
with those in the neighborhood of the town. They are upon that
account the greatest of all improvements." Internal improvements "encourage the cultivation of the remote," and "by breaking down the
monopoly of the country in its neighborhood, . . . they open many
new markets to its produce."[12] Gallatin's proposals for internal improvements and a state teachers' academy had an obvious kinship with
Smith's economic theory.

Perhaps Smith was at his ambiguous best in dealing with tariffs and
commercial regulations. Because of their tendency to distort market
forces he disliked restrictions on commerce. The less productive might
be sustained; the industrious suppressed. England's relative advancement in industry accorded it a substantial advantage in a free trade
situation. Removal of tariff barriers would only enhance this advantage, in allowing capital to be shifted from less productive areas to
those where productivity and profits were greater. Moreover, many
English tariffs and labor restrictions grew out of parliamentary log-

rolling or survived as quasi-feudal remnants where the "clamour and sophistry" of special interests had won concessions without any sense of national policy.[13] Neither of these circumstances was operative in America. Thus Smith's proscription of protection on these grounds did not apply to a nation in America's situation.

Another consideration in levying protective tariffs was defense. It "will generally be advantageous," Smith wrote, "to lay some burden upon foreign, for the encouragement of domestic industry . . . when some particular sort of industry is necessary for the defence of the country." He construed defense in a very broad sense, citing, as an example, the English navigation laws. These laws "very properly endeavor to give the sailors and shipping of Great Britain the monopoly of their own country, in some cases, by absolute prohibitions, and in other by heavy burdens upon the shipping of foreign countries." Since defense "is of much more importance than opulence" (i.e., wealth is meaningless if it can be easily stolen), "the act of navigation is, perhaps, the wisest of all the commercial regulations of England."[14] An exception to free trade of this magnitude might be construed to disprove the rule.

Another aspect of trade, not strictly defense-related, which Smith discussed, was commercial discrimination. "The case in which it may sometimes be a matter of deliberation how far it is proper to continue the free importation of certain foreign goods, is, when some foreign nation restrains by high duties or prohibitions the importation of our manufactures into their country." He concluded that "there may be good policy in retaliations . . . when there is a probability that they will procure the repeal of the high duties or prohibitions complained of. The recovery of a great foreign market will generally more than compensate the transitory inconveniency of paying dearer during a short time for some sorts of goods." Even after repeal of the offending nation's levies, "a good deal of reserve and circumspection" was required before lifting the retaliatory duties to avoid injuring manufactures created as a result of those duties.[15] Republican efforts to coerce Britain with nonimportation and embargo—indeed, Jefferson's commercial proposals of 1793—accorded with Smith's thoughts on tariffs and trade. Although it is wrong to construe Smith as protectionist, it is equally misleading to say he opposed all protective measures—particularly if his policy assumptions are applied to a country such as early-nineteenth-century America.

Students of economic thought have now by and large interpreted Smith's political economy as one much less dependent on unbridled competition than was earlier believed. Indeed, they often emphasize Smith's concern for guidance of individuals in their social interactions.[16] The need for its restatement arises out of the way some scholars dealing with the early national period have interpreted Jefferson and the Republican political economy. Linking him and the party to a laissez-faire philosophy of government, they sometimes point to Adam Smith's economic liberalism to support their interpretation. To explain the steps antithetical to laissez-faire that Jefferson and the Republican leaders took while in office, these scholars are compelled to conclude that their "idealism" was compromised by the "realities" of governance. World view becomes irrelevant, expediency is elevated, and any effort to find consistency in the Republicans' political economy is rendered academic. This interpretation is incorrect. Holders of the liberal world view never denied the need to mold policy to circumstances or to be responsive to the interests of propertied citizens. Laissez-faire was a tactic; nonimportation was a tactic; free trade was a tactic; embargo was a tactic; and war itself was a tactic. They were all means to an end: a powerful, independent, and prosperous nation. What was problematic from the statesman's point of view was the creation of a political consensus among the various propertied interests on appropriate government actions to achieve this end. Without a consensus the various economic interests would be allowed to act alone.

The essential role of a republican political system was to assure propertied citizens the ultimate authoritative sanction on government. In this system the statesman assumed the position of mediator among the various interests within the society, their collective right to determine government policy, and his own understanding of the best means to further those interests. Important policy questions, Gallatin insisted, could not be decided "by considerations of immediate profit," particularly when only a few citizens benefited at the expense of the rest. Joyce Appleby captures an essence of Republican policies when she writes, "What was distinctive about the Jeffersonian economic policy was . . . a commitment to growth through the unimpeded exertions of individuals whose access to economic opportunity was both protected and facilitated by government."[17] The long-term viability of the economic system and its continued ability to provide an environment favorable to the livelihood of all citizens were the chief criteria of policymaking.

Gallatin sought to devise a program that would fulfill these criteria and stabilize a newly independent nation. On the one hand, this program would mean constructing a viable national economy apart from—indeed, in defiance of—Great Britain. On the other, it would involve welding together different economic interests whose basis for political cohesion had been only recently state governments and, earlier, the British empire. "Experience," he reflected, "has proven that states . . . though they may be united by one common interest to form a league, will separate as soon as that interest ceases." He concluded that "the only way to prevent dissipation is to increase the conformity of the people['s interests] as much as possible."[18]

To forge an enduring national interest through the creation of a political-economic system that insured all citizens the opportunity to acquire and exchange property came to be Gallatin's overarching concern. If he could construct a national market system in which the pursuit of property would be readily open to all citizens, then political cohesion and stability would follow from the mutual exchange of the fruits of each citizen's property. The manufacturer would buy raw materials and food from the farmer, who, in turn, would buy the manufacturer's goods. The merchant would move supplies to areas of demand and transport any surplus abroad for sale. Individuals in every business would be drawn together, and a popular "conformity" would manifest itself in a consensus for the government's development of the national market system. The corresponding labor specialization would increase the nation's wealth. Not incidentally, domestic manufacturing would free America from dependence on Britain. Again, it was Smith's political economy that best expressed the conceptual basis for Gallatin's system.[19]

Smith's theory of economic development had roots in Humean psychology and the liberal theory of political cohesion. Smith combined self-interest in man and scarcity in nature to explain "a certain propensity in human nature . . . to truck, barter, and exchange one thing for another." This propensity gave rise to the division of labor, which caused "the greatest improvement in the productive powers of labour." Since exchange "gives occasion to the division of labour, so the extent of the division must always be limited . . . by the extent of the market." Without a market for the surplus "no person can have any encouragement to dedicate himself to one employment." It was the market system that created the conditions in which self-interest could be given sway to produce private wealth and public opulence.[20]

For Smith the domestic market was "the most important of all": it "affords the greatest revenue, and creates the greatest employment to the people of the country." Nevertheless, "when the produce of any particular branch of industry exceeds what the demand of the country requires, the surplus must be sent abroad, and exchanged for something for which there is a demand at home. Without such exportation, a part of the productive labour of the country must cease, and the value of its annual produce diminish." Particularly, "the perfection of manufacturing industry . . . depends altogether upon the division of labour; and . . . is necessarily regulated . . . by the extent of the market." In addition to economic development the market system performed a significant social and, by implication, political function. "Commerce . . . among individuals, is a bond of union and friendship." The market system was so potent a force for union that, in the absence of artificial restrictions and geographic impediments, it could unite all economic interests regardless of their nature or location. "Were all nations," Smith concluded, "to follow the liberal system of free exportation and free importation, the different states into which a great continent was divided would so far resemble the different provinces of a great empire."[21]

Both among individuals and among states on a continent like North America the market system could produce union and prosperity. Smith's presentation of the market system as an instrument of political cohesion might have only limited applicability among nations where unrestricted trade meant economic hegemony. But within a continent undivided by independent (white) nations, where the majority owned property, political cohesion based on the market was possible. In this respect Smith's market system could become the centripetal force countering the centrifugal forces of American federalism integral to Hume's and Madison's method of controlling factions. Extending the political sphere might forestall a faction from seizing power, but expansion loosened the bonds of political affection and national unity. A strong market system might reintegrate otherwise divergent groups and individuals. Moreover, extension of the market meant economic development and national prosperity.

The market became, in Gallatin's political economy, an instrument of social stability. Operating on these premises he could integrate individual freedom, national development, and political stability. If government refrained from serving any particular economic interest — that is, any faction — to the detriment of the rest, it could work to link all economic interests into a national market system, develop each, and expand all. The market system could function not only as the means to national prosperity and independence, but also as the instrument of political cohesion in a society (and continental empire) based on private, individual acquisition of property.

Gallatin recognized the tension inherent in government efforts to build an independent market system. In America the different economic interests and their tendency to be divided sectionally placed a heavy burden on national leadership. He rejected Hamilton's efforts to build the power of some merchants at the expense of agricultural, manufacturing, and other mercantile interests. In Congress he attacked any measure that "operated partially upon other parts of the

Union, though it might operate in favor of his constituents." Congress was "representative of the whole union" and should not "throw a burden upon one part of the union, because the part in which they were most particularly interested, would escape it."[22] Later, as Treasury secretary, he told Jefferson that Republican rule "should rest on the broad basis of the people, not on a fluctuating party majority."[23] Each branch of government, particularly the executive, had to create policies that balanced the general interest of the nation with the various interests of its parts. In all his efforts to promote economic development Gallatin never lost sight of the fact that in America's "half consolidated, half federalistic form the government . . . the bond of Union if made too tight would snap."[24]

II

Gallatin advanced comprehensive proposals for development of a national market system in the areas of internal improvements and central banking. While the timing of each proposal was linked to events during the Republican administration's first decade in office, they all related to demands the various interest groups within the party had made over the years. Each promised economic development based on theories, elaborated by Adam Smith, of the market system and the division of labor. More important, all Gallatin's proposals reiterated the function of the market system as a bond of union. Indeed, political stabilization through economic development is unquestionably the central element of his political economy.

The first area, transportation, developed directly out of the need to integrate the western United States into political and economic union with the East. Gallatin broached his ideas for a national transportation network in February 1802, when he submitted suggestions for internal improvements to William B. Giles, House majority leader. Gallatin proposed that 10 percent of the proceeds from land sales be used to build turnpikes between navigable waterways and less accessible areas. The extension of the market system would "contribute towards cementing the bonds of Union between those parts of the United States whose local interests have been considered as most dissimilar."[25] His annual Treasury report to the House of December 1806 looked forward three years toward the release of "the public revenues from every incumbrance." At that time they would be "applicable to such new objects of general improvements or national defense, as the Legislature might direct, and existing circumstances require."[26] The following year his report stressed "internal improvements, which, while increasing and diffusing the national wealth, will strengthen the bonds of union."[27] What made these improvements "national objects" and how they "strengthen the bonds of union," Gallatin explained to the House in a letter on the Cumberland Road. "The road can only be considered as a national object only if completed as a turnpike, whereby all the flour and other produce of the western adjacent counties may be brought to a market on the Atlantic shores; and the transportation of all salt and other commodities and merchandise whatever, imported from the Atlantic ports to Western country."[28] To Jefferson he again affirmed the road "as a national object of great importance (particularly as a bond of Union)."[29]

Politically, a federally constructed transportation network was important to the Republican constituencies of rising entrepreneurial groups. To these merchants, farmers, and manufacturers, development of the market system meant new outlets for trade and expansion of production facilities. within the states the Republican party often championed internal improvements.[30] In new areas of settlement the extension of the market meant prosperity and economic growth.[31] More subtly, internal improvements speeded the metamorphosis of subsistence farming into market-oriented agriculture. Since strong Federalist sympathies frequently persisted among the nonmarket farmers, the development of transportation would tend to disrupt this political alignment and integrate these farmers into the Republican coalition. Internal improvements supplemented the rhetorical appeal of "noble yeoman" with the concrete opportunity of new markets.

Directly related to the extension of the market was the Louisiana Territory and Gallatin's efforts to insure the federal government's role in developing its potential. The investment of several million dollars required some federal commitment to insure a return for the money. Settlement and cultivation of the land could not be separated from transportation facilities for marketing the consequent output. Gallatin planned to set aside a portion of the land sale proceeds for these facilities. But his proposals for massive infusions of federal money awaited the extinction of the debt, which still consumed two-thirds of the federal budget. He refused to borrow money to finance internal improvements because contemporary economic theory taught that every dollar loaned to government was one less dollar available to invest in private enterprise. Moreover, in peacetime, government borrowing was an unwarranted infringement on individual liberty and economic freedom. Despite his fervent desire to build a nationwide transportation network, he made no comprehensive proposals until 1808, when the extinction of the debt was at hand.

Gallatin issued his Report on Roads and Canals in April 1808. Prodded by his Treasury report of December 1806, the Senate requested the study in February 1807. In the covering letter of the report Gallatin restated his belief that "a general system of improvements intended to connect the most distant parts of our extensive territory [was] one of the strongest bonds of Union which can be superadded to those which already connect the several states."[32] The report began by asserting the unquestioned utility of roads and canals in increasing national wealth. It detailed several major commercial routes in need of development, including the future Erie Canal and the western access routes of future railroads. The core of his program was direct federal aid of at least $20 million over a ten-year period in loans to and partnerships with private development companies. He argued that private and state resources simply were not adequate to the task. Then he turned to the market system.

Opening new outlets for trade, Gallatin explained, would "stimulate the spirit of enterprise so conspicuous in the American character." National roads and canals "will shorten distances, facilitate commercial and personal intercourse, and unite, by a still more intimate community of interests, the most remote quarters of the United States." In America's business society the market system was the nexus of political cohesion and national community. Any government operation which facilitated commercial intercourse strengthened the nation by strengthening its market system. "No other single operation," he concluded, "within the power of Government, can more effectually tend to strengthen and perpetuate that Union which secures external independence, domestic peace, and internal liberty." Carter Goodrich has aptly labeled this report "one of the greatest planning documents in American history."[33]

Although the Senate request for the report passed 22 to 3, little action resulted from its receipt. A committee formed to consider it suggested 1,200 copies be printed and distributed to members of Congress and the public. International crises drew attention away from internal improvements. Not until January 1810 was any bill introduced in the Senate to implement Gallatin's suggestions for federal aid. It incorporated Gallatin's major suggestions for federal subscription of up to one-half the capital stock of any eligible canal or turnpike corporation. The federal stock would bear 6 percent interest secured by a land reserve in the Northwest. The legislation named thirteen specific locations for internal improvements. Finally, the bill accorded the president one-third of the votes in any corporation the government aided. The following month a similar bill was also introduced in the House. Although there was sporadic debate on the measure, a final bill never came to a vote in either chamber before or during the War of 1812.[34]

All Gallatin's plans for federal aid depended on a comprehensive banking system to work with the government and private enterprise to provide credit and facilitate loans. The expansion of economic activity required credit facilities to discount bills and concentrate capital for production and distribution. A central banking system was integral to the execution of these extensive government activities in the economy. It would also support private, local banks and mediate the pace of economic activity. The Bank of the United States had the potential for this role, but it would have to transcend partisan biases. It needed to assume a role much like that of the government, an impartial overseer and promoter of all business activities. From his first days as Treasury secretary Gallatin sought to transform the bank into this type of institution.

In dealing with the bank Gallatin assumed the role of mediator between the strong antibank wing of the Republican party, including Jefferson, and mercantile and banking interests, Republican and otherwise, which supported the institution. As a Pennsylvania legislator, he had helped to charter a bank in that state along lines similar to the federal bank. In his *Sketch of the Finances* he had approved the bank, regretting only its abuse by excessive government borrowing. When he took office as Treasury secretary, Gallatin informed the bank's president, Thomas Willing, that "it is equally in the interest of this department and of the Bank of the United States mutually to observe the most liberal spirit of accommodation towards each other." He felt "disposed to show on every occasion the sincerity of my wishes for the prosperity and advantage of the institution," and he did not doubt its "support and accommodation" for the "public good." In deference to party sentiments, Gallatin asked that this letter and others to follow be kept "perfectly confidential . . . especially as it relates to a monied institution."[35]

The desire for privacy stemmed from his wish not to antagonize the antibank members of his party. His correspondence with Jefferson revealed precisely such a disagreement over the banking issue. In June 1802 Gallatin asked the president's approval to contract with the Bank of Pennsylvania, which he had helped to create, part of the repayment of the Dutch debt. By placing the funds for the payment in this bank, the contract would provide temporary support for repayment of its notes discounted (paid and held) by the United States Bank. He explained that the Bank of Pennsylvania "chiefly supports retail shopkeepers," while the United States Bank "generally discounts importers." He wanted to aid the former without antagonizing the latter, which served a useful purpose in the national revenue system and as a source of loans to government.[36] Jefferson denied him permission to support the state bank on the ground that more deposits would only aggravate the problem of overextension. "The monopoly of a single bank is certain an evil," Jefferson explained, "The multiplication of them was intended to cure it; but it multiplied an influence of the same character with the first." He concluded that the banks had supplanted "the precious metals by a paper circulation [and] between such parties the less we meddle the better."[37]

Jefferson often expressed his desire to make "all banks Republican by sharing deposits among them in proportion to the dispositions they show." Such partisanship could have disrupted the functions of the United States Bank while fostering pro-Republican banking institutions.[38] Gallatin would not acquiesce in Jefferson's desire to use government deposits to Republicanize banks. He knew that government revenues held in the Bank of the United States were integral to its solvency, its support of federal fiscal operations, and its loan operations. He disagreed with the president over the utility of the bank, pointing out that it supplied safe repository for government deposits, eased revenue transmission, and increased monetary circulation through its credit and lending activities, which aided revenue collection. The administration, he insisted, had nothing to fear; the bank was "completely in our power and may be crushed," if necessary.[39] Despite these arguments Jefferson still considered the bank to be "one of the most deadly hostile existing, against the principles and form of our constitution." He feared that "an institution like this, penetrating by its branches every part of the Union, acting by command in phalanx may in a critical moment upset the government."[40] Years later Gallatin wrote that Jefferson "lived and died a decided enemy of our banking system generally, and specially to a bank of the United States."[41]

It is significant that the president's personal sentiments did not disrupt the administration's monetary policy nor lead it to any serious political assaults on the banking system. On the contrary, under Gallatin's auspices relations between the administration and the bank flourished. In May 1804 Gallatin arranged government revenue deposits to prevent a specie shortage, "equally injurious to commerce and our revenue."[42] This was not the first time he interceded on behalf of the bank and its commercial clients. Two years earlier he sold the government's bank stock to the House of Baring in London to make a debt payment to the Dutch rather than come into the domestic commercial paper market. To the bank's president, Willing, he explained that "I have been less guided by the facility thereby given to the Government operations, than by the general relief it will afford to the

commercial interest." In closing he hoped that the liquidation of federal holdings in the bank "will no degree affect the friendly & liberal
relations which have heretofore subsisted between Government &
Bank, which it will ever be my duty to promote & increase."[43]

Gallatin established a branch of the bank in Washington and
pressed for another branch in New Orleans to transmit tax revenues
and serve "as a bond of union between the Atlantic and Mississippi
interests."[44] He was also careful to insure good relations between the
Bank of the United States and state banks. Gallatin warned David
Lenox, Willing's successor, to check any causes for complaint concerning the loan policies of the bank's Baltimore branch. Local banks
would often borrow from the U.S. Bank to finance their commercial
activities. If these loans fell due before a ship voyage financed by it had
been completed, the local bank would lack the money to repay the
loan. Repayment pressures exerted by the bank on local banks caused
them to ask that government revenues collected locally be deposited in
their banks. They could then repay the loans with the federal revenues
and then cover the federal account when their loans to merchants or
retailers were repaid. Gallatin did not want federal revenue spread
among the less stable banks. He reminded Lenox that no use of the
bank's power "ought certainly be made to [the state banks'] injury
beyond what is necessary for the safety" of the bank itself. Both the
interest of the public and the interest of the bank required prudence in
the exercise of the latter's power—particularly since these local banks
were generally owned by prominent Republicans.[45] Here again Gallatin endeavored to mold the bank into an institution responsible to
the entire economic system and not to any particular interest.

When the time approached for the 1811 renewal of the bank's charter, Gallatin prepared a comprehensive report on its function and an
audacious plan for its reorganization. In this report to Congress he
surveyed the origins and financial structure of the institution. Employing simple, straightforward language, no doubt designed to demystify
its operations in the minds of antibank Republicans, he explained its
discounting and note-issuing procedures and its profits. After this explanation and a detailed description of present bank stock ownership,
property holdings, and outstanding loans, he concluded that "the
affairs of the Bank of the United States, considered as a moneyed
institution, have been wisely and skillfully managed." He listed four
chief advantages the government derived from the bank: safekeeping
of the public monies, collection of the revenues, transmission of government funds, and availability of loans to government. Only a central
bank could adequately provide those advantages. To counter the

charge of foreign influence Gallatin pointed out that foreign share-
holders had no vote. Moreover, he suggested retiring their $7.2 million
in stock through an equal subscription to American citizens, thereby
eliminating the problem. Then he presented his plan for the reorganization of the bank.[46]

As a first step, Gallatin proposed expanding the bank's capital
threefold to $30 million through a new stock issue. State governments
would be encouraged to subscribe to the new issue, and in return for
their subscription, the bank would open a branch within their boundaries. To those participating states and the federal government, he
offered "some share" in the bank's direction. His report suggested two
further changes: interest payments on excess government revenue on
deposit and an expanded obligation to lend the government two-thirds
of its capital. Reorganized in this manner "the bank itself would form
an additional bond of common interest and union, amongst the several states."[47]

Gallatin's plan was an excellent illustration of his political economy. Various interests represented in state governments were to be
incorporated into the central monetary organ of the market system.
The plan would inhibit any self-serving, abusive activities by the bank
and maximize its role in economic development. It would mobilize
both state and federal revenues in this development and lay a sound
foundation for national growth. Ultimately the growth and development of the national market system would bond the particular interests of the country into a mutual interest. The bank and the government would stand as the twin pillars of national economic expansion.
In this plan for the reorganization of the bank Gallatin's political
economy reached an apotheosis.

Gallatin's efforts to recharter and reorganize the bank proved futile.
The recharter legislation did incorporate his suggestion for enlarging
the bank's capital, but only to $20 million. States were accorded the
right to purchase shares and to establish branches within their boundaries. The legislation provided for a greater federal and state role in the
bank's direction. In letters to Congress Gallatin pleaded for the bank's
recharter. "It is impossible," he told William Crawford in January
1811, "that an institution which circulates thirteen millions of dollars,
and to whom the merchants owe fourteen, should terminate its operations . . . without giving a serious shock to commercial banking and
national credit." Nonetheless, the vested interests of some powerful
legislators and their constituents in state banks and their belief that a
lucrative business from the government and merchants might befall
them defeated the bank's renewal in the Senate.[48] Although Gallatin's
and the bank's subsequent efforts mitigated most of the harmful reper-

cussions of its demise, the fiscal chaos of the War of 1812 and the postwar years proved correct his predictions of dire consequences. Congress finally created a second Bank of the United States in 1816.

III

Prior to the War of 1812 Congress implemented none of Gallatin's plans for economic development. Indeed, Gallatin himself allowed his proposals, with the exception of that for the bank, to slide. There are several reasons for their failure to pass Congress. Primarily, the revenue and spending impact of Republican foreign policy eliminated the funds to implement Gallatin's proposals. Whenever he offered suggestions for new government spending, there were two caveats: that the debt be eliminated and that military preparations be unnecessary. His reasons for according priority to the debt have been explained in detail. As Graph 10 illustrates, international problems drained federal revenue. The embargo and nonimportation reduced tariff revenues. Without internal taxes, federal revenues were inadequate to finance internal improvements. Increased military outlays simply commanded all available funds and postponed Gallatin's loan program. "Gallatin himself," Carter Goodrich explains, "was forced to modify his position and finally lay aside the advocacy of internal improvements in order to protect the strength of the Treasury."[49]

There was another significant element in Congress's failure to enact the reports' recommendations: the interests of many Republicans in state aid to enterprises. This interest was most salient in the failure to recharter the Bank of the United States. Confronted in the 1790s by Federalist-controlled banks, the rising entrepreneurs, who constituted the nucleus of the Republican party, fought bitterly to extract state charters for their new banks. Often the bulwark of the Federalist banking establishment was a branch of the Bank of the United States. Samuel Smith, Stephen Girard, John Jacob Astor, Jacob Crowinshield, Aaron Burr, and other pillars of the Republican party had led this battle against Federalist dominance of banking. Despite Gallatin's efforts to recast the Bank of the United States into an institution without partisan demeanor, the antipathies remained and blocked the recharter. Too much money and emotion were at stake in 1810 to overcome partisan opposition to the recharter effort.[50]

State aid to internal improvements had a less obvious impact on Gallatin's plans. Although states had been financing internal improvements, similar federal aid did not represent competition as did the United States Bank. Recipients welcomed all government aid. Thus state aid did not preclude constituent requests for federal funds. Certainly interstate roads and canals were chiefly a federal concern. Although state desires for federal incentives were undiminished by state aid, congressional willingness to provide such incentives might have been. Representatives from the South, where transportation facilities were very good, might have been less inclined to finance canals or roads in the West or the North. On the other hand, many smaller farmers in the South owned lands in less accessible regions and welcomed federal or state aid. The precise impact of state aid on Congress's failure to enact Gallatin's proposals is not clear. It appears that the absorption of federal resources by war preparations and foreign policy obstructed his plans for a transportation system.[51]

Madison and Jefferson were not always in perfect accord with all Gallatin's proposals for economic development. Gallatin once observed that he was "not quite so orthodox . . . as my Virginia friends [on] the U. States Bank & internal improvements."[52] It is significant that Gallatin did *not* include the promotion of manufactures among his differences with Jefferson and Madison. In the case of the bank, Madison joined Gallatin in the 1810 recharter fight and signed the 1816 recharter legislation into law. Jefferson disliked the bank, but the economic necessity of banking, which Gallatin stressed constantly to him, wrought his acquiescence if not his enthusiasm. Jefferson did, as Gallatin later observed, die an enemy of banking and the United States Bank. Nevertheless, while in power, he deferred to Gallatin's judgment on banking issues.

Internal improvements enjoyed much greater support from Jefferson. Whenever he spoke of the liberation of American revenues from debt service, he offered internal improvements as an object for congressional consideration. They would, he explained, open "new channels of communication . . . between the States; the lines of separation will disappear their interests will be identified and their union cemented by new and indissolvable ties."[53] Madison, too, agreed with Gallatin on the utility of a better transportation network built with federal funds. Both presidents did have some constitutional reservations about congressional authority in this area. Madison vetoed an internal improvements bill in 1816, questioning the design of the program and the constitutional authority of Congress. His constitutional scruples reflected two concerns. He wanted to avoid expanding the implied powers within the document in the absence of a national emergency. Secondly, he believed that the larger the federal intervention into the economy, the more extensive the political consensus had to be. A constitutional amendment would require precisely such an extensive consensus for ratification.[54] Gallatin, on the other hand, thought the approbation of Congress an adequate measure of popular volition.

More significant than their differences is the cohesion with which they confronted these issues of economic development. Unlike their predecessors in the first administration, Jefferson's secretaries of state and treasury did not openly split and carry their causes into partisan politics. Though the rank-and-file party members often quarreled among themselves and occasionally with their leaders, the principals — Gallatin, Jefferson, and Madison — managed to maintain their rapport in policymaking. And in the most critical arena of all, foreign affairs, they led decisively and without mutual dissension. Such a feat was remarkable considering the bitter partisanship of the decade they succeeded.

CHAPTER NINE

The Republicans in Power
Political Economy and Foreign Policy

The future destinies of the Missouri Country are of vast importance to the United States.
—Gallatin to Jefferson, April 13, 1803

The conduct of the nation against whom this resort [of war] has been proclaimed left no choice but between that & the greater evil of a surrender of our Sovereignty on the Element, on which all nations have equal rights, and in the free use of which, the U.S. as a nation whose agriculture & commerce are so closely allied, have an essential interest.
—Madison, July 25, 1812

The Republican administration's foreign policy had its roots in the positions Jefferson, Madison, and Gallatin adopted in the 1790s. During their tenure, the major focus of American foreign policy was on Europe and the Americas. The Republicans' interest in these areas had a common root in the domestic economy's dependence on foreign commerce and markets. Linked with their efforts to build a national market system, foreign markets insured the exchange of surplus products and provided the country with commodities necessary for its economic well-being. When commercial property went to sea, so too did the government's obligation to protect it. The most important foreign markets were in Europe, Latin America, and the Caribbean islands.[1] An analysis of Republican foreign policy thus requires an examination of the assumptions the triumvirate made about government's role in commerce and of the trade patterns of American merchants.

I

The triumvirate understood that free trade was Chimera and that unrestricted access to world markets could only be wrought through

government intervention. Madison articulated their common understanding in a letter to Clarkson Crolius. "There are practical exceptions to the Theory [of free trade], which sufficiently speak for themselves. The Theory itself requires a similarity of circumstances, and an
equal freedom of interchange among commercial nations, which have
never existed."[2] The greatest impediment to unrestricted commerce
was England. If, Gallatin observed, "an enlightened policy should induce both governments to throw trade perfectly open . . . it cannot be
denied that it will give us a very great share of their carrying trade."[3]
Britain's carrying trade was financially important to its merchants and
a labor reserve for its navy. Since America's chief maritime rival would
not curb its commercial restrictions, the Republican leadership could
not consider a laissez faire commercial policy. To do so would mean
economic subordination to England.

In place of free trade the Republican leaders developed commercial
discrimination and reciprocity treaties. England resisted reciprocity
and thus became the target of commercial discrimination designed to
restrict the flow of its manufactured exports to America. As early as
1791 Jefferson had explained the dialectical relationship between domestic manufactures and British hegemony. If England restricted
American markets abroad, America would develop manufactures to
absorb its raw materials at home. Jefferson's Report on Commerce
and Madison's commercial resolutions of 1794 were early expressions
of this policy. Nonimportation and the 1807 embargo also rested on
commercial discrimination. "If [the English] repeal their orders, we
must repeal our embargo," Jefferson told Madison, "If they keep up
impressments, we must adhere to non-intercourse, manufactures and
a navigation act."[4] Commercial discrimination had two functions: to
coerce Britain and to foster domestic manufactures. Domestic manufactures, in turn, would provide a market for American raw materials
and render the nation less dependent on British goods.

It is analytically inadequate to examine only the patterns of American foreign trade in order to understand Republican foreign policy.
Nonetheless they are significant. Although the British empire consistently received more of America's domestically produced goods than
any other nation, its share of aggregate American trade never exceeded
one-half. Thus, British markets were not as important as *aggregate*
non-British markets. Politically, too, the non-British markets were
significant owing to the involvement in that trade of the Republican
party's constituencies of merchants and commercial farmers. During
wartime Britain's share of America's export trade dropped approximately from 45 percent to 25 percent. Consequently, in the first decade
of the nineteenth century the war-spawned carrying trade reduced the

importance of British markets to American merchants by roughly one-half (see Graph 11). As it had in the 1790s, Europe's war radically altered the economic interests of American merchants. The same dynamic that had nearly resulted in war in 1794 operated in 1804-7 and 1808-12: British seizures of American ships trading outside its empire.

The magnitude of foreign trade and its effects on the domestic price level had a major impact on economic interest groups in America. Agrarian interests were most affected by farm prices, and merchants, by trade volume. Graphs 12 and 13 illustrate the impact of foreign trade. The brief peace in Europe (1801-3) caused prices of farm products and manufactured goods to fall in the aftermath of a precipitous decline in commerce. The American economy derived little benefit from a pacific Europe. Once the war resumed, however, a spectacular rise in international commerce and in the prices of all products again brought substantial prosperity to the United States. All interest groups, including some manufacturers (especially the shipbuilders), benefited from the high prices and heavy trade. This prosperity ceased with the imposition of the embargo at the end of 1807.

Several facts are salient in the period prior to the embargo. Agricultural prices peaked in 1805 and then declined steadily during the two years before the embargo. From 1805 to 1807 farm prices declined by 13 percent; in the year of the embargo they fell 23 percent. Assuming a price decline consistent with the 1805-7 period during 1808, one would have predicted a 6.5 percent decline. Although the net decline in price attributable to the embargo was 16.5 percent—no small amount—the farmers were somewhat conditioned to a weak market by two years of falling prices. Since their expectations were lower, their perceived loss was less. The merchants were another matter. During the same two-year period before the embargo, they had experienced a 12.5 percent increase in trade. When the embargo took hold, their trade dropped by 80 percent. Again projecting a continuation of prior trends into 1808, one would have predicted a 6 percent increase in trade. Thus, the net loss in trade attributed to the embargo was 86 percent. Merchants, then, perceived and experienced a far greater loss than farmers from the embargo and their expectations of growth made the loss all the more traumatic. They attributed this loss to their government's policy (the embargo) and not to English actions, while the farmers looked more toward the actions of foreign governments as the cause of their declining prices in the pre-embargo period.

The merchants had little reason to desire such a commercially devastating foreign policy move, and as Anne Clauder observes, they were in fact generally quiescent about British seizures in the months before the embargo.[5] Their initial political acceptance of the move was based on its pacific nature, as earlier embargoes had been, and not on its use as a weapon to starve England into submission. The farmers, on the other hand, had more reason for anger against English actions and were more likely to accept further hardships. Two years of lower prices also cushioned them to some extent against the further price decline the embargo wrought. Alone among the major interest groups, manufactures reaped great benefits from the embargo: new capital from merchants, a steep rise in the prices of manufactured goods, and decline in raw material costs.

This situation contrasts with 1810–11. In the two years before Madison's call for war, farm prices again experienced a decline of 10 percent after a swift rise following the termination of the embargo. The consequent agrarian discontent has been well documented by George R. Taylor.[6] This time, however, the merchants too experienced a 9 percent decline in their trade. More significantly, the reexport or carrying trade fell off by one-third between 1810 and 1811. This decline in reexports occurred in Europe as a result of the British blockade of the Continent. Unlike the year before the embargo, the year before the war saw both farmers and merchants suffering serious economic dislocations as a direct result of British actions. Both groups looked toward non-European markets to offset the effects of blockade. This situation underscored the growing importance of America's trade with Latin America, which, in 1811, accounted for 15 percent of the total American export trade and 31 percent of its carrying trade.

Changes in commercial patterns loomed large politically for two reasons. First, since the party's inception, the core of Republican support among merchants had come from those individuals involved in the carrying trade to non-British markets in Europe and Latin America. The generally Federalist merchants trading with the British empire were less affected by the decline in the carrying trade. Exports of domestically produced goods to the British empire and areas under its hegemony, such as the Iberian Peninsula, actually rose in the 1810–11 period. Thus, the decline in trade afflicted principally Republican merchants. Secondly, America's chief commercial rival in Latin America was England. Not only was the Royal Navy seizing American ships bound for Europe, but it was also obstructing the carrying trade to Latin America—by far the largest market in that trade (see Graph 14). Whatever depredations Napoleon might inflict on American commerce to Europe paled before Britain's unequaled assaults on U.S. commerce in Europe and in Latin America. Arthur P. Whitaker's emphasis on the Anglo-American conflict in Latin America as a principal economic cause for war appears unmistaken.[7]

The intensity of this conflict is underscored by the British experi-

ence during the embargo. With American ships at bay and its markets
closed, English mercantile houses turned toward Latin America to
compensate for the loss. Their move was highly successful in warding
off economic disaster. When the Republicans reinstituted their commercial discrimination policy in 1811, it coincided with a cyclical
downturn in the English economy. The result was a deep depression,
and as in 1808, British business again looked toward Latin American
markets for relief. In this respect, Anglo-American competition for
these markets was an extension of the coercion intended by the Republican nonimportation policy. Moreover, the conflict over Latin American markets was fast becoming a centerpiece of American foreign
policy concerns. Madison connived in private business efforts to abet
revolutionary movements in South America.[8] American commerce
with its southern neighbors, then, was significant beyond mere quantitative measure.

As the complexities involving the Latin American trade demonstrate, simple commercial data alone do not explain foreign policy.
They are best understood as the context which provoked the Republican leaders to act without determining their policy. Policy is a response
to conditions. Its precise character is molded by ideology, political
interests, and practicality. That prominent Republicans such as Samuel Smith and Stephen Girard were losing their Latin American markets to British merchants protected by British warships undeniably had
an influence over the triumvirate's policy toward Britain. In the absence of conflicts over trade and markets there would have been no
nonimportation, no embargo, and no war—in short, no foreign policy
to analyze. Political economy is the key—the translation of the fundamental commercial context into policy. It relates the interests of a
political constituency to the overall aims of government policy. British
interference with American commerce did not evoke the same response from Hamilton as it did from the Republican leaders. Their
concept of the national interest—their political economy—was
different from his. Essentially, it was the Republican concept of the
national interest as it related to the patterns of commerce mentioned
above that molded their foreign policies.

II

It is sometimes forgotten that American westward expansion was part
of foreign policy. This lapse in memory is due in part to the sense of
inevitability retrospection accords past events. The sense of inevitability was prospective as well. The founders firmly believed that the
United States would dominate, if not settle, the Americas. Their belief

was rooted in more than economic necessity; it was ideological and cultural as well. In the spirit of Bishop George Berkeley's early-eighteenth-century pronouncement that "westward is the course of empire," European civilization and its offspring had looked toward the setting sun for trade, plantation, and empire. Their sense of inevitable expansion is important in that it allowed Americans to wait with confidence for the continent and shifts the explanatory burden for policies on more immediate concerns.[9]

There were concrete socioeconomic elements in American expansion: the need to make property available to a growing population, the development of natural resources for economic growth, and the political stability afforded by a large republic. Widespread property ownership or at least the promise of such ownership was essential to a democratic republic. Voters had to be independent in their livelihoods and sound in their basic interests. Cheap, abundant, and fecund land was America's greatest resource in the early nineteenth century. Foodstuffs and cotton were its largest exports, and their availability reduced raw-material and labor costs. Political stability from a large republic found its first expression in Madison's Tenth *Federalist*. Jefferson, too, insisted that Montesquieu's doctrine, which held small territory integral to republican government, was false. As late as 1821 he wrote, "I still believe that the Western expansion of our confederacy will ensure its duration, by overruling local factions, which might shake a smaller association."[10]

The greatest example of territorial expansion in this era, the Louisiana Purchase, is very much linked with these concerns. Spain's cession of Louisiana to France in early 1801 set the purchase in motion. Republican leaders considered Spain a decadent empire, slowly collapsing under the weight of its lethargy. They could tolerate Spanish custodianship until natural forces ended the interregnum. France, however, was another matter. The spectre of Napoleon's armies invading North America and confining the United States east of the Mississippi River was frightening and intolerable. In a statement extraordinary for its belligerence and threat of Anglo-American alliance, Jefferson ordered Minister of France Robert Livingston to warn Talleyrand that "there is on the globe one single spot, the possessor of which is our natural and habitual enemy." The spot was New Orleans, "through which the produce of three-eighths of our territory must pass to market, and from its fertility it will ere long yield more than half our whole produce and contain more than half our inhabitants." He concluded with some exaggeration, "The day that France takes possession of New Orleans . . . we must marry ourselves to the British fleet and nation."[11]

In analyzing this policy statement we must make some allowance for diplomatic hyperbole. Jefferson was after all only threatening Napoleon with a British alliance and war. Nevertheless, the statement reveals a great deal about the political economy of Republican foreign policy. Jefferson's basic concern stemmed from New Orleans's role as an outlet to foreign markets. The necessity of exchanging the products of property compelled government to protect markets as an adjunct to securing property in general. Over one-third of American exports, potentially much more, depended on passage through New Orleans. Any French obstruction of that route was the equivalent of the British naval blockades, only more dangerous and effective. Continued settlement of the continent depended on access to markets. Upon the extension of the market system rested economic development and national independence. Little wonder Jefferson threatened to ally America with England. Access to market, he told Monroe, would determine "the future destinies of this republic."[12]

Privately, to his manufacturing friend Pierre DuPont, Jefferson equated the New Orleans "crisis" to that of the Revolutionary War. Any "power" holding "the country east of the Mississippi becomes our natural enemy." He concluded that "peace and friendship with our neighbors" were possible only "*if our rights of navigation and deposit are respected.*" The emphasis was his.[13] Madison was no less belligerent. He instructed Livingston and Monroe, the special envoy, to contact the English government on the assumption "that war is inevitable" if France refused to relinquish New Orleans.[14] Gallatin, ever wary of Britain, suggested seizing New Orleans and all of Louisiana to preclude English occupation should Anglo-French hostilities commence.[15] The purchase resolved the crisis in America's favor and avoided war. On no previous occasion did the triumvirate express such immediate and uncompromising determination to make war rather than acquiesce. They "were sensible," Jefferson told Congress after the purchase, "that the continuance of that privation would be more injurious to our nation than any consequences which could flow from any mode of redress."[16]

The Lewis and Clark expedition reinforced the strong link between western settlement and commerce. Gallatin suggested to Jefferson that the expedition collect detailed information on all major rivers and tributaries "for the purpose of examining the communication with the Pacific Ocean."[17] Jefferson echoed his suggestions in instructing Lewis to discover a commercially viable northwest passage. "The object of your mission is to explore the Missouri river and such principal streams . . . [as] may offer the most direct and practicable water communication across this continent, for the purposes of commerce."

Jefferson's instructions to Lewis were virtually identical with those he gave another western explorer a decade earlier.[18] The New Orleans crisis and Louisiana Purchase illustrate several points about Republican foreign policy. Economic considerations were primary, as they were in Hamilton's acceptance of Jay's Treaty. Insofar as western expansion and settlement played a direct role, they too were mediated by economic factors. Without a market for surplus products, significant enduring settlement was not feasible. War was an extension of national economic policy. National honor and national interest were indistinct. "We are firmly convinced," Jefferson told his countrymen, "and we act on that conviction, that with nations, as with individuals, our interests soundly calculated, will ever be found inseparable from our moral duties."[19]

The West Florida controversy followed on the heels of the New Orleans crisis.[20] West Florida was a strip of land running between the Deep South and the Gulf of Mexico from present-day Florida to New Orleans. The rapidly developing cotton and rice cultivation in that area depended on an extensive river network through West Florida to the gulf. Although not a crisis of New Orleans's magnitude—the Spanish, not the French, controlled West Florida—it did present a problem to the administration. Madison explained to Monroe and Livingston that "settlements . . . are beginning; and the people have already called on the Government to procure the proper outlets to foreign markets."[21] The subsequent negotiations with Spain failed, but pressure for an American occupation of West Florida persisted. Repeatedly Gallatin reminded Jefferson and Madison of its extreme importance to increasing American trade. More than once he suggested seizing it by military force, though he preferred negotiation. Either way, "the natural growth of the United States . . . [will] enforce the claim to its full extent."[22] Jefferson constructed a more legalistic argument for seizure and by 1807 concluded that East Florida should be taken as well. As long as Spain remained France's ally, the United States could occupy the Floridas in reparation for French and Spanish depredations on American commerce. He also feared English intervention in Spain's name if the Spanish rebels managed to unseat Napoleon's brother from the Madrid throne. Ultimately, when America seized West Florida and "purchased" the peninsula, money was not exchanged between the two governments. As Jefferson suggested, the United States government merely imputed a payment based on commercial seizures attributed to Spain.[23]

Madison had the most direct dealings with the problem of the Floridas as secretary of state and president. By 1806 he described East Florida as "important" and West Florida as "essential" to U.S. inter-

ests.[24] In a most revealing passage Madison touched on the connection
between domestic political concerns and foreign policy. The "obsti-
nacy of the Spanish authorities in vexing and obstructing the use of
the Mobille [sic] by our Citizens living on its Waters, and having no
other channels of communication with the sea, is kindling a flame
which has been with difficulty kept under, and must in a short time
require force to resist." The "time is approaching when the [govern-
ment] may have no other choice, than between a foreign and an internal conflict."[25] In other words, Spain was obstructing the access of
American citizens to foreign markets. These citizens were demanding
that their government take action to secure their property and markets. Both principle and practicality dictated that the government
fulfill its basic function to protect property and respond to its citizens'
legitimate demands. Failure to do so would invite popular action in
defiance of the government — a defiance justified by natural right. Foreign policy was not a power game played by diplomats, but an extension of domestic political and economic exigencies.

Given the choice between domestic strife and foreign conflict, the
government would make war. War, however, became unnecessary. Local property holders, encouraged by agents of the federal executive,
seized West Florida from the Spanish in 1810. Under Madison's executive authority, state militia entered the area and secured it for the
United States. Madison justified the invasion on national security
grounds to preclude "foreign interference with W.F. or . . . internal
convulsions, more especially if threatening the neighboring tranquility
[and] to take care of the rights & interests of the U.S."[26] It was the first
time agents of the executive aided in toppling a foreign government
from power as a prelude to American economic and, in this case,
political penetration.

As West Florida became U.S. territory, the Republican leaders focused on the Caribbean and Latin America. Writing to Charles Pinckney in Spain, Madison expressed the administration's determination to
retain West Florida, acquire East Florida, and keep Britain out of
both. Beyond the Floridas, the "position of Cuba gives the United
States so deep an interest in the destiny, even of that Island, that . . .
they could not be a satisfied spectator at its falling under any European Government, which might make a fulcrum of that position
against the commerce and security of the United States."[27] In 1811 he
proposed an embryonic Monroe Doctrine by recommending that Congress declare "that the United States could not see without serious
inquietude any part of a neighboring territory in which they have in
different respects so deep and so just a concern pass from the hands of

Spain into those of any other foreign power." Madison subsequently offered South American revolutionaries "good wishes for success."[28]

The significance of Latin America lay, as Arthur P. Whitaker observes, not only in its growing importance as an American marketplace, but also in the fact that England alone competed with America for that market.[29] Gallatin provided the most succinct analysis of this situation. Britain, he wrote Madison, planned to assume control of the Spanish empire and crush the Latin American "revolutionary movements." The "English interest and prejudices against us arising from that source will therefore be the principal obstacles to our [commercial] views in that quarter." He anticipated "new sources of collision" over any "undue British ascendency" there. After reaffirming Florida's and Cuba's importance, he explained that Havana "may become a central point of communication both of Mexico and the Caracas Coast."[30] To whatever extent France might equal Britain's assault on America's European commerce, only England interfered with U.S. commercial penetration into Latin America—a fact the administration did not overlook.

III

When the European War resumed in 1803, conflict over commerce and markets remained in most aspects the same as in the 1790s. America's carrying trade, the reexport of goods from non-European sources to the Continent, boomed when the British navy drove the merchant marine of France and its client states from the oceans. American goods found their markets expanded by war. The heavy demand for naval seamen weakened Britain's merchant marine and induced its sailors to flee to American ships to avoid press gangs. In an effort to retain the lucrative carrying trade as much as to blockade Napoleonic Europe, England seized American ships, condemned cargoes, imposed legal sanctions, and impressed American seamen. French privateers and customs officials also interfered with neutral commerce, but France impressed no American sailors, stayed out of Latin America, and seized only 60 percent of the shipping that Britain did.[31] The Republican leaders believed that England, not the inherently unstable Napoleonic empire, was the real threat to American independence.[32]

Republican policy toward Great Britain encompassed three areas: the carrying trade, impressment, and foreign markets. The carrying trade was the weakest cause of conflict. At various times Jefferson, Madison, and Gallatin had expressed their unwillingness to make war solely over a trade that was of marginal benefit to the economy apart from the reexporting merchants and was a constant source of international conflict. In the late 1790s Gallatin, especially, was wary of military action to protect this trade.[33] However, the trade was very important to America's balance of payments. In his report on Anglo-American commerce, Gallatin noted the severe trade deficit America ran with Britain. "As that balance must necessarily be paid out of the proceeds of the exports of the United States to other countries, . . . the quantity imported, either for home consumption or reexportation, must be affected by every obstruction to the commerce of the United States with other countries."[34] In other words, America's trade deficit with England required income from the carrying trade to maintain the balance of payments and avoid a drain on capital resources. The triumvirate also took great umbrage at British efforts to restrict reexports. "Lessening the competition with, and thereby favoring the price of British and other Colonial productions reexported by British Merchants," Madison railed, "has no origin or plea but those of commercial jealousy and monopoly."[35] By "admitting a trade with her enemies in her own behalf, and subjecting neutrals to special licenses and to tribute, [the English] prove that retaliation is a cover for usurpation and monopoly."[36] The Republican leaders found restrictions on even the carrying trade an unacceptable expression of British hegemony.

Impressment of Americans had a long and odious history dating back to colonial days. It outraged whole coastal towns then, and no less so in the nineteenth century.[37] Each seaman impressed from an American ship was a brutal reminder of national weakness. Pique, however, was peripheral; what was central was control of the seagoing labor force. Although estimates vary, foreign, mostly British, seamen manned between one-half and one-third of America's merchant fleet. These foreign sailors supplied the labor for the huge increase in American commerce following the resumption of war in 1803. The British wanted the laborers back, not only for their navy, but to exert control over the world's commerce by controlling the allocation of the maritime labor force. When Madison suggested that the government return these foreign sailors in exchange for English concessions on trade and impressment, Gallatin balked. "An engagement on our part to employ no British sailor," he warned Jefferson, "would materially injure our navigation, much more indeed than any restrictions which . . . they could lay upon our commerce." No English concession could compensate America "because the curtailing of our navigation by that measure would effectually prevent our enjoying the advantages which might otherwise result from such modifications." In other words, America would lack the seamen to man the ships necessary to take advantage of

British trade concessions. Jefferson instructed Madison "to suspend all propositions respecting our non-employment" of foreign seamen.[38] The conflict over impressment was a contest over commerce.

The third major area of policy was foreign markets for American exports. This area was most critical of all in that it integrated the three largest and most powerful propertied groups in the nation: farmers, planters, and merchants. Britain interfered with America's growing Latin American markets. Geographical location and their strategic neutralization by British naval power insured the West Indian market for American exports. In Europe, however, the English continued their efforts to force all Continental trade through English ports and blockade it where Napoleon prohibited British merchants. Every time the Royal Navy closed a European port, the demand for American exports decline and the domestic clamor for retaliation rose. Year after year Gallatin, Jefferson, or Madison reported a fresh blockade that "will naturally affect us until another channel of communication can be opened with the north of Europe; the price of American and West Indian produce being low and unsteady in England."[39] One or the other recounted the damage to the economy by "the losses sustained by our commerce in the Continental ports, and by the fall of prices in our produce at home, under a limitation of the market to G. Britain."[40]

The issue of war became a question of whether the Republican leaders would acquiesce in the British government's regulation of foreign markets for the benefit of its propertied citizens or would resist that regulation and fulfill their obligation to America's propertied citizens. National independence meant having a government that responded to the interests and demands of its citizens, not those of another nation. Madison interpreted this question as a choice between war and "the greater evil of a surrender of our Sovereignty on the Element, on which all Nations have equal rights, and in the free use of which, the U.S. as a nation whose agricultural & commerce are so closely allied, have an essential interest."[41] Honorable statesmen fulfill their obligation to serve the economic interests of their nation's citizens. In international affairs, as in life, one must occasionally draw one's sword to protect one's purse.

Jefferson explained the threat to independence posed by commercial hegemony. While lauding John Jacob Astor's efforts to secure the Indian fur trade from the British, he observed that "nothing but the exclusive possession of the Indian commerce can secure us their peace."[42] The "exclusive possession" of commerce was tantamount to colonial subordination. Jefferson had noted this fact in this Report on Commerce of 1793. As the control of an individual's livelihood obviated his independence, the control of a nation's commerce made it a

colony. Upon the independent market system and its foreign extensions rested the Republican leaders' plans for political stability and
economic growth; English neocolonialism threatened that vision.
They would risk their empire in war before accepting British hegemony. Unlike Hamilton, they realized they could not have both.

The triumvirate employed three principal policies against Great
Britain: nonimportation, embargo, and war. Nonimportation was
rooted in Jefferson's and Madison's proposals for American foreign
policy in the early 1790s: commercial discrimination and the Report
on Commerce. Throughout this period, nonimportation and related
discriminatory legislation were intended to coerce Britain and develop
American industry. Jefferson and Madison might have believed, and
probably preferred, that coercion would budge English commercial
policy before America industrialized sufficiently to replace the British
market. Nonetheless, they proposed commercial coercion in 1793 and
1794, and implemented it in 1807 and 1810 fully cognizant of its potential, indeed ineluctable, impact on American manufactures if England remained adamant. Dictated both by their assumptions about
national independence and by their evaluation of the world situation,
their foreign policy course was essentially formulated by 1793, though
not implemented until 1807. Actual power was not an independent
causal variable in their foreign policy decisions. More precisely, power
was an *intervening* variable which accorded them the ability to implement their plans for commercial coercion when circumstances akin to
those of 1793 again made it opportune to strike against English economic hegemony.

To understand the embargo of 1807 it is perhaps useful to employ a
contemporary concept of policy analysis, the policy repertoire—that
is, a range of prepared alternatives available to decisionmakers.[43] A
policy repertoire of sorts helps to explain the initial embargo decision
of December 1807. Embargo was, after all, the traditional mechanism
of protecting American merchant ships against superior foreign na-
vies.[44] Nonetheless, as the response evolved from a prelude to a decision about the proper policy course into a major policy, the stimulus
to domestic manufactures and the coercive effect on England became
the principal justification for its continuance. This shift in the embargo's purpose from protecting commerce during a decisionmaking
process to effecting economic change at home and coercion abroad
illustrates the importance of particular political economies. In 1794
Hamilton also achieved the imposition of an embargo to protect shipping and gain time to prepare a policy response to British seizures, in
this case, Jay's peace mission. Thus, the similarity in repertoire explains only the basic mechanism of embargo; it does not explain what

results from the time gained by the initial response. Only the respective political economies of the Republicans and Hamilton can explain the final policy. In this instance, the policy repertoire, too, acted as an intervening, not an independent, variable.

By April 1808 the embargo had been linked to strong measures of nonimportation. At that point the policy ceased to be a hiatus for decisionmaking and became a deliberate instrument for commercial coercion and the development of manufactures.[45] Madison wrote as much to William Pinkney on April 30, 1808. He linked the policy to the "wrongs" of English and French edicts against neutral commerce, and the realization "that we are less unripe for manufacturing establishments than had been supposed." Experience had, he added, admonished the nation "to lessen our dependence for supplies on foreign nations."[46] As the policy's failure to coerce England became evidence, its salutory impact on manufacturing became its principal justification.[47]

Finally, there was the decision for war. Increasing conflicts with England over Latin America markets and neutral rights, and the declining prices of agricultural products, again created a policy crisis in the administration. Nonimportation had been reimposed in 1810 when England refused to repeal its Orders in Council after Napoleon revoked his commercial edicts. Regardless of the authenticity of the French action, in the minds of the Republican leaders Britain had always been the chief threat to American commerce. If England acquiesced, France could be compelled to follow. Thus, Madison and Gallatin were willing to accept Napoleon's word, if only to insure that their retaliatory measures against Britain were rooted in an even-handed neutrality. The crucial question in the first months of 1812 was whether nonimportation could succeed. In April Madison requested and received a sixty-day embargo. On April 3 he wrote Jefferson that the continued tenure of Perceval at Whitehall indicated England preferred "war with us, to repeal of their Orders in Council. We have nothing left," he concluded, "but to make ready for it."[48] Unwilling to submit to English restrictions and believing that nonimportation had failed, he asked for and received a congressional declaration of war in June.[49]

In his war message to Congress Madison encapsulated the reasons for this decision to make war. British conduct was "hostile to the United States as an independent and neutral nation." First, he condemned impressment, the emotional issue involving control of the seagoing labor force. Then he addressed the issue of open markets: "Our commerce has been plundered in every sea, the great staples of our country have been cut off from their legitimate markets, and a

destructive blow aimed at our agricultural and maritime interests."
The crucial economic link between agriculture and shipping, foreign
markets, was the chief cause of conflict. For Britain to assault American trade and markets was to attack the whole nation. Agricultural
interests were unquestionably at stake; the prices of their commodities
were declining as a result of British restrictions. Madison attributed
these restrictions to "the monopoly which [Britain] covets for her own
commerce and navigation" over world trade. He mentioned British
manipulations of Indian tribes on America's frontiers—the only reference in his message to domestic territorial matters. The crux of the
conflict was foreign markets and English claims "to regulate our external commerce in all cases whatsoever." In concluding he warned
France that continued interference with American trade might demand
a military response as well.[50]

Although support in Congress for war has been variously attributed
to "land hunger" and sectional politics, subsequent examinations have
found these explanations untenable in light of the support for war
among members of Congress from each part of the nation.[51] As an
alternative, "party unity" is stressed as a causal variable,[52] but problems persist in this explanation. Recently, the party unity explanation
has been subjected to a devastating criticism by Rudolph M. Bell.
Employing a statistical game-theory approach to the analysis of legislative voting patterns, Bell concludes that "party unity had existed, at
least within the legislature, for years and therefore cannot have *determined* war in 1812 any more than it had determined peace before
1812." In its place he points beyond the party per se to its role "as a
vehicle for the political expression of salient socioeconomic and geo-
graphically circumscribed forces."[53] Party unity was, in other words,
another intervening variable and not independently causal.

Bell returns to more basic economic causes for support of the war,
and his analysis yields results consistent with this essay's overall interpretation of the era's political-economic conflicts. He points toward
the earlier explanations stressing interdicted markets and declining
prices of agricultural goods. More significantly, he finds strong support for the war, and for Republican foreign policies in general, among
"surplus agricultural areas, and undeveloped regions with an eye to
future prosperity and participation in expanding American trade." Urban areas divided into "declining New England districts" and "Middle
Atlantic and southern commercial centers." The latter were pro-war.[54]
These divisions accord with the areas of Republican political strength
since the mid-1790s. The economic issue was not a matter of occupational pursuits, of farmer versus merchant. It involved whether their
fortunes lay, whether in newer non-British markets and trade or in

older commercial patterns and subsistence agriculture. Republican foreign policy decisions, like all Republican policies, can be explained through political-economic analysis. This analysis, however, is complex, requiring sophisticated causal models. Whether based on narrow sectional and occupational determinism or mistaken attributions of causality to power, party unity, or idealism, alternative explanations of policies have proven unsatisfactory.

When the war that caused the Anglo-American conflict ended, so too did the conflict. Napoleon's defeat allowed restoration of the status quo ante bellum and ended English interference with neutral commerce. Twenty-two years of European war had enabled America to double its territory, its population, and in all probability, its gross national product. Manufactures had prospered in what amounted to eight years of constant interruptions in Anglo-American trade. By avoiding defeat, the United States had been victorious. Canada remained English, but New Orleans and New England remained American. The Spanish empire in the Americas was an empty shell. East Florida became, in effect, a spoil of war. Most importantly, "the war," as Gallatin explained, "has renewed and reinstated the national feelings and character which the Revolution had given, and which were daily lessened."[55] With the Federalists discredited permanently, the war and then the peace came to be the prologue for an American system which might realize the goals of the Republican political economy.

CHAPTER TEN

The Republican Triumvirate and Manufacturing

An Overview

Want of capital appears to be the greatest if not the only obstacle to [manufactures'] progressing more rapidly.
— The Collector of Portsmouth, New Hampshire, reporting to Gallatin on the state of manufacturing, December 30, 1809

Since . . . want of capital is the principal obstacle to the introduction and advancement of manufactures in America, it seems that the most efficient and most obvious remedy would consist in supplying that capital. . . . The United States might create a circulating stock, bearing a low rate of interest, and lend it at par to manufacturers . . . [;] five millions of dollars a year, but not exceeding, in the whole, twenty millions, might be thus lent.
— Gallatin in his Report on Manufactures, April 19, 1810

I have always considered it as among the happiest of circumstances of my administration that the harmony and cordiality which subsisted among all it's [sic] members amalgamated us into one mind. We never had a question who had a right to the merit or demerit of any particular measure; for in truth all measures of importance were the measures of all.
— Jefferson to John Minor, July 10, 1809

Since one major thesis of this essay is that Hamilton was not an advocate of American manufacturing, it is important to draw together the positions of the Republican triumvirate on manufacturing. With the work of Merrill Peterson, E. James Ferguson, and others the anti-manufacturing image of the Republican leaders has been shaken severely, though it still lingers in subdued form.[1] Three facets of the manufacturing issue require examination: the demands and political allegiances of the manufacturers, especially after 1800; the policies and proposals offered by the administration to meet those demands;

and the attitudes of the triumvirate toward manufacturing. In the last we must deal with the question of household versus factory production.

I

As they had in the 1790s, manufacturers in the early 1800s persisted in petitioning Congress for aid. On the whole, their petitions followed the pattern of earlier years. They complained of foreign, generally English, competition. They requested protective tariffs, prohibitions, relaxation of duties on raw materials, and federal loans. There were also petitions from the merchants and mechanics of New York and Newburyport, Massachusetts, opposing any relaxation in the navigation laws. Such relaxation, the New York mechanics explained, would endanger the employment of "that numerous class of mechanics, who are concerned in either building or equipping of vessels."[2] The brief hiatus in the European conflict from 1801 to 1803 lowered the prices of imported manufactures, causing iron producers to complain. On the other hand, Philadelphia's calico printers believed that commercial capital displaced from the carrying trade might flow into their manufactures if heavier duties on dyed muslins were levied.[3]

Beyond these more traditional concerns with imports and other difficulties, manufactures in New York City and Philadelphia exhibited a marked growth in the sophistication of their political economy. New York's "mechanics and manufacturers" constructed an elaborate plea for protective tariffs. Machinery would assuage labor shortages. American merchants could carry American manufactures as British merchants carried English products. Manufacturing also offered an outlet for merchant capital safe from the depredations of foreign powers. The "internal intercourse it will occasion, will tend to assimilate and strengthen the empire." The manufacturers concluded that "so long as we remain a nation of farmers and merchants merely, we shall be tributary to the Europeans."[4] Their link of the development of manufacturing to the national market system and economic independence was similar to the basic assumptions of Gallatin's political economy.

Philadelphia's "subscribers, artisans and manufacturers" were more elaborate in their arguments for manufacturing. They requested protective tariffs, an end to duties on raw materials, and an assured market for their products to attract substantial capital investment. They explained that interregional population flows (New England to New York and Pennsylvania) had increased the labor supply. They denied that manufacturing towns in themselves bred vice. Only in Europe, "where the Government, the law and the employer, are all in combination, or rather conspiracy, against the employed," were poverty and vice endemic to industry. England, they asserted, was a great nation because of its manufacturing—an argument Gallatin had once made in Congress. The manufacturers offered a comprehensive statement on the impact of industry on the nation's economy: "New sources will be laid open for the employment of capital in the interior; the coasting trade and internal commerce will receive a new impulse; domestic industry will put to shame idleness and dissipation; foreign nations will lose their influence over our councils." Not to overlook the agricultural interests, they added, "The fertile lands of America will rise to their just value, by bringing a market to the door of the farmer."[5]

The symmetry between the manufacturers' presentation of manufacturing's role in the American market system and the Republican leadership's concept of its role is remarkable. National independence and unity were the consequences which both of them attributed to manufacturing. This *sympatico* becomes more evident in Gallatin's proposals, detailed below, for federal aid to manufacturing. It is instructive to assess first the impact of the Republican nonimportation policy on manufacturers as reflected in their petitions and reports on their development.

Without exception the petitions of manufacturers after 1807 praised in one form or another the salutory affect of Republican commercial policies on their businesses. Never before had petitioners in nonshipbuilding industries lauded any federal policy relating to their manufactories with such unanimity. Manufacturers still requested protective tariffs to insure their markets against any renewed flow of English imports and additional capital for expansion. In this context Kentucky manufacturers praised Gallatin's proposal for federal loans to manufacturers. There was a new emphasis in these petitions on protecting what *had* developed during the commercial interruptions rather than on affording the conditions necessary to begin that development. As much as tariff protection, these manufacturers asked for capital to expand.[6]

The Republican administration and Congress had responded to their manufacturing constituency. On taking office the administration repealed the hated excise taxes on manufactures, though the tariff increases sought by manufacturers did not come so quickly. Merchants and farmers, whether Federalist or Republican, were not very supportive of high tariffs, and their opposition in Congress prevented increases for a period. However, problems with the Tripolean pirates allowed the triumvirate to increase the tariff. Unlike the Federalists, who when faced with a similar need for revenue chose to tax manufacturers, the administration prevailed on Congress to add 2.5 percent to all ad valorem duties in 1804, and used the revenue, the "Mediterranean Fund," to finance expeditions against the Barbary Pirates. This increase brought the average tariff on manufactured imports to between 15 and 17.5 percent—the highest rates imposed to that time. Congress doubled the tariff rates in 1812 and kept them in the 20 to 25 percent range after the war. More importantly, the prices of imported goods rose steadily during the decade owing to wartime demand in Europe. Higher prices raised the effective protection of duties calculated ad valorem. For example, assuming a 17.5 percent ad valorem rate, a 10 percent increase in the cost to a merchant of an item would translate into a nearly 12 percent increase in the selling price of the item. Ad valorem duties were more protective in the inflationary situation during the Napoleonic wars.

As illustrated in Graph 15, the most effective protection to manufactures that the administration offered was nonimportation. In November 1806 Congress passed a prohibition on the importation of several major categories of British goods: footwear, cordage, nails, hemp, glass, leather, clothing, and specific types of woolen and cotton manufactures. Enforcement of the prohibition was sporadic, but imported goods did increase in price. A year later the embargo and rigorous enforcement of nonimportation choked off manufactured imports. After a brief hiatus in 1809, nonimportation was reimposed against Britain in 1810. Not only did these prohibitions give exclusive possession of the American market to domestic producers for nearly a decade, if the war years are included, but commercial interruption released millions of dollars in merchant capital to alternative pursuits, particularly manufacturing, and lowered the costs of raw materials and labor.

Letters written in 1809 for Gallatin's Report on Manufactures from Treasury agents throughout the nation affirmed the growth and development of domestic industry under the nonimportation and embargo policies. They wrote of the introduction in New England factories of cotton machinery, itself built in America. Not all ventures were immediately successful, but each report stressed the continued efforts to achieve success. Areas in the South reported a growth in household manufactures as well as in large enterprises. In Virginia there was a symbiotic development of household production of clothing and factories for cording and spinning cloth. Thus, household manufactures and factory production were not, at this stage, antagonistic developments, but often mutually reinforcing. In contrast to the refusal of some manufacturers to respond to Hamilton's requests for information on manufactures a decade and a half earlier, no manufacturers refused to cooperate for fear of being taxed.[7]

It is not surprising that Republican policies aided manufacturers. Mechanics and manufacturers had been, to some extent, part of the Republicans' political constituency since the 1790s. Manufacturers were in the forefront of the rising entrepreneurial groups who, particularly in the North, constituted the nucleus of the coalition. The triumvirate continued close relations with leading American manufacturers and advocates: Tench Coxe, Pierre DuPont, and Eli Whitney. In 1810 Pennsylvania's manufacturing output exceeded the combined production of New York and Massachusetts, the next two largest manufacturing states. Republican support there was particularly strong among manufacturers and mechanics. Indeed, the embargo and nonimportation treated the state less harshly than others because of the rapid expansion of manufactures.[8] Republican strength also increased in Delaware among manufacturers along the Brandywine River, who constituted practically the whole party in that state.[9]

In a report to Gallatin on Providence manufactories, Thomas Coles, the port collector, attested to this transformation under Republican rule. "It is impossible," he explained in November 1809, "to obtain from the proprietors of the cotton mills a statement of their profits. Every one however is assured that they are ample—and this may be considered as one principal cause, that so many have entered of late into this business. The Embargo, I have heard mentioned by some of the manufacturing gentlemen, has having determined many, to place their dominant capital into manufacturers." Federal policy had progressed a long way from the days when manufacturers complained of Hamiltonian fiscal policies diverting capital from their enterprises.[10]

II

Of all the principal policymakers at the national level in this period Gallatin alone owned a manufactory. He hired his glassmakers from those skilled workers thrown out of work when John Amelung's Maryland glassworks failed.[11] It was William Smith of South Carolina, Hamilton's chief spokesman in the House of Representatives, who defeated the bill providing a federal loan to aid Amelung in 1790. Gallatin's factory in western Pennsylvania also produced munitions for the state militia.[12] During his tenure in the Treasury Department, he supported the development of manufacturing consistently but cautiously. He was aware that American manufactures were concentrated outside the South. Unlike internal improvements, industry required protective tariffs, which aided the manufacturer at the expense of the farmer and merchant. He was conscious of both the need for industry to achieve economic independence and the danger federal aid posed to the internal peace of the union. His proposals for massive federal aid to manufactures awaited two conditions. First the debt had to be reduced to release government revenues from servicing principal and interest. As with internal improvements, borrowing money to aid manufactures was an unacceptable means of government finance. Second the international trade situation had to deteriorate sufficiently to convince the less industrially oriented political constituencies that manufacturing was the only alternative to foreign hegemony. These conditions were met gradually during the first decade of the Republican rule.

January 1804 marked the beginning of Gallatin's policy recommendations for federal aid to manufacturers. In his annual Treasury report he proposed alterations in the tariff to ascertain "with precision, the amount consumed in the United States of each class" of imports. This knowledge "would hereafter, enable the Legislature, without risk to the revenue, to introduce, from time to time, such modifications as might appear most favorable to the agricultural and manufacturing interests of the Country."[13] Gallatin wanted neither to appear to be dictating to Congress, nor to incite any sectional or interest-group conflicts. Nonetheless, he realized the importance of manufacturing and continued to press it in his November 1807 report. In describing the various means to finance a war he noted that "a great portion of the surplus of agricultural products necessarily requires a foreign market." He pointed out that a maritime war would interdict those markets and require larger government revenues. A doubling of the tariff rates in that contingency would increase revenues and result directly in an "increase of domestic manufactures. . . . in itself a desirable object."[14] Not incidentally, increased manufacturing would provide an outlet for those agricultural products whose foreign markets would be blocked by war.

Gallatin understood that embargo and nonimportation could serve not only to coerce Britain into reopening foreign markets to American goods, but also to stimulate manufactures by reducing imports and rechanneling mercantile capital. Domestic manufactures would reduce America's need for British goods and foreign markets to dispose of surplus commodities. After a year of embargo, Gallatin discussed explicitly its impact on manufactures. He cited the great quantity of "redundant unemployed capital" and a glut of unexported produce as the proper environment for the growth of manufactures. He then advocated "a permanent increase of duties on articles selected with the view to those which may be manufactured in the United States."[15] Such a tariff system would insure investors that their capital flowing into manufacturing would be secure regardless of international vicissitudes.

Gallatin articulated his plans for systematic protection of manufacturing in a letter to Thomas Newton, chairman of the House Committee on Commerce and Manufactures, in June 1809. He distinguished three stages of manufacturing development: industries too little advanced for protection, such as silks, fine muslins, and cutlery; advanced industries needing only nominal duties for protection, such as sugar, carriages, cabinets, and some window glass; industries at a crucial point requiring immediate and substantial protection, such as woolens, cotton products, flax, hemp, paper, leather, iron goods, and several other metal products. Cotton goods industries, particularly, should be protected because of their role in providing a market for raw domestic cotton.[16] In strongly advocating protection for textile and iron production he was laying the groundwork for two key sectors in the industrialization process. He believed that their protection was important for the rapid development of manufacturing. He followed this brief letter with an extensive Report on Manufactures ten months later.

In the Report on Manufactures he pointed out that American manufactures, currently valued at $120 million, "create a home market not inferior to that which arises from foreign demand." Commercial depredators "have broken inveterate habits, and given a general impulse . . . forcing industry and capital in other channels" and causing "the great increase of manufactures during the last two years." America's "perfectly free and unfettered" industry contributed to this increase. To preserve and promote manufacturing "the most obvious means are bounties, increased duties on importations, and loans by Government." Gallatin discounted aid in the form of bounties as "more applicable to articles exported than to those manufactured for home consumption." Though careful to mediate his call for protection with the need to maintain competition and avoid a "less profitable" use of capital, he still envisioned duties of 17.5 to 25 percent and a "total prohibition of East India cotton goods." The size of the duties depended on the domestic manufacturers' abilities to meet the expanded demand and the government's ability to prevent smuggling.[17]

The "want of capital," Gallatin explained in the report, "is the principal obstacle to the introduction and advancement of manufactures in America." Thus, "the most efficient, and most obvious remedy would consist in supplying that capital. For," he continued, "although the extension of banking may give some assistance in that respect, their operation is limited to a few places, nor does it comport with the nature of those institutions to lend for periods as long as are requisite for the establishment of manufactures." To supply capital he suggested direct federal loans. These loans would be in the form of a "circulating stock, bearing a low rate of interest," lent "at par to manufacturers." This stock could total $20 million advanced in annual increments of $5 million. Then the banking system could discount these stocks and provide funds for production and distribution. The $5 million for manufactures (and the $2 million for internal improvements) would be financed out of the revenues previously allocated for debt service.[18]

It is instructive to compare briefly Gallatin's Report on Manufactures with Hamilton's and Coxe's.[19] Overall, one is impressed by the similarity between Gallatin's and Coxe's reports, and the differences between these and Hamilton's. Gallatin and Coxe advocated direct loans to manufacturers and a federally constructed internal transportation network; Hamilton did not. All three suggested protective tariffs of varying levels, but Hamilton stressed bounties while Gallatin and Coxe rejected them as inappropriate. They were, Gallatin contended, chiefly aids given to encourage exports. Neither Gallatin nor Coxe believed banks to be useful sources of capital for manufacturers, while Hamilton did. Banks, Gallatin pointed out, did not lend "for periods as long as are requisite for the establishment of manufacture." Finally, the responsiveness of Gallatin's report to the demands of the manufacturers themselves, particularly for capital, stands in stark contrast to Hamilton's lack of sympathy with the needs and problems articulated to him by manufacturers. Empathy and political constituency appear to place Gallatin in the midst of the manufacturers, while Hamilton stood among his British-trading merchants and speculators.

Although Republican policies in general aided manufacturing far beyond anything Hamilton did (or is purported to have done), the specific proposals of Gallatin's report met with little success in Congress. House supporters of manufactures had seized Gallatin's June 1809 letter to Newton to propose protective legislation. In part the request for his Report on Manufactures represented the members' need for guidance and information on the subject; in part it also served as a delaying tactic. The report request passed by a lopsided 93 to 38 vote, but receipt of the final document in April 1810 prompted no congressional action. The press of international affairs, the support commercial interruptions afforded manufactures, and the failure of members to produce a tariff bill acceptable to the merchant-farmer majority preempted any further protective legislation prior to the war. Although important, manufacturers lacked the political weight within the Congress to push through stronger protective measures, even with Gal-

latin's support, until the war. Tariff rates rose during the conflict and
were sustained at protective levels into the postwar era. Gallatin's loan
proposal, however, never achieved fruition.[20]

III

That the Republican triumvirate supported domestic manufactures is
now acknowledged by some historians. A nouveau issue has become
what sort of manufactures they supported. In a recent treatment of the
issue, Drew McCoy argues that one cannot neglect the "different types
of manufacturing"—specifically household and factory. It was the
household variety, he concludes, that the Republican leaders advocated.[21] There are several problems with McCoy's and similar interpretations. First of all, the distinction between household and factory
(more precisely, manufactory) production in the early nineteenth century was not clear as, for example, between a homemaker's sewing a
personal garment and a modern factory. Secondly, philosophical preferences notwithstanding, there is good reason to doubt whether any of
the three Republican leaders were definitive about supporting household over factory production. Finally, given the twofold function of
domestic manufactures, it is difficult to accept that household production alone could absorb America's raw material output and eliminate
the need for English imports.

Gallatin presents the greatest obstacle to the household interpretation. He owned a factory producing munitions and glass, and could
hardly be said to find his own business repugnant. Moreover, in his
Report on Manufactures, he clearly advocated large-scale production
facilities. Indeed, his $20 million loan proposal could have capitalized
a manufacturing company larger than the SEUM every six weeks for
four years—over thirty-three factories the size of the SEUM in a mere
forty-eight months. Only by totally ignoring Gallatin's Report on
Manufactures can one construe the Republican political economy as
exclusively or even chiefly supporting household manufactures. Mc-
Coy and others do ignore him.

Madison also presents difficulties for the household interpretation.
His 1794 commercial propositions represented a comprehensive protective tariff system whose effects on manufactures would have not
been limited to household producers. In the midst of the embargo he
observed that nonimportation would continue, "especially as the idea
gains force daily, that we are less unripe for manufacturing establishments than has been supposed." Having "shut our markets against
[England's] manufactures," he concluded a few months later, America
"stimulates and establishes permanent substitutes of our own."[22] His

annual presidential message in December 1810 lauded "a highly interesting extension of useful manufactures, the combined products of *professional and household* industry, . . . [which are] more than a recompense for those privations and losses resulting from foreign injustice which furnished the general impulse required for its accomplishment." He called for protective tariffs in this and subsequent state of the union addresses.[23] As if to silence all doubts concerning the potential extent of America's industrial development, he spoke at the end of 1813 of the commercial interruptions that had "cherished and multiplied our manufactures so as to make us independent of all other countries for the more essential branches . . . and is even rapidly giving them an extent which will create additional staples in our future intercourse with foreign markets."[24] A nation does not export household necessities; large-scale enterprises alone could provide the manufactured "staples" for "foreign markets."

Jefferson evinced a somewhat ambivalent attitude toward large-scale manufactures. Unquestionably he "preferred," as Merrill Peterson observes, to keep the "factories and workshops" in Europe. Nonetheless, Peterson adds, they "would the more likely result from his commercial system."[25] An intellect of Jefferson's sophistication would no doubt have anticipated this outcome to some extent. Although he tied manufacturing development to England's "conquest over our navigation and commerce" and limited it to an output "sufficient for our own consumption, of what we raise the raw material (and no more)," these were in fact pseudolimitations.[26] Manufacturing could not be turned on and off depending on British actions. There had to be ever-expanding domestic production to absorb ever-growing agricultural production.

To compensate for the loss of the British export market some $27 million worth of raw materials—including foodstuffs, cotton, and lumber—would require a domestic outlet. At the outset of the embargo Jefferson himself speculated that the $80 million and twenty to thirty thousand seamen that American merchants could no longer employ in international commerce would "furnish a great capital, much of which will go into manufactures." Capital and labor in this quantity could supply only large-scale manufactories. He explicitly acknowledged the implication of this goal: "For the finer goods we much resort to the larger manufactories established in the town."[27] Indeed, massive infusions of capital and labor accounted for a manufacturing boom in the northeastern states and in seaport cities, especially Philadelphia. In the interior and the South household manufactures predominated, but throughout the nation entrepreneurs began small factories.[28]

Moreover, there is some evidence that Jefferson supported *state* loans and other aid to manufacturers. In his Report on Commerce he wrote of "the State governments . . . opening the resources of encouragement which are under their control and extending them liberally" to manufacturers. As early as December 1791, he wrote an opinion supporting a loan of $2,500 by the state of Virginia to a woolen manufactory.[29] Although the question of his preference for state instead of federal aid remains open, Jefferson's support for manufacturing is clear. He believed that "the claims of agriculture attract every being who can engage in it" and that workers, therefore, might be hard to find and keep.[30] Nonetheless, in 1813 he wrote, "I have not formerly been an advocate for great manufactories. . . . But other considerations entering into the question have settled my doubts."[31] Perhaps Merrill Peterson best summarizes Jefferson's position on manufactures when he writes, "The American System, generally, was the legitimate offspring of Jefferson's mature politics."[32]

Undeniably, neither Jefferson nor Madison nor the manufacturers themselves wanted an impoverished urban industrial working class. Yet the exigencies of economic independence, the prospects of avoiding an English-model working class, and the threat of commercial wars led them to put aside their apprehensions and support the development of large manufactories.[33] They had reason to believe an impoverished urban class could be avoided by the use of women in factories, the location of factories in rural settings, the availability of western lands, and the education of propertyless to be good citizens. Even in the early nineteenth century there were a small but growing urban working class, a "seagoing proletariat," and slaves. Despite their existence social order and political society had been maintained.[34] In expressing gratitude for his recent election to a manufacturing society, Madison presented what might be a balanced view of his and Jefferson's policy toward manufactures: "Altho' I approve the policy of leaving to the sagacity of individuals, and to the impulse of private interest, the application of industry & capital, I am equally persuaded, that in this as in other cases, there are exceptions, to the general rule. . . . Among these exceptions is the policy of encouraging domestic manufactures, within certain limits, and in reference to certain articles."[35] The political economy of the Republican leaders was a question of circumstances as well as philosophical preferences. Between 1790 and 1812 circumstances wrought their active, effective support of manufacturing.

One could argue that the federal policies benefited manufacturers principally by chance — unintended effect: that is, the increase in tariff rates, nonimportation, embargo, and war were foreign policy phenomena, and any stimulus to manufacturing was coincidental. This argument would ignore Gallatin's extraordinary proposal for aid: $20 million in capital loans to a sector of the economy that yielded only $120 million in gross output. Yet, it must be granted that Congress failed to enact his proposal. Hence, the unintended effects argument still survives. There is, however, a larger question of cause and effect at issue here. While commercially coercive foreign policies were means to open international markets to American goods, the open markets were themselves means to the end of an independent and prosperous nation. That end was the leitmotif of the Republican political economy, the source of their political appeal, and the basis for the support the party and its leaders received from the rising entrepreneurial groups in their coalition. They promised equality of opportunity both in the political process and in a growing economy. It was this promise that they strove to fulfill during their rule. Throughout the early national era, the triumvirate held economic independence most dear. Implicitly then, the development of manufacturing was never alien, but always integral, to their political economy. Regardless of their philosophical preferences, Jefferson, Madison, and Gallatin advocated and pursued policies which successfully advanced American manufacturing.

CHAPTER ELEVEN

Political Economy and Policymaking

The most important element in any analysis of political or economic phenomena is the hypothesis to be tested. Without some overarching hypothesis even the most intensive examination of data is a pointless exercise. The advancement of knowledge rests as much on the synthesis, as the discovery, of fact. To study a particular policy or policymaker, a sense of the overall context is necessary to weight the significance of various elements in the decisionmaking process. Certain defensible assumptions about the structure of policymaking must be made and then used to assess the myriad of variables entering into the policy process. In this book I have identified political economy as the basis for these assumptions and have linked the political economy of the period's policymakers to private property, commercial development, social stability, and a concept of freedom. To substantiate these assumptions I have reconstructed the world views of the leading policymakers. This methodology involves no value judgment beyond the belief that reason preponderates in effecting a set of ends through policy. Chance, the random nature of circumstance, was excluded as a primary policy determinate because, like the lust for power, chance is ahistorical. It explains no more (and no less) about the early national era then it explains about ancient Greece.

The exclusion of chance as a significant causal variable is an important methodological assumption. Often in scholarship where such things are considered, the chief counterproposition to a political-economic analysis of policy is a tacit assumption of randomness: what happens happens to happen.[1] An analogy is sometimes drawn between an individual's life, where chance or luck appears to play such an awesome role, and the history of a particular event. Aside from the dubious anthropomorphic analogy, events often interpreted as products of luck are generally the realization of probabilities inherent in a particular individual's background, skills, and aspirations. To make a crude analogy: not every thoroughbred horse wins the Kentucky Derby, but every Derby winner is a thoroughbred. The issue is not that a particular outcome *must* occur versus any outcome may occur, but that a particular outcome will *probably* occur versus another outcome will *probably* not occur. Political-economic analysis explains what is probable and why it is probable. Certainty is always a retrospective inference; probability alone is prospective. Chance has little explanatory role in the history of policymaking. At best, chance extends the realm of acknowledged probability. At worst, it is an excuse for poor analysis.

Another variable occasionally accorded causal power is the behavioral pattern of large organizations, unique to no single political economy.[2] This bureaucratic inertia should be considered in any explanation of policy—particularly in crisis situations where general policy parameters admit more than one possible response. In this early national era, however, large organizations simply did not exist. Though there were policy repertoires, their impact was, in all probability, limited to the embargo decisions. In these instances they served as intervening variables and were not independently causal. The ultimate decisions, in other words, were dependent on the political economy of the decisionmaker.

There are several other interpretations which hold one or another variable as the key causal element in the policymaking of this era. Most often these interpretations tend to stress ideology or interests as primary policy determinants. At least insofar as it involves the policymakers of this period, the dichotomy between ideology and interest is artificial. Inherent in these leaders' world views was the right of propertied citizens to determine government policy. Economic interests were integral components, not alien interpositions, in their ideologies. Reason (or ideas) served to help the passions realize their objects. As Madison noted in the *Federalist,* enlightened self-interest or the reason of citizens should govern the government, and government leaders should govern the passion of their citizens in the polity.[3] There were in the minds of Madison and other leaders no profound antagonisms among economic interest, ideology, and political policy; they necessarily interacted. In the context of changing circumstances, an inevitable tension did exist among different ideas and interest groups. Political leaders had an obligation to resolve this tension according to national interests; the way in which a leader chose to do so and the reasons for his choice constituted his political economy.

Policymaking has three elements: a perception of the world as it is, a vision of how it should be, and a strategy based on political constituency and world view for creating the ought out of the is. A private property system and its political, economic, and social implications pervaded the thought and actions of the early national leaders. Their concepts of freedom and independence were inextricably bound up with individual ownership of productive property. Although property lay at the root of political controversy, it was never the object of it. A particular *expression* of the property system, such as slavery or contract, might be challenged by a "radical," but never the system as a whole. Even these few "radical" challenges the ruling groups rebuffed and then strengthened the political structure against them.

The underlying assumption of the sanctity of private property helps to explain two glaring inconsistencies in the American leaders' commitment to freedom: slavery and Indian removals. Although slavery increasingly became a southern, cotton-producing phenomenon during this period, in the beginnings of the 1790s a few property owners in the North still owned slaves. Concerns over slavery voiced during the Revolution were largely muted by the political coalition that created the Constitution. In the early nineteenth century, there was some tenuous basis for Jefferson's and Madison's belief that economic change and moral rectitude might lead to voluntary emancipation and transportation of the black population out of the country. Moreover, slaves were a form of property and during this period enjoyed an immunity to political controversy similar to other forms of property. It is important to remember that slavery became an inseparable element of the South's political economy *during* these years. The conflict was postponed until slavery became the distinguishing fact of the South's existence.[4]

If blacks were without political rights because they were property, Indians were without rights because they failed to acknowledge the liberal concept of property. Their presence obstructed westward expansion. Not only were they uncivilized in the most profound liberal sense; the Indian way of life impeded the extension of property ownership and the market system across the continent. If they had surrendered their way of life and settled on 160-acre plots, the Republican leaders might have tolerated their existence. The vast bulk of their land would then be opened to settlement. When they resisted this assimilation, the Republican leaders took steps that would one day mean their cultural extinction. It was not their culture that repelled the Republican leadership. (In later life, for example, Gallatin became an ethnologist specializing in Indian customs and languages.) It was their mode of production, their hunting economy, which interfered with the expansion of the market system, that mandated their destruction. Had they ceased to hunt and begun to farm, had they shown more enthusiasm for the Indian 'factories' that entrepreneurs created to facilitate the marketing of their goods, then they might have survived individually. Their mode of production, however, was doomed.[5]

Although the political leaders agreed on property, contract, the ultimate ends and origins of political society, and some form of republican government, they exhibited undeniable differences in political economy and policies. Madison offered the traditional explanation of this difference: "The distinction [between the parties] has its origin in the confidence of the [Republican Party], in the capacity of mankind for self Govt. and a distrust of it by the other or by its leaders."[6] In any assessment of Madison's view it is paramount to recognize that his explanation represents only part of the story and contains significant implications for differences in policies and programs. Hamilton's distrust of small property holders and his efforts to bribe the larger ones entailed policies that subordinated America to Britain, restricted commercial expansion, and retarded manufacturing. The triumvirate's reliance on a national system and responsiveness to the economic interest of all property holders to bring political stability led them to resist British domination, expand commercial opportunity, and foster manufacturing. Their respective political economies generated a myriad of conflicting policies and were fundamentally divergent.

It is likewise too simplistic to argue that, once in power, the Republican leaders became "Federalist" in their policies. This argument is based on a misunderstanding of Federalist policies, at least under Hamilton, and an equal misapprehension of the Republican critique of those policies. The linchpin of this argument is the legend that Hamilton was an economic nationalist. His nationalism extended only to formation of a central government; otherwise, he sought commercial alliance with Britain, which effectively precluded economic independence. Remove the pin and the interpretative mechanism grinds to a halt. Indeed, the argument could better be reversed. Hamilton's policies would have maintained an agrarian America, though under the control of a merchant faction, while the policy proposals of Jefferson, Madison, and Gallatin in the early 1790s would have advanced economic independence through expanded foreign markets and some degree of industrialization. It was not the Republicans who became more "Federalist" after 1800 but the Federalists who became more Republican under John Adams after 1796. However, the 1797–99 conflict over national independence was with France, and the neocolonial Federalist faction had been on the side of Britain against France, while their Republican opposition had been on the side of France against Britain. These complexities obscured the turn in Federalist policy under Adams.

More significantly, every policy the Republican leaders advanced while in office they had proposed in some form *prior* to their election. Jefferson and Madison had advocated commercial discrimination through tariffs and nonimportation in the early 1790s. Gallatin had promoted a state bank and internal improvements while in the Pennsylvania legislature. Their policies, like Hamilton's, cannot be construed to be products of their office. They were rooted in a political economy conceived years before their ascent to power. Indeed, their political economy was in large measure a *cause* of that ascent and of their continued rule over the next decade and a half.

Nonetheless, Hamilton's use of fiscal policy to garner political support and justify English hegemony did have an impact on Republican policies during their administration. The triumvirate's attacks on his excessive reliance on federal fiscal policy to insure stability often spilled over into attacks on his ostensive economic goals. Hamilton's use of federal power instilled in them a wariness of that power. Consequently, a reticence developed among Republican leaders about federal intervention in the economy. Perhaps this reticence evinced itself most significantly in the relationship among the executive branch, Congress, and the Constitution.

To anyone who had heard his speech in the Constitutional Convention, it was no secret that Hamilton wanted a much stronger central government than the convention created. Nor was there any doubt that many members of Congress and their business associates profited from funding and assumption. Hamilton was quite candid about the need for some corruption of the legislature to give the fledging executive government more power. The prominence of corruption in the Hamiltonian system made it the focus of Republican political attacks. Both to distance themselves politically from his policies and to avoid any appearances of replication, the triumvirate consistently shied away from exerting strong pressure on Congress for economic development or straying too far from constitutional strictures. There were also undeniable economic tensions within the Republican coalition. Thus, while the leadership did support economic development and the constitutional expansion of federal power, they were circumspect in that support. Gallatin was the boldest in his proposals for economic development through internal improvements, the central bank, and manufactures, but even he did not attempt to bring the pressure to bear on Congress that Hamilton did for his programs.

The three leaders agreed that internal improvements were necessary for development of the market system. Constrained by the reduction of the debt and by repugnance at Hamilton's practices, they moved slowly toward proposing new roads and canals. Jefferson, who in 1800 feared the "bottomless abyss" for money, placement, and corruption that federal roads represented, wrote five years later that "the increase of revenues is a pleasing circumstance, as it hastens the movement of liberating our revenue, and of permitting us to begin upon canals, roads, colleges, etc." A constitutional amendment would have to authorize these objects, and each state could manage its improvements using federal revenues.[7] As president, Madison suggested to Congress "a general system of internal communication and conveyance." Such a system "will have the effect of drawing more closely together every part of our country by promoting intercourse and improvements and by increasing the share of every part in the common stock of national prosperity." Years later he expressed his belief that Congress lacked the constitutional authority to build a transportation network. Nonetheless he supported an amendment to provide proper authority.[8] Jefferson leaned toward a constitutional amendment and a state-constructed network with federal funds. Madison also retained this constitutional scruple, but unlike Jefferson, he sought federal supervision of construction and locations. Gallatin, on the other hand, assumed Congress was competent to authorize a network and wanted the federal government to work directly with private companies to construct it. All three, however, left the final decision to Congress, which contained the often opposing interests within the party.

The Bank of the United States was the second area where Hamiltonian policies tainted Republican initiatives. Gallatin and Madison strongly supported the recharter effort. Although he allowed Gallatin to assist and even expand the bank, Jefferson never overcame his disaffection. Since Gallatin demurred from a role in the recharter fight beyond suggestions and warnings, the opposition blocked recharter. Had he entered the fray with the intensity that Hamilton had in 1790, the results might have been different. His reorganization proposals certainly would have provided the credit expansion that the antibank forces desired. As it was, the administration could not maintain sufficient party discipline to have Vice-President George Clinton break the Senate's tie vote in favor of recharter. Only in foreign policy did the triumvirate act with the forceful, effective leadership that Hamilton had demonstrated.

The Republican leaders' effectiveness in foreign as opposed to domestic policy reveals several things about their philosophy of government and their political coalition. Above all, foreign affairs were unquestionably within the purview of the executive. No scruples concerning strong presidential direction to Congress or the states constrained the triumvirate's initiatives—a fact amply demonstrated by the embargo, nonimportation, and the Louisiana Purchase. Secondly, the essential thrust of their foreign policies—the protection of America's access to markets—enjoyed universal support among interest groups within the party. Indeed, if Jefferson can be said to have been elected on a platform, its main plank was economic prosperity based on a commerce unencumbered by foreign powers. The administration's commitment to this principle surfaced in each major foreign policy decision: the Barbary War, the Louisiana Purchase, nonimportation, embargo, the seizure of West Florida, and the War of 1812. In domestic policy per se (as opposed to the domestic ramifications of foreign policy), a strong agreement among party supporters on the proper policy was absent. The triumvirate deferred more to Congress and at times to strict constitutional construction. When they expressed their preferences, as in the case of the bank, the divisions within their party thwarted them. The importance of the political agreement among propertied citizens on government actions cannot be overemphasized in explaining why the triumvirate acted as they did.

In his "Autobiographic Sketch" of 1849 Gallatin observed that "the principal questions in which I was engaged related to constitutional construction or to the finances[,] though not quite so orthodox on the first subject as my Virginia friends (witness the United States Bank & internal improvements)."[9] Besides reinforcing the previous analysis, this statement is revealing for its exclusion of manufacturing. Perhaps because manufacturing was an integral part of foreign policy, perhaps because they never considered Hamilton's activities in this area significant or genuine, the triumvirate concurred in the necessity of developing domestic industry through prohibitions and tariffs. Gallatin alone advocated loans. According to reports received by the Treasury, a tenfold increase in manufacturing could be attributed directly to the nonimportation and embargo policies of the Republican administration. In New England, for example, there were four cotton mills in 1804; five years later there were eighty-seven.[10] Because of the link in foreign policy between national independence and manufacturing, the triumvirate succeeded in the promotion of manufacturing while they fell short in internal improvements and banking.[11]

Gallatin and his two compatriots rested their hopes for a strong union and a fully independent nation on a national market system. Toward that end they directed their policies, domestic and foreign, and advanced their proposals. Theirs was a bold and imaginative stabilization program. Hamilton's political economy relied on the English model; in this respect, it was timid and mundane. He, not they, sought to freeze political society in time. The triumvirate's political economy, particularly Gallatin's, was dynamic—the economics of Adam Smith, not James Steuart. They did not believe that progress over time meant inevitable decay. They believed that time could be mastered through an expanding market system. Although the frontier was the chief metaphor of this expansion, it was only a metaphor. The expansion of the market system involved much more than settling a continent.[12]

The Republican political economy, as Merrill Peterson observes, came to be the American System. Glyndon Van Deusen could have been writing of Gallatin's Republican system when he explained:

Only through the agency of the national government [could Henry] Clay's American System . . . really come into being. With that system in operation, the tariff, by stimulating the manufacturing interest, would build up a market for agriculture and provide a great impetus to internal commerce. . . . Internal improvements would create a veritable commercial revolution . . . by facilitating marketing of agricultural and industrial goods in all sections of the country. The chartering of a new national bank would provide the stabilization, at desired levels, of currency and credit. Thus would be provided, through governmental activity, a harmonization of interest and a fructification of national wealth and power.[13]

This is not the legacy of men who would proscribe economic progress.

In their later lives Jefferson, Madison, and Gallatin retreated somewhat from the policies which they had advanced while in power. This retreat represents no fundamental shift in their political economy; rather, it reflects a change in circumstances. The consistent sanction on government activity was the consent of the governed. The people should be guided by their leaders, but leaders had a fundamental obligation to follow the mandates of their propertied citizens. Both the rapid expansion of the economy after 1820 and the growing sectionalism undercut the political consensus for federal regulation and intervention. Without that consensus the Republican leaders believed the various economic interests should be allowed to act alone. Had their market system succeeded, this political dissension and consequent laissez-faire might have been avoided. Andrew Jackson's challenge and ultimate victory over John Quincy Adams was symbolic of the loss of political consensus for a comprehensive federal role in economic development. Thus, in 1820 Jefferson railed against a revival of "Federalism" during the Missouri Crisis; in 1831 Gallatin penned an extended polemic against protective tariffs; and, a few years later, Madison warned of the snake of disunion sneaking into the American Eden.[14]

Because they feared the disruption of the union, they could not condone the exercise of federal power without the consent of the majority of property holders. Their earlier vision of federal development of the market system, in which the nation as a whole might develop manufacturing, was obscured by the cotton bales of the South. The market system, which would have created a political consensus on federal programs, did not come to pass. Southern leaders refused to bear the cost in protective tariffs and federal transportation projects for developing manufacturing largely in the Northeast and Midwest. The growing sectional character of the American polity frightened the triumvirate. If the federal government acted to advance the development of manufacturing or internal transportation in one section of the nation to the detriment of another, it became an agent of a faction. Since they would brook no revival of the Hamiltonian politics of corruption and faction, the three former leaders backed away from their support of federal aid.

Beyond political changes wrought by economic development, the triumvirate simply grew older and less bold in their projects. They were apprehensive about the union that they had worked so hard and so long to establish. They could still recall thirteen separate colonies struggling to unite, while many of the rising leaders remembered only a nation growing into a continent. Undisciplined by wise statesmen, economic expansion could become as destructive to political stability and national cohesion as, in earlier years, it had been necessary. "The energy of this nation," Gallatin observed in 1836, "is not to be controlled: it is at present exclusively applied to the acquisition of wealth and to improvements of stupendous magnitude. . . . I would have proposed a gradual, slow; & more secure progress. I am however an old man; and the younger generation has a right to govern itself."[15] It is to their everlasting tribute that, despite their apprehensions for the future, they still affirmed the right of a people to determine their own destiny. In this respect, the traditional image of the Republican leaders as torchbearers of the Revolution remains vivid.

Despite its ultimate outcome, the political economy of the triumvirate stands as a more comprehensive and effective expression of liberal economic nationalism than Hamilton's vigorous but flawed efforts to procure a strong union through a highly centralized government tied to Britain. At the center of the Republican political economy was the market system in which all its essential elements found expression: economic development, political stability, social cohesion, and national independence. Insofar as the expansion of territory and markets was integral to it, their political economy was an imperial project. Jefferson labeled it "an empire of liberty." Within their understanding of the word "liberty"—the independence and self-determination accorded by property ownership—their political economy would maintain the majority's independence and, through expansion, promise that same independence to others with the capability and the desire to acquire property. The propertyless—blacks, wage-laborers, tenants, Indians, women—were for the time being excluded by law and circumstance. Nevertheless, the Republican leaders wrought an unprecedented expansion of human freedom, the progeny of which was the American System. The American Revolution had created the freest society on earth, and the triumvirate worked to make it freer and economically independent. In their political economy capitalism and political democracy were first reconciled.

A Note on Commercial Discrimination

Commercial discrimination is fundamentally war by nonmilitary means. After the inauguration of the federal government, Jefferson, Madison, and Gallatin proposed it three times and implemented it twice. Ostensibly it failed both times and was not implemented the third time for fear of failure. Some assessment of the tactic remains necessary for two reasons. First, its probable failure in 1794 has become the chief justification for Hamilton's acquiescence in the Jay Treaty. Second, in 1807 the Republican leaders had an opportunity to accept a settlement with Britain on terms better than those Jay accepted. They rejected it for several reasons: its failure to ban impressment, its restrictions on the reexport trade, and its limitations on export markets. At the core of their rejection was the firm belief that commercial discrimination could exact better terms from England.[1] This belief led to the embargo, the nonimportation of British goods in 1810, the extraordinary expansion of domestic manufactures over these years, and, ultimately, war.

Embargo should be distinguished from nonimportation. The former was essentially a defensive, if not pacific, tactic whose purpose was to protect American ships from seizure in the absence of a navy and reduce the chances of a *casus belli*. Usually lasting for sixty days, embargoes were imposed four times during this period: 1794, 1798, 1807, and 1812. Their nonbelligerent nature is aptly illustrated by Hamilton's successful effort to have one imposed in 1794 in lieu of Madison's nonimportation resolutions. From 1807 to 1809 the embargo tactic merged with nonimportation to compel English repeal of its seizure and condemnation policy. This use of an embargo, however, was an aberration.

Nonimportation and the embargo of 1807–9 failed to affect Britain's policy. Several factors assuaged the economic impact of losing American markets and exports. Anglo–Latin American commerce rose precipitously on the credit extended by English merchants to finance their sales. Tobacco and cotton were adequate because of accumulated supplies and new sources of cotton in Egypt and India. A decline in English manufacturing offset reduced supplies as market mechanisms adjusted to the situation. Foodstuffs were short, but reductions in liquor distillation and a good harvest compensated for the shortage. England managed to send some foodstuffs to its West Indian colonies to stabilize the area most seriously affected by American sanctions. Moreover, the influence of the West Indian planters over London was on the decline. Canada helped to meet English lumber requirements, and smuggling provided a trickle of needed American commodities. Overall, strategic necessity and the belief that domestic dissension would soon overcome America's will to continue the sanctions forestalled Whitehall's acquiescence.[2]

That the Republican leadership again employed nonimportation against Britain in 1810 is not surprising. Despite its failure a year earlier, it remained the only weapon, short of war, America possessed to combat English aggression. Although much is made of Napoleon's duplicity in repealing his decrees against American trade merely to invite reprisal against England, in Madison's and Gallatin's view England remained the chief threat to independence and commerce. If Britain acquiesced, Napoleon's continued violations could be dealt with effectively. Indeed, if Britain ceased to search, seize, and force America's European trade through its ports, most of France's restrictions would become moot. The administration was not fooled; it merely recognized the practical aspects of the situation. If England gave way, France would cease its random assaults or face a de facto Anglo-American alliance.

In 1812 nonimportation finally succeeded. A bad harvest, the collapse of the Latin American markets due to the overextension of credit, an effective French blockade of the Continent, and the continued drain of the war combined with the loss of the American market to cause the most severe British depression in fifteen years. Labor riots, the political pressure of merchants and manufactures, and Whitehall's fear that war with America would only worsen the slump led to the repeal of the coercive British policy against the United States in July 1812.[3] There was, however, a two-month delay in transmitting the news. The administration remained skeptical, in large part because of London's repudiation of a similar agreement negotiated in 1809 by their minister David Erskine. They believed that the repeal was merely a ruse to undercut the war effort. Thus, there was no change in the decision for war.[4] Decades later Gallatin speculated that more "timely repeals of the orders in council would have prevented the war."[5] Commercial discrimination, then, had succeeded one time out of two.

Returning to the 1794 case, Madison's and Jefferson's insistence that commercial discrimination in the form of nonimportation would have succeeded appears to have more weight in light of future events. The question of its efficacy in that time is of two parts: First, could the American economy and political structure have sustained the loss of revenue and commerce for a year or two of nonimportation? And second, would the economic pressure on Britain's economy have been sufficient to provoke an effective political movement for repeal? Although there are numerous variables, two appear most pertinent to answering these questions: the duration of nonexportation and the business cycle in Britain. In 1797 England experienced a depression unequaled until the 1811 contraction. The nonimportation policy, had it been enacted, would probably have taken hold in America by the middle of 1794. If the American government and economy could have sustained that policy until the 1797 depression, then it might have succeeded as the 1810 policy succeeded when an equivalent depression struck England. Two and a half years, however, would have been a long time for an economy much weaker than the one that could endure only fifteen months of nonimportation and embargo in 1807 and 1810. Perhaps nonimportation might have precipitated a British depression sooner. The question is by no means resolved either way, and to charge that Jefferson and Madison were "idealistic" in proposing that American resist English hegemony in 1794 is as yet unproven.

A Note on Statistical Sources

The graphs in Appendix C and other statistical data cited in the text are drawn from a variety of sources. The principal sources are the annual reports of the Treasury Department on finances, commerce, and navigation included in the *New American State Papers: Commerce and Navigation,* ed. Thomas C. Cochran, 47 vols. (Wilmington, Del., 1973) and the *New American State Papers: Public Finance,* ed. Thomas C. Cochran, 32 vols., (Wilmington, Del., 1972–73). Most of the material within these reports is collected in Timothy Pitkin, *A Statistical View of the United States of America* (Hartford, Conn., 1816), and Adam Seybert, *Statistical Annals of the United States, 1789–1818* (Philadelphia, 1818). The most comprehensive modern collection of these data, though it is not as inclusive as the earlier ones, is the *Historical Statistics of the United States: Colonial Times to 1970* put out by the U.S. Department of Commerce, Bureau of the Census (1976). The *Historical Statistics* also includes price data for the major cities. For stock prices and general business indicators I consulted Walter B. Smith and Arthur H. Cole, *Fluctuations in American Business, 1790–1860* (Cambridge, Mass., 1935).

Possibly the most interesting data are the customs records of destination and cargo for each major port. Such information would be invaluable, but, sadly, all records that collected this data for the Treasury Department have been destroyed by fires. The alternative is the painstaking reconstruction of trade patterns from individual merchants or foreign port records. Another promising alternative is the British Foreign Office Records of its agents' reports on American commercial activity. This information, which is massive and difficult to access, is not reflected in the statistical materials offered in this study.

Graphs

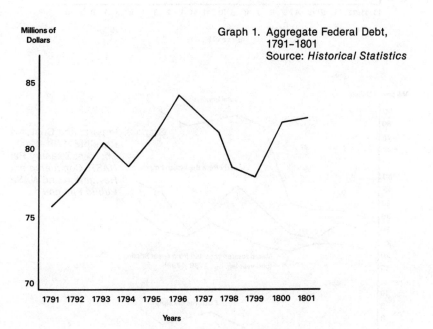

Millions of
Dollars

Graph 1. Aggregate Federal Debt,
1791–1801
Source: *Historical Statistics*

85

80

75

70

1791 1792 1793 1794 1795 1796 1797 1798 1799 1800 1801

Years

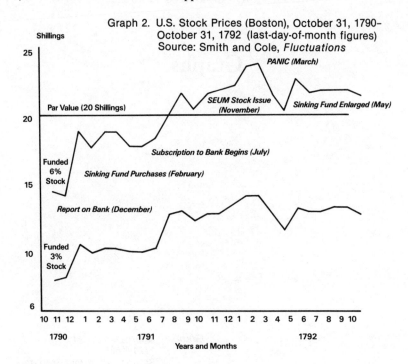

Graph 2. U.S. Stock Prices (Boston), October 31, 1790–
October 31, 1792 (last-day-of-month figures)
Source: Smith and Cole, *Fluctuations*

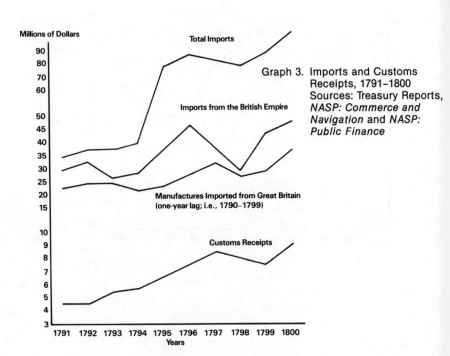

Graph 3. Imports and Customs
Receipts, 1791–1800
Sources: Treasury Reports,
*NASP: Commerce and
Navigation* and *NASP:
Public Finance*

Graph 4. U.S. Trade in Millions of Dollars, 1790–1800
Source: Treasury Reports, *NASP: Commerce and Navigation*

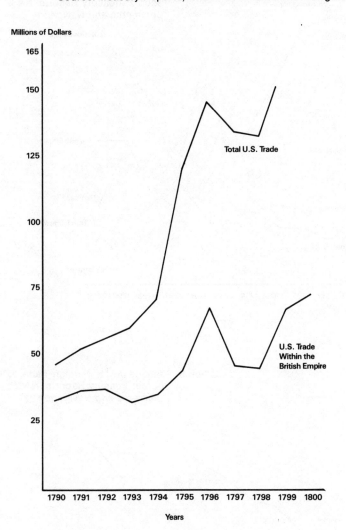

Millions of Dollars

165

150

125

Total U.S. Trade

100

75

50

U.S. Trade
Within the
British Empire

25

1790 1791 1792 1793 1794 1795 1796 1797 1798 1799 1800

Years

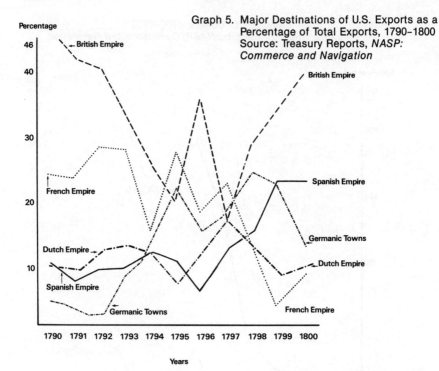

Graph 5. Major Destinations of U.S. Exports as a Percentage of Total Exports, 1790–1800 Source: Treasury Reports, *NASP: Commerce and Navigation*

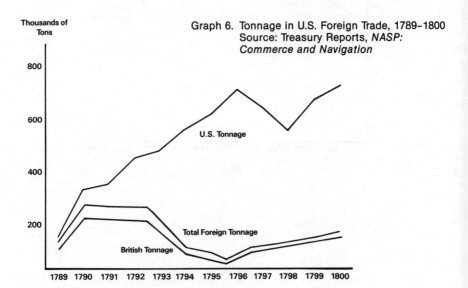

Graph 6. Tonnage in U.S. Foreign Trade, 1789–1800 Source: Treasury Reports, *NASP: Commerce and Navigation*

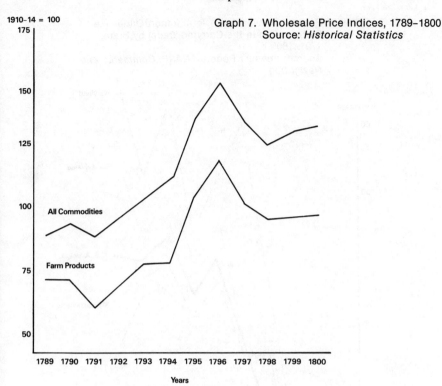

1910–14 = 100

Graph 7. Wholesale Price Indices, 1789–1800
Source: *Historical Statistics*

All Commodities

Farm Products

Years

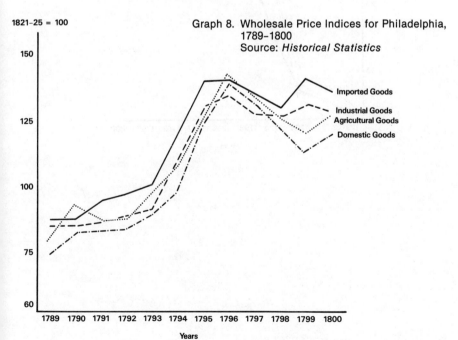

1821–25 = 100

Graph 8. Wholesale Price Indices for Philadelphia,
1789–1800
Source: *Historical Statistics*

Imported Goods

Industrial Goods
Agricultural Goods

Domestic Goods

Years

Graph 9. Ratio of Drawbacks to Total Import Duties (i.e.,
          Participation in the Carrying Trade) by State,
          1791–1800
          Source: Treasury Reports, *NASP: Commerce and
          Navigation*

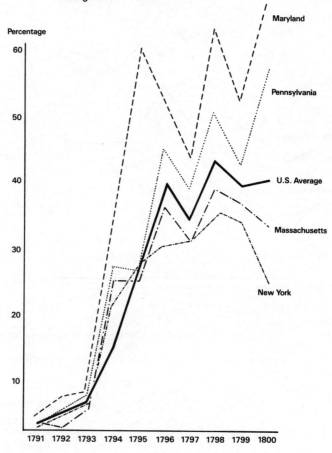

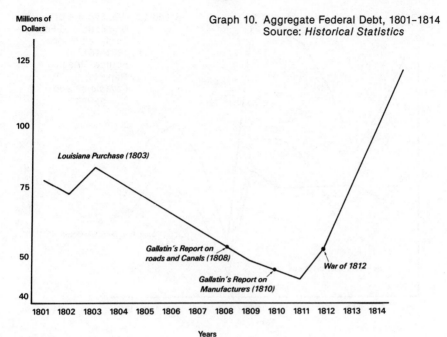

Millions of Dollars

Graph 10. Aggregate Federal Debt, 1801–1814
Source: *Historical Statistics*

Louisiana Purchase (1803)

Gallatin's Report on
roads and Canals (1808)

Gallatin's Report on
Manufactures (1810)

War of 1812

Years

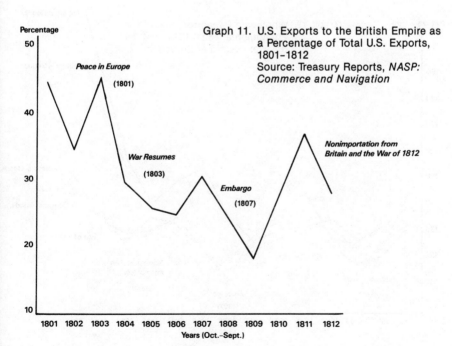

Percentage

Graph 11. U.S. Exports to the British Empire as
a Percentage of Total U.S. Exports,
1801–1812
Source: Treasury Reports, *NASP:
Commerce and Navigation*

Peace in Europe

(1801)

War Resumes

(1803)

Embargo

(1807)

Nonimportation from
Britain and the War of 1812

Years (Oct.–Sept.)

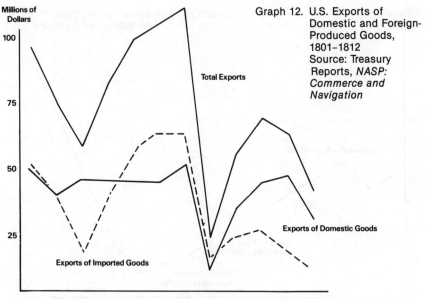

Graph 12. U.S. Exports of Domestic and Foreign-Produced Goods, 1801–1812
Source: Treasury Reports, *NASP: Commerce and Navigation*

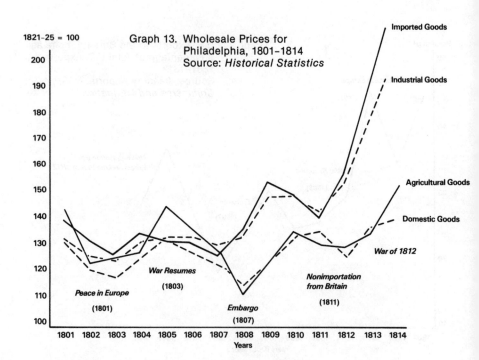

Graph 13. Wholesale Prices for Philadelphia, 1801–1814
Source: *Historical Statistics*

Graph 14. U.S. Exports and Reexports to Latin America as a
Percentage of Total U.S. Export Trade, 1805–1811
Source: Treasury Reports, *NASP: Commerce and
Navigation*

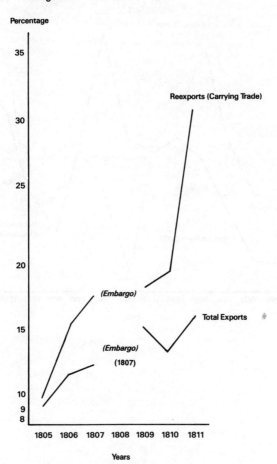

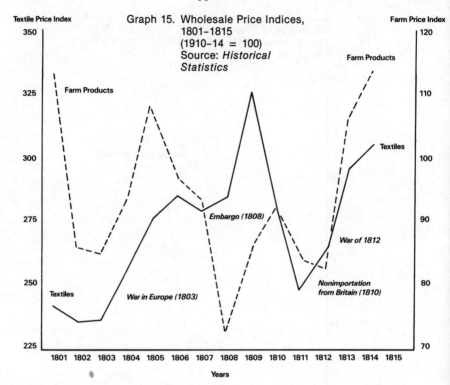

Graph 15. Wholesale Price Indices,
1801–1815
(1910–14 = 100)
Source: *Historical
Statistics*

Textile Price Index

Farm Price Index

Farm Products

Textiles

Embargo (1808)

War of 1812

War in Europe (1803)

Nonimportation
from Britain (1810)

Years

Notes

The following abbreviations have been used in the notes:

Annals | *The Debates and Proceedings in the Congress of the United States,*
of | *1789-1824.* Comp. Joseph Gales. 42 vols. Washington, D. C., 1834-56.
Cong.

ASP | U. S. Congress. *American State Papers.* Ed. Walter Lowrie and Matthew S. Clarke. 38 vols. Washington, D. C., 1832-61.

NASP | *New American State Papers.* Gen. ed. Thomas C. Cochran. Wilmington, Del., 1972-.

PAG | *The Papers of Albert Gallatin* (microfilm). Ed. Carl Prince. Philadelphia, 1970.

PAH | *The Papers of Alexander Hamilton.* Ed. Harold C. Syrett. 26 vols. New York, 1961-78.

PTJ | *The Papers of Thomas Jefferson.* Ed. Julian P. Boyd. Princeton, 1950-.

WAG | *The Writings of Albert Gallatin.* Ed. Henry Adams. 3 vols. New York, 1960.

W&MQ | *William and Mary Quarterly*

WJM | *The Writings of James Madison.* Ed. Galliard Hunt. 9 vols. New York, 1900-1910.

WTJ | *The Writings of Thomas Jefferson.* Ed. Paul L. Ford. 10 vols. New York, 1892-99.

Chapter 1
America in 1789: An Overview

1. For two of the best discussions of paradigms see Thomas A. Kuhn, *The Structure of Scientific Revolutions* (Chicago, 1970), and J.G.A. Pocock, *Politics, Language, and Time* (New York, 1973), 3-4, 273-91. Although Thomas Hobbes, John Locke, and William Petty are discussed briefly in this chapter, the focus of the discussion is David Hume. Father of the Enlightenment, preeminent philosopher, political theorist, and political economist, Hume embodied much of the liberal tradition in Anglo-American thought. However, this sketch of the Anglo roots of American liberalism is not intended to identify specific intellectual influences on particular founders, nor to assess a founder's concurrence or lack of concurrence

with one or another of Hume's ideas, nor to elevate Hume above all other strains of liberal thought. Hume simply expresses as well as anyone (and better than most) the commonality of perspective, the liberal world view, shared by men of affairs in this period. Hume understood all the essential elements of the conceptual paradigm of his era. His only deficiency, if it may be labeled such, was his failure to recognize it as a historically specific paradigm. Douglass G. Adair's classic article, "That Politics May Be Reduced to a Science: David Hume, James Madison, and the Tenth *Federalist*," *Huntington Library Quarterly*, 20 (August 1957), 343–60, accords Hume a central role in Madison's thinking. More recently, Roy Branson's "James Madison and the Scottish Enlightenment," *Journal of the History of Ideas*, 40 (April–June 1979), 235–50, reaffirmed the link to Hume and Locke, but observed that the circumstances in the new nation molded Madison's thought. James Conniff provides a detailed evolution of Madison's thought as molded by political and economic conditions to the Tenth *Federalist* in "The Enlightenment and American Political Thought: A Study of the Origins of Madison's *Federalist* Number 10," *Political Theory*, 8 (August 1980), 381–402. Conniff does point toward Francis Hutcheson, rather than Hume, as a major influence on Madison. I regard the differences between Hume and other liberal thinkers to be less significant than their similarities.

2. John H. Randall, Jr., *The Career of Philosophy*, 2 vols. (New York, 1962), 1:460–562; C. B. MacPherson, *The Political Theory of Possessive Individualism* (Oxford, 1962), 9–106; Christopher Hill, *The World Turned Upside Down* (New York, 1972); and Ernest Cassirer, *The Philosophy of the Enlightenment* (Princeton, 1951), v–xii, 3–92.

3. Cassirer, *Philosophy of the Enlightenment*, 93–133. He summarizes this characteristic of modern thought: "We may ascend to the highest heavens or descend to the deepest abyss, yet we shall never transcend the bounds of our ego, since we shall always encounter ourselves and our own thoughts" (118).

4. MacPherson, *Possessive Individualism*, 9–106; Hill, *World Turned Upside Down*, 313–19.

5. See my as yet unpublished paper, "William Petty's Theory of Economic Progress."

6. John Locke, *Two Treatises of Government*, ed. Peter Laslett (Cambridge, 1960); MacPherson, *Possessive Individualism*, 194–262.

7. Hume's role in the Enlightenment, though clear in Cassirer's work, is more explicitly presented in Peter Gay's *The Enlightenment: An Interpretation*, 2 vols. (New York, 1969). Cassirer stresses Leibniz's role where Gay stresses Hume's.

8. David Hume, *A Treatise of Human Nature*, ed. L. A. Selby-Bigge (Oxford, 1968), xxi. The discussion of Hume's philosophy is aided by *Hume: A Collection of Critical Essays*, ed. V. C. Chappell (Garden City, N.Y., 1966), particularly Robert Paul Wolff, "Hume's Theory of Mental Activity," 99–128, and F. A. Hayek, "The Legal and Political Philosophy of David Hume," 335–60. See also Randall, *Career of Philosophy*, 1:563–983. In "From Applied Theology to Social Analysis: The Break between John Locke and the Scottish Enlightenment," in *Wealth and Virtue: The Shaping of Political Economy in the Scottish Enlightenment*, ed. I. Hont and M. Ignatieff (Cambridge, 1983), John Dunn stresses the differences between Locke and Hume et al., especially with regard to Hume's atheism. Again, these discontinuities seem to me less significant than the continuity in liberal thought. The father of all modern thought, René Descartes, held "God" to be a concept interchangeable with the "order of nature."

9. Hume, *Treatise*, 275–82, 414–18.

10. Ibid., 295–96, 414–15, 457–62, 470–75, 574.

11. Ibid., 464–65, 471–84.

12. Ibid., 484–501.

13. Ibid., 491–92.

14. Ibid., 534–39; *David Hume's Political Essays,* ed. Charles W. Hendel (New York, 1953), 49–50, 60. By the time Hume wrote, the commercial property classes in England controlled the government more securely than in Locke's and Petty's era. He was, therefore, less insistent on a popular (propertied) representative government than were either of them. The more integral property became to the social order, the less of an issue it was. This explanation accords with the "nondecisionmaking" paradigm employed by modern policy analysts, but originally, it was Hegel's insight. See, for example, Peter Bachrach and Morton S. Baratz, *Power and Poverty: Theory and Practice* (New York, 1970), 39–51, and Matthew A. Crenson, *The Unpolitics of Air Pollution: A Study of Non-Decisionmaking in the Cities* (Baltimore, 1971), esp. 177–84.

15. Hume, "Of the Independence of Parliament," "Of Refinement in the Arts," and "Idea of a Perfect Commonwealth," *Political Essays,* 68–71, 128–29, and 147–54. The notion of "corruption" and the "country" versus the "court" party is a leitmotif of the "ideological" school interpretation of the American Revolution and Constitution by Bernard Bailyn, Gordon Wood, J.G.A. Pocock, Drew McCoy, and others. They place the founders in a classical republican, as opposed to a liberal republican, mold; Pocock describes the Revolution as "the last great act of the Renaissance" in *The Machiavellian Moment: Florentine Political Thought and the Atlantic Republican Tradition* (Princeton, 1975). Through several fine studies, Joyce Appleby has gone far toward restoring political economy and liberal republicanism to a central place in the founders' intellectual heritage. See her *Capitalism and a New Social Order: The Jeffersonian Vision of the 1790s* (New York, 1984); *Economic Thought and Ideology in Seventeenth-Century England* (Princeton, 1978); and especially, "What Is Still American in the Political Philosophy of Thomas Jefferson," *W&MQ,* 39 (April 1982), 287–309. In a recent article, Donald Winch reviewed Appleby's work ("Economic Liberalism as Ideology: The Appleby Version," *Economic History Review,* 37 [1985], 287–97). Unlike Winch, I find Appleby's effort compelling. As Winch suggests, intellectual historians may exhibit "promiscuous habits," but Appleby's effort to synthesize the ideas and economic activities of the founders represents an advancement over the "ideological" school, which fell into the Nietzschean trap of looking *and* thinking backwards, i.e., asserting the primacy of idealized notions over political economic realities. Historiographic reviews which stress the unexplained over the explained without explaining it have an incestuous flavor which Hegel aptly characterized in his *Philosophy of History*: "Instead of writing history, we are always beating our brains to discover how history ought to be written."

16. Hume, "Of Commerce," *Political Essays,* 130–41.

17. Hume, "Of Parties in General," and "Of the Coalition of Parties," ibid., 77–84, 93–100.

18. Hume, "Idea of a Perfect Commonwealth," and "Of Parties in General," ibid., 147–48, 78.

19. *Federalist,* no. 54 (Madison), in Alexander Hamilton, John Jay, and James Madison, *The Federalist* (New York: Modern Library Edition, n. d.).

20. Ibid., no. 12 (Hamilton).

21. Ibid., no. 85 (Hamilton).

22. Ibid., no. 51 (Madison).

23. Ibid., no. 10 (Madison).

24. Ibid., no. 51 (Madison).

25. Ibid., no. 49 (Madison).

26. MacPherson, *Possessive Individualism*, 279–92. In a letter to James Sullivan, John Adams explained why women, children, and the propertyless were excluded from the political system: "Is it not equally true, that men in general, in every society, who are wholly destitute of property, are also too little acquainted with public affairs to form a right judgement, and too dependent on other men to have a will of their own?" May 26, 1776, in *The Works of John Adams,* ed. Charles F. Adams (Boston, 1850–56).

27. MacPherson, *Possessive Individualism*, 279–92. Christopher P. Hill summarizes best the effect on England's propertyless classes of the ascension to power of the propertied and their ideology: "The rich inherited the earth." Hill, *The Century of Revolution, 1603–1714* (New York, 1961), 151. In other words, conditions changed very little for the general populace with the rise of a new elite.

28. Jackson T. Main, *The Social Structure of Revolutionary America* (Princeton, 1965), 156, 194.

29. E. James Ferguson, *The Power of the Purse: A History of American Public Finance, 1776–1790* (Chapel Hill, 1961), 333. In his seminal work, Ferguson estimates that the Revolution cost between $154 and $164 million; federal expenditures between 1790 and 1812 were about $154 million.

30. Robert R. Palmer, *The Age of the Democratic Revolution* (Princeton, 1959), 188.

31. George R. Taylor, "American Economic Growth before 1840: An Exploratory Essay," *Journal of Economic History,* 24 (1964), 427–44.

32. Douglass C. North, *The Economic Growth of the United States, 1790–1860* (Englewood Cliffs, N.J., 1961), 41–42. American merchants carried 59% of their pre-Revolutionary trade in 1790.

33. See Appendix B, "A Note on Statistical Sources."

34. Ferguson, *Power of the Purse,* 109–29, 156–67, 209–10, 228–41.

35. Ibid., 66–249; Curtis P. Nettels, *The Emergence of a National Economy, 1775–1815* (New York, 1962), 30–79; and Merrill Jensen, *The New Nation* (New York, 1950), 41–325.

36. This is essentially Beard's argument, refined by Ferguson, *Power of the Purse,* and Forrest McDonald, *We the People: The Economic Origins of the Constitution* (Chicago, 1958).

37. Jensen, *New Nation,* 323–26.

38. This interpretation of the social origins of the Constitution accords somewhat with Gordon S. Wood, *The Creation of the American Republic, 1776–1789* (New York, 1969), 393–467.

39. Madison's two discussions of the "propertyless" illustrates this direction: "Observations on the Draft of Virginia's Constitution," November 1788, *WJM,* 5:286–87, and the *Federalist,* no. 10.

40. See Charles Sydnor, *Gentlemen Freeholders* (Chapel Hill, 1952).

41. Madison to Phillip Mazzer, October 8, 1788, *WJM,* 5:267.

42. Madison to Jefferson, October 17, 1788, *PTJ,* 14:19.

43. Speech before the Virginia Ratifying Convention, June 5, 1788, *WJM,* 5:26.

44. Hamilton to Washington, July 3, 1787, *PAH,* 4:224.

45. Speeches on May 31, 1787, in Max Farrand, *The Records of the Federal Convention of 1787,* 4 vols. (New Haven, 1937).

46. Speech before the Constitutional Convention, June 1787, *PAH*, 4:193–95, 198–202, 219.

47. This summary is derived from the *Federalist*, nos. 1, 6–8, 10–12, 49, 51, 85; and Madison to Jefferson, October 24, 1787, *PTJ*, 12:276–79. Hamilton linked economic stagnation to rebellion in the *Federalist*, no. 6. Gordon S. Wood develops an interpretation of the Constitution along these lines, but neglects the role of political economy in his *Creation of the American Republic*.

48. Alfred Young, "Conservatives, the Constitution, and the 'Spirit of Accommodation,'" in *How Democratic Was the Constitution?*, ed. Robert Goldwin and William Scham (Washington, 1980), presents a very perceptive discussion of the elite-popular molding of and support for the Constitution. For Hamilton's discussion of this issue see "Conjectures about the New Constitution," September 17–30, 1787, *PAH*, 4:275.

49. Harry Ammon, "The Formation of the Republican Party in Virginia, 1789–1796," *Journal of Southern History*, 19 (1953), 285.

50. Norman K. Risjord, "Virginia Federalists," ibid., 33 (1967), 496–97.

51. Ibid., 498; *The Debates in the Several State Conventions, on the Adoption of the Constitution*, ed. Jonathan Elliot, 5 vols. (Philadelphia, 1836), 3:453–623.

52. Lisle A. Rose, *Prologue to Democracy: The Federalists in the South, 1789–1800* (Lexington, 1968), 16–18, 55; Richard Walsh, *Charleston's Sons of Liberty: A Study of Artisans, 1763–1789* (Columbia, S.C., 1959), 135–37.

53. Mark L. Renzulli, Jr., *Maryland: The Federalist Years* (Rutherford, N.J., 1972), 72–77, 98–99.

54. Ibid., 68, 98–101.

55. Roland M. Bauman, "The Democratic-Republicans of Philadelphia: The Origins, 1776–1797" (Ph.D. diss., Pennsylvania State University, 1970), 101–11, 123, 163; Robert L. Brunhouse, *The Counter-Revolution in Pennsylvania, 1776–1790* (Philadelphia, 1942), 195ff.

56. Staughton Lynd, "The Mechanics in New York City Politics, 1774–1788," *Labor History*, 5 (1964), 241–45; Alfred F. Young, *The Democratic Republicans of New York: The Origins, 1763–1797* (Chapel Hill, 1967), 66–82, 91–100, 156–57.

57. Paul Goodman, *The Democratic-Republicans of Massachusetts: Politics in a Young Republic* (Cambridge, 1964), 11–19, 27, 42.

58. Ibid., 11–44.

59. Jackson Turner Main, *The Antifederalists: Critics of the Constitution* (Chapel Hill, 1961), 40, 69–70, 261–79, and *Political Parties before the Constitution* (Chapel Hill, 1973), 321–74.

60. Renzulli, *Maryland*, 94.

Chapter 2
The Political Economy of Alexander Hamilton: Theory and Practice

1. In his biography of Hamilton, *Alexander Hamilton: Portrait in Paradox* (New York, 1959), John C. Miller resorts to paradox to "explain"—that is, subsume—the inconsistencies revealed by the topical-eventful approach. Paradox, however, *subsumes* ostensible inconsistencies; it does not resolve them. Broadus Mitchell's biography, by far the most comprehensive, suffers less from this approach; see *Alexander Hamilton*, 2 vols. (New York, 1957–62). However, Mitchell appears to be writing to affirm a particular past in which Hamilton plays the role of beneficent statesman bringing private economic power to heel for national pur-

poses. Using Hamilton as a precedent for a contemporary planned economy creates problems for an analysis of the historical figure. Despite his resort to paradox, Miller's recognition of the difficulties of making Hamilton's political economy analytically coherent is, in many respects, superior to Mitchell's icon. In the most recent biographical effort, *Alexander Hamilton* (New York, 1982), Jacob E. Cooke explicitly acknowledges the problem with past biographies and offers an "eclectic" approach relying "most heavily on Freudian theory." His intent and erudition notwithstanding, Cooke fails to analyze satisfactorily the most fundamental elements of Hamilton's political economy and policymaking.

2. Joseph Dorfman, *The Economic Mind in American Civilization*, 2 vols. (New York, 1946); Louis M. Hacker, *Alexander Hamilton in the American Tradition* (New York, 1957); and E.A.J. Johnson, *Foundations of American Economic Freedom* (Minneapolis, 1973). Ferguson's *Power of the Purse* does integrate the economics and politics of the national debt in a very satisfactory manner.

3. Hamilton, "The Farmer Refuted," February 23, 1775, *PAH*, 1:92–95, and speech before the Constitutional Convention, June 19, 1787, *PAH*, 4:216.

4. Defense of the Funding Systems, July 1795, *PAH*, 19:59–60; and Hamilton to James Bayard, April 1804, *PAH*, 25:605.

5. Opinion on the Constitutionality of the Bank, February 23, 1791, *PAH*, 8:66, 98. This analysis is based on Hamilton's transposition of terms and phrases in his drafts of this document.

6. "Tully: Number 3," August 28, 1794, *PAH*, 17:160.

7. Hamilton to Edward Carrington, May 26, 1792, *PAH*, 11:443; Hamilton spoken to Jefferson, August 13, 1791, *PAH*, 9:34; Hamilton to Timothy Pickering, September 16, 1803, *PAH*, 26:148–49; and convention speech, June 20, 1787, *PAH*, 4:219.

8. Hamilton, "The Farmer Refuted," February 23, 1775, *PAH*, 1:97.

9. Hamilton to Carrington, May 26, 1792, *PAH*, 11:443; Hamilton to ?, December 1779–March 1780, *PAH*, 2:242.

10. Hamilton to John Jay, November 26, 1775, *PAH*, 1:176; Hamilton to Robert Morris, August 13, 1782, *PAH*, 3:135; "Tully: Number 2," August 26, 1794, *PAH*, 17:150.

11. These quotations and the analysis are drawn from Hamilton's speeches and notes during the Constitutional Convention, June 18, 1787, *PAH*, 4:192ff.

12. Madison's version of Hamilton's Speech, June 26, 1787, ibid., 218; Yates's version, ibid., 219n; Lansing's version, ibid.

13. See Madison's speech and notes in the Virginia constitutional convention, December 2, 1829, *WJM*, 9:358–64, 358n–60n.

14. Convention speech, June 26, 1787, *PAH*, 4:218–19n.

15. The plan was presented June 18, 1787, ibid., 188–92, 196–98, 202–3, 205–6.

16. Ibid., 208–9.

17. Alfred F. Young, *Democratic Republicans of New York*, 82, notes that Hamilton's speech represented the views of New York's conservatives.

18. Hamilton to Gouverneur Morris, February 29, 1802, *PAH*, 25:544; Hamilton to Carrington, May 26, 1792, *PAH*, 11:444; Hamilton to Jefferson, August 13, 1791, *PAH*, 9:34.

19. Hamiltons "Fact: Number 2," October 16, 1792, *PAH*, 12:571.

20. Hamiltons Remarks in the New York Assembly, January 27, 1787, *PAH*, 4:29; Defense of the Funding System, July 1795, *PAH*, 19:52; "Continentalist: Number 5," April 18, 1782, *PAH*, 3:77.

21. Hamilton, "Vindication: Number 3," May–August 1792, *PAH,* 11:470–72; see also Defense of the Funding System, July 1795, *PAH,* 19:50–71.

22. Ferguson, *Power of the Purse,* 109–44.

23. Hamilton to James Duane, September 30, 1780, *PAH,* 2:401–8, and to Issac Sears, October 12, 1780, ibid., 472.

24. Hamilton to ?, December 1779–March 1780, ibid., 244.

25. Hamilton to Duane, September 30, 1780, ibid., 414–15.

26. Hamilton to ?, December 1779–March 1780, ibid., 254–60, and to Duane, September 30, 1780, ibid., 415; "Continentalist: Number 4," August 30, 1781, ibid., 670–74.

27. Hamilton to Morris, April 30, 1781, ibid., 635; Morris to Hamilton, May 26, 1781, ibid., 654–64.

28. Morris to Hamilton, October 5, 1782, *PAH,* 3:178–79; *Federalist,* no. 35 (Hamilton).

29. "Letter from Phocion to the Considerate Citizens of New York," January 1–27, 1784, *PAH,* 3:494. See also Hamilton's speech in New York City, April 21, 1802, *PAH,* 25:610–11, and "The Farmer Refuted," February 25, 1775, *PAH,* 1:106–7.

30. Hamilton, "Continentalist: Number 5," April 18, 1782, *PAH,* 3:78–79; Hamilton to Robert Morris, April 30, 1781, *PAH,* 2:617.

31. Ferguson, *Power of the Purse,* 284–86.

32. Hamilton, Report on Public Credit, January 1790, *PAH,* 6:80.

33. Hamilton to Washington, March 27, 1792, *PAH,* 8:223.

34. Hamilton, Defense of the Funding System, July, 1795, *PAH,* 19:5, 31–32. For the positions of Jefferson, Madison and Gallatin on the debt, see below, Chapters 5 and 7. Hamilton shielded his political use of the debt with the sanctity of public credit because it was an unassailable argument.

35. Hamilton, Speech in the Continental Congress, January 28, 1783, *PAH,* 3:246; Speech and Notes in Constitutional Convention, July 1787, *PAH,* 4:166, 216.

36. For Hamilton's extensive discussions of the army's role in politics, see his letters to Washington, February 13, 1783, *PAH,* 3:254–55; to Thomas S. Lee, September 18, 1794, *PAH,* 17:246; to Theodore Sedgwick, February 2, 1799, *PAH,* 24:202; and his speech before the Continental Congress, February 19, 1783, *PAH,* 3:262.

37. Hamilton to McHenry, January 27–February 11, 1798, *PAH,* 21:345–46.

38. Hamilton, Report on Public Credit, *PAH,* 6:70–74.

39. Ibid.

40. Stephen Higginson to Hamilton, November 11, 1789, *PAH,* 5:511. Ferguson observes that the prefunded debt hovered around 50% of par value. *Power of the Purse,* 257.

41. The method of speculation is drawn from several sources: Gouverneur Morris to Hamilton, January 31, 1790, *PAH,* 6:239; James Jervis to Hamilton, February 16, 1790, ibid., 254; and Young, *Democratic Republicans of New York,* 221–23.

42. Report on Public Credit, *PAH,* 6:70–73; Thomas Willing to Hamilton, March 22, 1790, ibid., 308.

43. Hamilton to Benjamin Lincoln, February 1, 1791, *PAH,* 8:1–2. See also his Report on Additional Supplies for the Ensuing Year, August 5, 1790, *PAH,* 6:524; Washington to Hamilton, August 28, 1790, ibid., 578; Report of the Commissioners of the Sinking Fund, August 28, 1790, *PAH,* 8:27; Hamilton to Short, April 13,

1791, ibid., 281–82; and Report Relative to the Loans, February 13, 1793, *PAH,* 14:30–33.

44. Report on a National Bank, December 13, 1790, *PAH,* 7:236–342.

45. Hamilton to Washington, *PAH,* 8:221–22. Emphasis added.

46. William Short to Hamilton, February 17, 1791, ibid., 52–53, and February 22, 1791, ibid., 60.

47. North, *Economic Growth,* 221, 228.

Chapter 3
Hamilton and Manufacturing: A Reexamination

1. Coxe to Jefferson, April 15, 1791, Jefferson Papers (microfilm), Library of Congress, Washington, D. C.

2. The original plan is in the Jefferson Papers at the Library of Congress in the older microfilm edition (Reel M-28), wrongly dated 1792. Compare it to the final Prospectus for a Manufacturing Society, August 1791, *PAH,* 9:145–48.

3. Hamilton to William Duer, April 20, 1791, *PAH,* 8:300–301n.

4. Rufus King to Hamilton, August 15, 1791, *PAH,* 9:60; Hamilton to King, August 17, 1791, ibid., 76; Hamilton to William Seton, August 16, 1791, ibid., 71–72; Hamilton to Duer, August 17, 1791, ibid., 75.

5. Prospectus for a Manufacturing Society, August 1791, ibid., 145–48.

6. *Laws of the State of New Jersey* (Newark, 1800), 105.

7. Hamilton to William Short, *PAH,* 9:547.

8. Jacob E. Cooke, "Tench Coxe, Alexander Hamilton, and the Encouragement of American Manufactures," *W&MQ,* 32 (1975), 380. In his biography of Hamilton, Cooke is surprisingly critical of the report, calling it a "less impressive achievement" than Hamilton's other state papers, "prolix," and derivative of Coxe's work. He does not place it in the context of Hamilton's fiscal policy nor link his interpretation of the report as a "inspiration for American economists of the next generation and beyond" to Hamilton's herculean efforts to establish federal credit. In essence, Cooke views the report as shining anachronism—an interpretation that is ahistorical. Cooke, *Hamilton,* 97-102. If, on the other hand, the report is viewed as a vehicle to elicit and reinforce investor interest in the SEUM and raise stock prices, it was a success: stock prices soared in the winter of 1791-92.

9. Arthur H. Cole, ed., *Industrial and Commercial Correspondence of Alexander Hamilton* (Chicago, 1928), 231-32.

10. Cooke, "Tench Coxe," 373.

11. See Hamilton's letters to Lincoln of January 25 and June 8, 1790, *PAH,* 6:207-8, 460; Cooke, "Tench Coxe," 370, 373; and Cooke, *Tench Coxe and the Early Republic* (Charlottesville, 1978), 158-63, 182-84.

12. In his very important and provocative essay on this period, "The Age of Mercantilism," William A. Williams also makes a point of the time lag. See *Contours of American History* (Chicago, 1966), 166-67. Responding to Williams, Cooke explains the hiatus as a product of Hamilton's "extensive research that went into [the report's] preparation, including hundreds of letters soliciting information on the state of manufactures in every part of the Union." "The Federalist Age: A Reappraisal," in *American History: Retrospect and Prospect,* ed. George A. Bilias and Gerald N. Grob (New York, 1971), 129-30n. There are several problems with Cooke's explanation. To begin with, there is no evidence beyond Hamilton's correspondence with Lincoln and his general circular immediately after the House directive of January 1790 that Hamilton did anything further concerning the report until

February 1791. He did not fruitfully solicit information until June 1791—eighteen months after the directive. As to the "hundreds of letters," there were only four different solicitations of manufacturing information, two by Hamilton and two by Coxe, and fewer than fifty responses to them, including enclosures in letters to Hamilton. Ninety percent of these responses were to the final solicitation in June 1791. Hamilton personally corresponded with no manufacturer concerning the report. In any event, Cooke himself observes that these letters from manufacturers "did not significantly influence" the final report. His explanation thus leaves the period from February 1790 to May 1791 a mystery.

13. For Coxe's requests for manufacturing information see Cooke, "Tench Coxe," 371, and *PAH*, 6:209n and 8:434. The Treasury received three letters in response to these inquiries: Lincoln to Hamilton, May 25, 1790, *PAH*, 6:430, 460; Hazard to Hamilton, March 9, 1791, ibid., 166-67; and Whipple to Hamilton, June 4, 1791, ibid., 434-36. Hamilton's June 1791 circular received some forty responses from Treasury agents. *PAH*, vol. 9, passim.

14. Coxe, draft of Report on Manufactures, *PAH*, 10:16-18, 20-22. Cooke argues that "when the lineage of the Report on Manufactures is traced, the major threads are found to lead to Tench Coxe." He also credits Coxe "with both the initial idea and plans for [SEUM's] actualization." "Tench Coxe," 380. Yet the differences between the Coxe draft and Hamilton's report far outweigh the similarities. In addition Hamilton did write several major drafts of the report that indicate his desire to create his own arguments for the type of manufacturing he wanted to see develop. With reference to the SEUM, Coxe's plan for a large manufactory proposed an *inland* location on the Susquehanna River "for inland trade and manufactures." There it would be insulated from foreign imports and removed from the speculative urban centers. Tench Coxe, *A View of the United States of America* (Philadelphia, 1794), 386, 395. Coxe also wrote Hamilton that the SEUM's "plan" had been "devised by you," that is, Hamilton. May 20, 1792, *PAH*, 11:406. For a concise discussion of the Coxe-Hamilton drafts, see *PAH*, 26:629-30.

15. Coxe, draft, *PAH*, 10:17-18, 20-21. For Coxe's loan proposal see the first draft of the report (ibid., 47-49), which Cooke has discovered to be part of Coxe's draft. Cooke, "Tench Coxe," 372n.

16. Hamilton, Report on Manufactures, *PAH*, 10:230-69. Although Coxe could find benefits for merchants exporting American manufactures and importing raw materials, and those engaged in the carrying trade along the coast, he could offer no inducement to merchants importing foreign manufactures to interest them in domestic development of industry. These importing merchants were central in Hamilton's stabilization program. Coxe, *A View of the United States*, 316-24.

17. Report on Manufactures, *PAH*, 10:269. Joseph Davis notes that "in the Report on Manufactures the tendency is to gloss over the failures and paint in glowing terms the successes in domestic manufactures." Davis, *Essays in the Earlier History of American Corporations*, 2 vols. (Cambridge, 1917), 1:358n.

18. Bray Hammond, "Long and Short Term Credit in Early American Banking," *Quarterly Journal of Economics*, 49 (1934-35), 79-81, 89 and *Banks and Politics in America from the Revolution to the Civil War* (Princeton, 1957), 75.

19. For example, as late as 1812 the New York Manufacturing Society sought a bank charter because of the difficulty of borrowing money from existing banks. Herman Krooss, "Financial Institutions," in *The Growth of the Seaport Cities, 1790-1825*, ed. David T. Gilchrist (Charlottesville, 1967), 124.

20. Report on Manufactures, *PAH*, 10:277-81.

21. Ibid., 275-76.

22. The clearest illustrations of this antagonism were the yearly reports of Phineas Bond, the British consul at Philadelphia, expressing the desire of the English to maintain their monopoly of manufactures and their concerns over possible American development, in the *Annual Report of the American Historical Association for 1896*, ed. J. Franklin Jameson, 2 vols. (Washington, 1897), 1:553–54, 581–82, 630–54.

23. Cf. Albert Gallatin, Report on Manufactures, U. S. Congress, *NASP: Manufactures,* 1:124–30. Indeed, it was Gallatin's Report on Manufactures and his Report on Roads and Canals, *NASP: Transportation,* 1:17–39, discussed below, which incorporated Coxe's plans for economic development.

24. Report on Manufactures, *PAH,* 10:291–92, 296–98.

25. Ibid., 336–37.

26. Gallatin, Report on Manufactures, *NASP: Manufactures,* 1:130.

27. Report on Manufactures, *PAH,* 10:300; emphasis added.

28. Ibid., 313–27.

29. Ibid., 306.

30. Ibid., 337.

31. Ibid., 310–11.

32. Ibid., 337–40. Coxe's proposal for a manufacturing board is drawn from the first draft, ibid., 47.

33. Hamilton, Report Relative to Additional Supplies for the Ensuing Year, *PAH,* 11:142.

34. Hamilton to Seton, January 18, 1792, *PAH,* 10:525.

35. Fisher Ames to Hamilton, July 31, 1791, *PAH,* 8:591.

36. ? to Hamilton, September–October 1791, *PAH,* 9:251–52.

37. Thomas Marshall to Hamilton, October 2, 1791, ibid., 268. Joseph Davis also questions the viability of the SEUM's site: "Truly natural conditions were excellent. But, 'thickly settled' must be interpreted with a large measure of 'relativity,' for on the present site of the city of Paterson there were not more than ten dwellings and a church. Potentially, indeed, communication with New York was 'easy,' but for the time being railroads were non-existent, roads were extremely poor, and the Passaic was not navigable within several miles of the Falls. . . . Enthusiasm for the site proved quite premature." *Essays,* 1:402–3, 408.

38. James Fillary to Hamilton, January 1791, *PAH,* 7:614–16.

39. Robert F. Jones concludes that Duer "viewed his official positions as accessories to his commercial and speculative activities." He "approached the SEUM as if it were yet another of his stock speculations." Jones, "William Duer and the Business of Government in the Era of the American Revolution," *W&MQ,* 32 (1975), 411–14.

40. Phillip Schuyler to Hamilton, March 25, 1792, *PAH,* 11:186; also 258n, 259n.

41. Hamilton to Duer, March 23, 1792, ibid., 171.

42. Hamilton to Phillip Livingston, April 2, 1792, ibid., 218–19.

43. Hamilton, Defense of the Funding System, July 1795, *PAH,* 19:62; see also Hamilton to Washington, August 18, 1792, *PAH,* 12:247–48.

44. Hamilton to Seton, May 25, 1792, *PAH,* 11:425.

45. Seton to Hamilton, June 25, 1792, ibid., 566–67. Herman Krooss states that "it is questionable whether the loans would have been made if Alexander Hamilton had not been involved." "Financial Institutions," 122.

46. Peter Colt to Hamilton, May 7, 1793, *PAH,* 14:420.

47. Broadus Mitchell's description of the SEUM's failure and Hamilton's role in

it affirms this problem: "Hamilton, unintentionally, had been the cause of costly errors, for his choice of chief mechanics, and of L'Enfant, proved in trial to be bad. His solicitude for the experiment was not matched by experience, judgment, or full focus on the complicated work in hand. He was too much engaged in establishing the national credit to allow him to organize an industrial enterprise (with a town attached) at the same time." He concludes that the industrial development of the nation would be better left in the private hands of small manufacturers. Mitchell, *Alexander Hamilton,* 2:192–93.

48. Davis, *Essays,* 1:450–51, 480; 2:269.

49. Hamilton to Washington, August 18, 1792, *PAH,* 12:244–53.

50. Draft of President's Fourth Annual Address to Congress, October 15–31, 1792, ibid., 565.

Chapter 4
Hamilton's Stabilization Program: The Question of Neocolonialism

1. Charles A. Beard, *Economic Origins of Jeffersonian Democracy* (New York, 1927); Samuel F. Bemis, *Jay's Treaty: A Study in Commerce and Diplomacy* (rev. ed., New Haven, 1962); and Paul A. Varg, *Foreign Policies of the Founding Fathers* (East Lansing, Mich., 1963).

2. See Short to Hamilton, May 4, 1791, *PAH,* 8:324.

3. "Continentalist: Number 5," April 18, 1782, *PAH,* 3:78–79. Hamilton reaffirmed this position in his Report on the Difficulties in . . . Laying Duties on Distilled Spirits, March 5, 1792, *PAH,* 11:85.

4. John C. Miller, *The Federalist Era, 1789–1801* (New York, 1960), 17–19, 222–25; Edward Stanwood, *American Tariff Controversies in the Nineteenth Century* (New York, 1903), 39–49; and Irving Brant, *James Madison, Father of the Constitution, 1781–1800* (New York, 1950), 246–47, 252–53.

5. Hamilton to George Beckwith, October 1789, *PAH,* 488. Smith also led the successful fight against a federal loan to John Amelung, a Maryland glass manufacturer, whose factory burned down. Some of Amelung's unemployed artisans later found work in Albert Gallatin's factory in Pennsylvania.

6. Ibid., 483, and Hamilton to Beckwith, July 15, 1790, *PAH,* 497–98.

7. Hamilton to Beckwith, September 26–30, 1790, *PAH,* 8:73.

8. Hamilton to Beckwith, January 19, 1791, *PAH,* 7:441–42, and June 15, 1791, *PAH,* 8:476.

9. Hamilton to Jefferson, February 16, 1791, *PAH,* 8:43–44.

10. Hamilton to Jefferson, January 13, 1791, *PAH,* 7:426.

11. Hamilton to William Short, May 9, 1791, *PAH,* 8:336.

12. Report Relative to Supplies, March 16, 1792, *PAH,* 11:139–40.

13. Report on the Difficulties, March 5, 1792, ibid., 84–86.

14. William Heth to Hamilton, October 14, 1792, *PAH,* 12:556.

15. View of the Commercial Regulations, 1792–93, *PAH,* 13:412–27.

16. Anna C. Clauder, *American Commerce as Affected by the Wars of the French Revolution and Napoleon, 1792–1812* (Philadelphia, 1932), 15–46; Varg, *Foreign Policies of the Founding Fathers,* 88–105.

17. Hamilton to Willard et al., August 12, 1793, *PAH,* 15:231.

18. See the reports of "significant" opinion sent to Hamilton from Stephen Higginson (Boston), April 10, 1793, *PAH,* 14:305–6; Rufus King (New York), April 24, 1793, ibid., 335–36; Edward Carrington (Virginia), April 26, 1793, ibid., 347;

Samuel Smith (Baltimore), June 16, 1793, *PAH*, 15:1; and William Heth (Virginia), June 14, 1793, *PAH*, 14:543.

19. James McHenry to Hamilton, April 14, 1793, *PAH*, 14:317.

20. See Hamilton to Washington, May 2, 1793, ibid., 405–7.

21. Of the foreign policy studies of this period touching on neutral rights, the classic remains Herbert W. Briggs, *The Doctrine of Continuous Voyage* (Baltimore, 1926).

22. Conversation between Hamilton and Hammond (recorded by Hammond), April 2–May 17, 1793, *PAH*, 14:273.

23. Commercial Propositions of January 3, 1794, *WJR*, 6:204–7.

24. Mitchell, *Alexander Hamilton*, 2:143. Mitchell is summarizing the general conclusion of Hamilton's numerous biographers.

25. "Number 2," February 7, 1794, *PAH*, 16:13.

26. Hamilton to Washington, April 14, 1794, ibid., 274–76.

27. Ibid., 273, and Willard et al. to Hamilton, July 1, 1794, ibid., 556.

28. "The Union" in the *National Gazette*, April 2, 1792, *WJM*, 6:104–5.

29. Remarks before the New York State Assembly, March 8, 1787, *PAH*, 4:126–27.

30. Hamilton to Washington, April 14, 1794, *PAH*, 16:278–79.

31. Hamilton to Washington, April 23, 1794, ibid., 322–23; see also Hamilton to Jay, May 16, 1794, ibid., 383, and his suggestions for a commercial treaty, April–May 1794, ibid., 357–58.

32. See n. 31 above.

33. Hamilton to Hammond, July 1–10, 1794, *PAH*, 16:548. See also his Conversation with Hammond of December 23, 1794–January 5, 1795, *PAH*, 18:459.

34. Willard et al. to Hamilton, January 1, 1795, *PAH*, 18:24. For Hamilton's general attitude toward popular rebellion, see his letter to James McHenry, March 18, 1799, *PAH*, 22:552–53.

35. See, for example, his Report on a Plan for the Further Support of Public Credit, January 16, 1795, *PAH*, 18:113.

36. Hamilton to Edmund Randolph, December 1–12, 1794, *PAH*, 17:409–10.

37. Remarks on the Treaty, July 7–11, 1795, *PAH*, 18:451–52.

38. "Number 2," July 25, 1795, ibid., 493–501.

39. "Number 6," August 8, 1795, *PAH*, 19:105–6.

40. "Number 19," October 14, 1795, ibid., 318–34, and "Number 25," October 30, 1795, ibid., 365–74.

41. "Number 31," December 12, 1795, ibid., 473–84.

42. Jefferson to Madison, September 21, 1795, *WTJ*, 7:31–33.

43. See Rufus King to Hamilton, April 18, 1796, *PAH*, 20:121–22; Hamilton to King, April 18, 1796, ibid., 123: Hamilton to Oliver Wolcott, April 10, 1795, *PAH*, 18:324; Wolcott to Hamilton, September 6, 1795, *PAH*, 19:295; and Jefferson to Madison, September 21, 1795, *WTJ*, 7:31–33.

44. Hamilton to Washington, March 28, 1796, *PAH*, 20:83–85.

Chapter 5
Jefferson, Madison, and Hamilton: A Parting of Ways

1. Jefferson's closest students—Merrill D. Peterson, *Thomas Jefferson and the New Nation* (New York, 1970); Dumas Malone, *Jefferson and His Time*, 4 vols. (Boston, 1948–70); and Julian P. Boyd, ed., *Papers of Jefferson*—have done much to dispel the largely artificial realist-idealist dichotomy so often imposed on him.

2. Three articles present a very balanced analysis of the vicissitudes of Jefferson's political economy: Merrill D. Peterson, "Thomas Jefferson and Commercial Policy, 1783–1793," *W&MQ*, 22 (1965), 584–610; William D. Grampp, "A Reexamination of Jeffersonian Economics," *Southern Economics Journal*, 12 (1946), 363–82; and Joseph J. Spengler, "The Political Economy of Jefferson, Madison, and Adams," in *American Studies in Honor of William K. Boyd*, ed. David K. Jackson (Freeport, N.Y., 1968), 3–59. See also Jefferson's letters to Thomas Randolph, Jr., May 30, 1790, *PTJ*, 16:449–50, and to Madison, November 18, 1788, *PTJ*, 14:188. In the former he accorded Locke, Hume, and Smith high marks for their philosophies, while Turgot and the Physiocrats received only a passing acknowledgement as "excellent books of Theory."

3. Jefferson to Monroe, June 20, 1790, *PTJ*, 16:537.

4. Jefferson to George Gilmer, June 27, 1790, ibid., 574–75.

5. May 9, 1789 *Annals of Cong.*, 352; Madison to Hamilton, November 19, 1789, *PAH*, 5:525–56.

6. Madison to Jefferson, February 4, 1790, *PTJ*, 16:147–50.

7. Madison to Hamilton, November 19, 1789, *PAH*, 5:525–26. For Madison's worries over prolonging redemption of the national debt, see his letters to Randolph, March 14, 1790, and to Henry Lee, April 13, 1790, *WJM*, 6:8, 11.

8. Mississippi Question, August 2, 1790, *PTJ*, 17:113.

9. Jefferson to Washington, July 12, 1790, and August 27, 1790, ibid., 109, 129; and Jefferson to Monroe, July 11, 1790, ibid., 25.

10. Julian P. Boyd, *Number Seven: Alexander Hamilton's Secret Attempts to Control American Foreign Policy* (Princeton, 1964). For a more extensive presentation of foreign policy issues see Joseph Charles, *The Origins of the American Party System* (New York, 1961), 8–37; Bradford Perkins, *The First Rapprochment* (Los Angeles, 1967), 11–26; and John C. Miller, *Alexander Hamilton*, 134, 388.

11. Hamilton to Jefferson, January 13, 1791, *PAH*, 7:426.

12. Report on the Fisheries, February 1, 1791, *PTJ*, 19:217–20 (emphasis added); Peterson, "Jefferson and Commercial Policy," 584–610; and Peterson, *Thomas Jefferson*, 171, 290, 304, 329–30, 428–29, 514–15.

13. Peterson, *Thomas Jefferson*, 514–15, and Jefferson to David Humphreys, June 29, 1791, *WTJ*, 5:344–45. Drew McCoy links Madison's foreign policy with Jefferson's in this respect, but he understates to the point of ignoring the implications of their policy for domestic manufacturing development. McCoy, "Republicanism and American Foreign Policy: James Madison and the Political Economy of Commercial Discrimination, 1789–1794," *W&MQ*, 31 (1974), 633–46. He compounds this error of interpretation in his book, *The Elusive Republic: Political Economy in Jeffersonian America* (Chapel Hill, 1980).

14. Jefferson to George Mason, February 4, 1791, and to Nicholas Lewis, February 9, 1791, *PTJ*, 19:241, 263. Emphasis added.

15. Madison to Jefferson, July 10, 1791, *WJM*, 6:55.

16. Jefferson to Monroe, April 17, 1791, *WTJ*, 5:318–20.

17. Jefferson to David Humphreys, August 23, 1791, and to Plumard De Rieux, January 6, 1792, ibid., 376, 420.

18. Madison to Jefferson, August 8, 1791, *WJM*, 6:58–59.

19. *The Complete Anas of Thomas Jefferson*, ed. F. B. Samuel (New York, 1903), February 29, 1792, 54–55; and Jefferson to Washington, May 23, 1792, *WTJ*, 6:1–6. Joyce Appleby places Jefferson's concern with corruption in proper context and distinguishes it from the notion of corruption in civic humanism: "To be fearful, as the Jeffersonians were, of the corruption they saw in public stock specu-

lation was not the same as making corruption part of the eternal human drama." "What Is Still American," 408.

20. "Spirit of Governments," February 20, 1792, *WJM*, 6:94, and "The Union," April 4, 1792, ibid., 104–5.

21. Coxe to Jefferson, April 15, 1791 and enclosures dated 1792, Jefferson Papers, Library of Congress.

22. Jefferson to Monroe, April 17 and July 10, 1791, and to David Humphreys, April 9, 1792, *WTJ*, 5:320, 353, 502.

23. Madison to Henry Lee, January 1, 1792, *WJM*, 6:81; Madison to Edmund Pendleton, February 21, 1791, ibid., 95; and Jefferson to Washington, February 29, 1791, *Anas*, 54–55.

24. "Republican Distribution of Citizens," March 5, 1792, in the *National Gazette, WJM*, 6:96–99.

25. Compare Madison's Commercial Resolutions, January 3, 1794, ibid., 204–7, and Jefferson's Report on Commerce, December 16, 1793, *WTJ*, 6:470–84, with Hamilton's tariff suggestions in his Report on Manufactures, December 1791, *PAH*, 10:313–27, and his Suggestions for a Commercial Treaty, April–May 1794, *PAH*, 16:357–58.

26. Jefferson to Thomas Pinckney, September 7, 1793, *WTJ*, 6:412–16.

27. Jefferson to Madison, March 1793, ibid., 192–93, and Madison to Horatio Gates, March 24, 1794, *WJM*, 6:209. Both men believed, however, that England would acquiesce rather than make war and that unrestricted markets, not manufacturing, would assure economic independence.

28. Report on Commerce, *WTJ*, 6:476–80.

29. Ibid., 480–82. See n. 13, above.

30. Ibid., 482–84.

31. Jefferson to Madison, September 21, 1795, *WTJ*, 7:31–33.

32. Madison to Robert R. Livingston, August 10, 1795, and to ?, August 23, 1795, *WJM*, 6:235–36, 239–47.

33. Jefferson to Madison, March 27, 1796, *WTJ*, 7:68–69.

34. For the political organization of the 1790s see Nobel E. Cunningham, *The Jeffersonian Republicans: Formation of Party Organization, 1789–1801* (Chapel Hill, 1957); David H. Fischer, *The Revolution of American Conservatism* (New York, 1965); and Nobel E. Cunningham, *The Jeffersonian Republicans in Power: Party Operations, 1801–1809* (Chapel Hill, 1963).

35. Leonard W. Levy's two works are very instructive on these points: see *Jefferson and Civil Liberties: The Darker Side* (Cambridge, Mass., 1963), and *Freedom of Speech and Press in Early American History: Legacy of Suppression* (Cambridge, Mass., 1960).

36. Jefferson to Pinckney, May 29, 1797, *WTJ*, 7:128.

Chapter 6
Economic Origins of the Republican Political Coalition

1. February 11, 1799, *Annals of Cong.*, 2862.

2. Richard B. Morris, *Government and Labor in Early America* (New York, 1965); Young, "The Mechanics and the Jeffersonians," 252ff; and Lynd, "Mechanics in New York," 241–45. A very detailed and useful exposition of the political and social changes in the cities is William B. Wheeler's "The Urban Jeffersonians, 1785–1809" (unpublished manuscript, Dept. of History, University of Tennessee). For the general role of nomenclature in political and social processes see Raymond

Williams, *Culture and Society* (London, 1959), esp. xiii–xvii. The building trades had a monopoly and were concerned with federal action only insofar as it affected the economy in general.

3. Petition to Congress, April 13, 1789, *ASP: Commerce and Navigation,* 1:5.

4. Petition to Congress, May 25, 1789, *NASP: Manufactures,* 1:35–36.

5. See, for example, the Boston shipwrights' Petition to Congress, May 4, 1789, *ASP: Commerce and Navigation,* 1:5–6.

6. Samuel Breck to Hamilton, September 3, 1791, *PAH,* 6:210; and the enclosures in National Gorham to Hamilton, October 13, 1791, *PAH,* 9:372–74.

7. Thomas Newton to Edward Carrington, enclosed in Carrington to Hamilton, October 4, 1791, *PAH,* 9:278.

8. Whipple to Hamilton, December 19, 1789, *PAH,* 6:210, and Neil Jamieson to Josiah Parker, June 18, 1790, *PTJ,* 16:523–27.

9. Petition of New York's mechanics and manufacturers to Congress, April 17, 1789, *NASP: Manufactures,* 1:34; Petition of Baltimore's tradesmen and mechanics to Congress, April 11, 1789, ibid., 33.

10. Enclosure to Hamilton, October 11, 1791, *PAH,* 9:354; enclosure to Hamilton, September 15, 1791, ibid., 339; enclosure to Hamilton, September 16, 1791, ibid., 339; enclosure to Hamilton, October 10, 1791, ibid., 444.

11. Enclosures to Hamilton, August 25–October 10, 1791, ibid., 170–71, 194, 346, 348, 360–361, 443–45; and petition of John Amelung to Congress, May 27, 1790, *NASP: Manufactures,* 1:39.

12. Enclosure to Hamilton, October 15, 1791, *PAH,* 9:436–38.

13. Enclosures to Hamilton, August 20, September 30, and October 10, 1791, ibid., 325, 360–61, 443; and memorandum to Daniel Stevens, October 1791, *Industrial and Commercial Correspondence,* 91. This problem confronted manufactures from Boston to Charleston.

14. Hammond, "Long and Short Term Credit," 79–81, 89; Redlich, *Modeling of American Banking,* 1:10–18.

15. Enclosure to Hamilton, July 21, 1791, *PAH,* 9:323–34. See also the enclosure to Hamilton, August 20, 1791, ibid., 327.

16. Report on Public Credit, *PAH,* 6:70–74.

17. Enclosure to Hamilton, October 13, 1791, *PAH,* 9:374.

18. Enclosures to Hamilton, August–October 1791, ibid., 162, 177–80, 275–76, 436, 446.

19. Enclosures to Hamilton, ibid., 193, 323, 337–38, 363; and "Juricola" (Tench Coxe), *Philadelphia Gazette and Universal Daily Advertiser,* July 31, 1795.

20. Constance Green, *Eli Whitney* (Boston, 1956); Aleine Austin, "Matthew Lyon: New Man of the Democratic Revolution, 1749–1822" (unpublished manuscript). State aid to business is discussed in Louis Hartz, *Economic Policy and Democratic Thought: Pennsylvania, 1776–1860* (New York, 1947), and Oscar Handlin, *Commonwealth: A Study of the Role of Government in the American Economy, Massachusetts, 1774–1861* (New York, 1947).

21. Victor S. Clark, *History of Manufactures in the United States, 1607–1860,* 3 vols. (New York, 1929), vol. 1.

22. Report Relative to Additional Supplies for the Ensuing Year, March 16, 1792, *PAH,* 11:142; and Report on the Difficulties in the Execution of the Act Laying Duties on Distilled Spirits, March 5, 1792, ibid., 84–86. Compare the latter with the Report on Manufactures, *PAH,* 10:336–37. See also the petition to Hamilton, May 10, 1794, *PAH,* 16:398–99; Carrington to Hamilton, October 8, 1791, *PAH,* 9:300; petition of Baltimore manufacturers to Congress, June 5, 1789, *NASP:*

Manufactures, 1:37: John C. Miller, *Federalist Era,* 155-57; and Eugene P. Link, *Democratic–Republican Societies, 1790–1800* (New York, 1942), 73-75, 93. Link states that his study "indicates, rather conclusively, that workmen and mechanics outnumbered all other classes in the popular societies."

23. "An Observer," *Philadelphia Gazette and Universal Daily Advertiser,* January 7, 1792; Davis, *Essays,* 1:450-51, 2:258, 269; and Link, *Democratic-Republican Societies,* 6-10.

24. George Logan, *Five Letters Addressed to the Yeomanry of the United States* (Philadelphia, 1792), 20-27; Davis, *Essays,* 1:437.

25. Young, "Mechanics and Jeffersonians," 251-54; Young, *Democratic Republicans of New York,* 201, 230.

26. Renzulli, *Maryland,* 158.

27. Link, *Democratic-Republican Societies,* x, 5-22; Young, *Democratic Republicans of New York,* 395, 402; and Baumann, "Democratic-Republicans of Philadelphia," 598-601.

28. Link, *Democratic-Republican Societies;* Young, *Democratic Republicans of New York,* 382, 405-6; Young, "Mechanics and Jeffersonians," 258-63; Harry M. Tinkcom, *Republicans and Federalists in Pennsylvania, 1790–1801* (Philadelphia, 1950), 81, 85-86; Goodman, *Democratic-Republicans of Massachusetts,* 70; and Baumann, "Democratic-Republicans of Philadelphia," 448-49.

29. See Young, *Democratic Republicans of New York,* 249, 395, 414, and Baumann, "Democratic-Republicans of Philadelphia," 448, 577-78, 598-601, for a discussion of merchant involvement in the Democratic Societies.

30. For the desertion of manufacturers to the Republican party see Goodman, *Democratic-Republicans of Massachusetts,* 70-77, 97-102; Young, *Democratic Republicans of New York,* 102, 345, 382, 405-6, 567-70; John A. Munroe, *Federalist Delaware, 1775–1815* (New Brunswick, N.J., 1954), 128-30, 200-207, 213-20; Tinkcom, *Republicans and Federalists in Pennsylvania,* 71; and Baumann, "Democratic-Republicans of Philadelphia," 451-79, 577-78.

31. The following discussion of the breakup of the constitutional coalition and formation of the Republican party among merchants and farmers is based on many sources: Tinkcom, *Republicans and Federalists in Pennsylvania,* 85; Baumann, "Democratic-Republicans of Philadelphia," 577-78; Young, *Democratic Republicans of New York,* 249, 346, 353, 365, 414; Renzulli, *Maryland,* 163-73; Goodman, *Democratic-Republicans of Massachusetts,* 56, 70-77, 97; Clauder, *American Commerce,* 15-21, 32-35; Risjord, "Virginia Federalists," 502ff.; Ammon, "Formation of the Republican Party," 289ff.; Malcolm C. Clark, "Election of 1796 in Maryland," *Maryland Historical Magazine,* 61 (1966), 229-30; Bemis, *Jay's Treaty;* Gerald A. Combs, *The Jay Treaty: Political Battleground of the Founding Fathers* (Berkeley and Los Angeles, 1970), 117; John S. Pancake, *Samuel Smith and the Politics of Business: 1752–1839* (University, Ala., 1972), 34-38, 50-51; and Gordon D. Ross, "The Crowninshield Family in Business and Politics, 1790–1830" (Ph.D. diss., Claremont Graduate School, 1964), 5-8, 12-23.

32. Information on the Crowninshields is drawn from Ross, "The Crowninshield Family," 5-16, 20-23, 141-74; and Goodman, *Democratic-Republicans of Massachusetts,* 105-9.

33. Young, *Democratic Republicans of New York,* 249, 285, 354-56, 373, 394, 449-53.

34. Baumann, "Democratic-Republicans of Philadelphia," 385, 577-78; Tinkcom, *Republicans and Federalists in Pennsylvania,* 85-86; and Link, *Democratic-Republican Societies,* 75.

35. Link, *Democratic-Republican Societies*, 75; Clauder, *American Commerce*, 33; Arthur P. Whitaker, *The United States and the Independence of Latin American, 1800–1830* (New York, 1962), 68–70.

36. Information on Smith is derived from Pancake, *Samuel Smith*, 34–97, 137; Whitaker, *Independence of Latin America*, 56; and Renzulli, *Maryland*, 164–65.

37. Douglass North, "Early National Income Estimates of the U.S.," *Economic Development and Cultural Change*, 9 (1960–61), 388–89.

38. Goodman, *Democratic-Republicans of Massachusetts*, 97.

39. For example, if over a year the aggregate demand for American wheat both domestically and abroad were $10 million and American farmers produced 20 million bushels, the price per bushel would be 50 cents. If Britain were to eliminate 10% of that market by blockading France, aggregate demand would fall by $1 million. The price per bushel would also fall five cents. The consequent loss of 10% of a wheat farmer's income could be the difference between a good year and a poor one. At some point the quantitative decline in price assumes a qualitative political character. Precise variations in price would of course depend on the elasticity of the demand and supply as well as other variables. See George R. Taylor's discussion of markets, farmers, prices, and political discontent in "Agrarian Discontent in the Mississippi Valley Preceding the War of 1812," *Journal of Political Economy*, 39 (1931), 471ff.

40. James A. Henretta, "Families and Farms: *Mentalité* in Pre-Industrial America," *W&MQ*, 35 (1978), 3.

41. Ibid., 11–19, 24–26, 30–32; also nn. 37 and 39, above. Joyce Appleby describes the assimilation of farmers into the market economy (and Republican policies) in "Commercial Farming and the 'Agrarian Myth' in the Early Republic," *Journal of American History*, 68 (March 1982), 833–49, esp. 839–44.

42. Henretta, "Families and Farms," 7–8, 22.

43. Renzulli, *Maryland*, 321; Munroe, *Federalist Delaware*, 213, 241.

44. Young, *Democratic Republicans of New York*, 568.

45. Tinkcom, *Republicans and Federalists in Pennsylvania*, 94–95.

46. Rose, *Federalists in the South*, 105–6, 112–15, 120–21; Ammon, "Formation of the Republican Party," 289–310; Risjord, "Virginia Federalists," 502.

47. Risjord, "Virginia Federalists," 507–17.

48. Paul Goodman, "Social Status of Party Leadership: The House of Representatives, 1797–1804," *W&MQ*, 25 (1968), 465–74.

Chapter 7
Gallatin as Critic: The Transition to Power, 1796–1801

1. Jefferson's life is ably and concisely handled by Merrill D. Peterson, *Thomas Jefferson*. For Madison consult Irving Brant, *James Madison*, 5 vols. (Indianapolis, 1950–61). For Gallatin there are Henry Adams' classic, *The Life of Albert Gallatin* (Philadelphia, 1880), Raymond Walters' *Albert Gallatin: Jeffersonian Financier and Diplomat* (Pittsburgh, 1969), and an excellent biographical dissertation by Edwin G. Burrows, "Albert Gallatin and the Political Economy of Republicanism" (Ph.D. diss., Columbia University, 1974). Burrows, however, contributes little to understanding the political economy of the Republicans and ends his thesis in 1800.

2. Draft of the Harrisburg Conference, September 3, 1788, *WAG*, 1:1.

3. Dumas Malone, *Jefferson and His Time*, 3:255–57; Wolcott to Hamilton, December 8, 1796, *PAH*, 20:436–37n.

4. Gallatin, *A Sketch of the Finances of the United States,* in *WAG,* 3:73–169. Surprisingly little attention is accorded to the *Sketch* despite its intrinsic importance and the fact that Jefferson and Madison prevailed on Gallatin to write it; Jefferson to Madison, March 6, 1796, *WTJ,* 7:61–62.

5. *Sketch, WAG,* 3:145.

6. Ibid., 131–33, 148.

7. Ibid., 143. Gallatin cited Adam Smith as the source of this assertion.

8. Ibid., 99–103.

9. Ibid., 135–36, 144–46.

10. Ibid., 146–47.

11. Ibid., 149–50.

12. Ibid., 149, 154. On the floor of Congress Gallatin synthesized his critique of Hamilton's program as antirepublican and pro-British: "To such doctrines avowed on this floor, to such systems as the plan of Government which the late Secretary of the Treasury (Hamilton) had proposed in the Convention, may perhaps be ascribed that belief . . . that there exists in America a Monarchio, Aristocratic Faction, who would wish to impose upon us the substance of the British Government." January 15, 1798, *Annals of Cong.,* 1136–38.

13. *Sketch, WAG,* 3:160–62.

14. Ibid., 91. The manner in which Gallatin expressed this consolidation proposal very nicely reflected the mediation of individual property rights and government intervention in the national interest. "It may be further observed that, however improper and dangerous it may be for government to pass laws with a view of giving a certain direction to industry and capital, it cannot be doubted that the effects of a provision which tended gradually and without any injury to property now vested in that species of property to diminish the immense number of small distilleries would prove favorable to the general wealth and to the morals of the community."

15. Ibid., 154–55.

16. February 28, 1796, *Annals of Cong.,* 340.

17. March 2, 1796, ibid., 411.

18. April 26, 1796, ibid., 1187–98.

19. Jefferson to Madison, March 27, 1796, *WTJ,* 7:68–69.

20. Charles, *American Party System.*

21. April 20, 1793, *Annals of Cong.,* 1509–19.

22. January, 1800, ibid., 355.

23. Gallatin to Hannah Gallatin, January 19, 1798, *PAG.*

24. Miller, *Alexander Hamilton,* 451–529; Alexander De Conde, *The Quasi-War: Politics and Diplomacy of the Undeclared War with France, 1797–1801* (New York, 1966), 124–30, 146, 254. The French did not have enough warships to blockade British ports so they would announce a blockade and begin checking the logs of neutral ships. Any ship which had visited a "blockaded" port would then be seized. (The British, of course, made sure any neutral ship entering its ports recorded that entry in its log.) The Franco-American Treaty curbed this practice.

25. Pancake, *Samuel Smith,* 52; Young, "Mechanics and Jeffersonians," 260, 266–67.

26. Munroe, *Federalist Delaware,* 207–13; Goodman, *Democratic-Republicans of Massachusetts,* 103–5, 114–24; Renzulli, *Maryland,* 168–70, 211; Tinkcom, *Republicans and Federalists,* 256, 271; and Manning J. Dauer, *The Adams Federalists* (Baltimore, 1953), 237–63.

27. Whitaker, *Independence of Latin America,* 4–23, 56. These merchants in-

cluded the Smiths of Baltimore, Stephen Girard of Philadelphia, David Parrish of New York, and the Crowninshields of Salem.

28. See Wheeler, "Urban Republicans," ch. 8, and Dauer's maps of voting patterns, *Adams Federalists,* app. 3.

29. David A. Bohmer, "Stability and Change in Early National Politics: Maryland and the Election of 1800," *W&MQ,* 36 (1979), 27–50.

30. Young, "Mechanics and Jeffersonians," William B. Wheeler, "The Baltimore Jeffersonians, 1788–1800: A Profile of Intrafactional Conflict," *Maryland Historical Magazine,* 66 (1971), 153–68; and Dauer, *Adams Federalists,* app. 3. Dauer's own evidence of party strength throughout the nation, from which the discussion of national trends in party strength is drawn, refutes his thesis that agrarian rejection of Federalist commercial policies caused Adams's defeat in 1800.

31. Henretta, "Families and Farms." See Chapter 6 above.

32. Paul Goodman, *The American Party Systems: Stages of Political Development,* ed. W. N. Chambers and W. D. Burnham (New York, 1967), 56–89.

33. Henretta, "Families and Farms," 32.

34. Cunningham, *Jeffersonian Republicans,* 222.

35. Stephen Kurtz, *The Presidency of John Adams and the Collapse of Federalism* (Philadelphia, 1957), 406–8. Much of the ensuing analysis of Adam's political fortunes accords with Kurtz's interpretation.

36. Hamilton to Miranda, August 22, 1798, *PAH,* 23:156. Compare Hamilton's earlier position on France expressed to Wolcott, November 22, 1796, *PAH,* 20:414, to his later position articulated to James McHenry, June 27, 1799, *PAH,* 23:227.

37. Miller, *Alexander Hamilton,* 513–29.

38. "Mine is an odd destiny," he wrote Gouverneur Morris in 1802. "Every day proves to me more and more, that this American world was not made for me." February 29, 1802, *PAH,* 25:544.

39. Peterson, *Thomas Jefferson,* 661.

Chapter 8
The Republicans in Power: The Political Economy of Albert Gallatin

1. Gallatin to Jefferson, February 12, 1805, *WAG,* 1:227.

2. Gallatin, *The Oregon Question* (1846), *WAG,* 3:535.

3. Gallatin to Jefferson, August 10, 1801, *WAG,* 1:33, and to Lafayette, May 12, 1833, *WAG,* 2:469.

4. Draft of the Harrisburg Conference, *WAG,* 1:1.

5. February 11, 1799, *Annals of Cong.,* 2862.

6. Gallatin to Jefferson, December 18, 1807, *WAG,* 1:368.

7. William D. Grampp, *Economic Liberalism,* 2 vols. (New York, 1955), 1:vii–xvi, 2:95; and William D. Grampp, *The Manchester School of Economics* (Stanford, 1960), 36.

8. Adam Smith, *The Wealth of Nations,* ed. Edwin Cannon (New York: Modern Library Edition, 1937), 423.

9. See Grampp, *Economic Liberalism,* 2:3–72, and Eric Roll, *A History of Economic Thought* (Homewood, Ill., 1974), 146–54.

10. It is not this essay's intention to assert that Adam Smith's *Wealth of Nations* was the bible of the Republican triumvirate and that their policies were merely exegeses of it. Grampp offers the best explanation of Smith's relationship to the Republican political economy: "I may not say [Smith] was the source of what they thought. I may say that his ideas explain that thought better than the ideas of

anyone else." Grampp, "Adam Smith and the American Revolutionists," *History of Political Economy*, 11 (1979), 180. Smith's role is similar to that of Hume's—an embodiment and exemplar of an intellectual tradition shared by many.

11. Smith, *Wealth of Nations*, 315, 325–29, 863, 882–83. In his attack on government indebtedness Smith noted that "a creditor of the public, considered merely as such has no interest in the good condition of any particular portion of land, or in the good management of any particular portion of capital stock." His point was that money lent to government was that much less capital available to individual enterprise. Beyond its individual owner's purview the money might be wasted and the national wealth reduced.

12. Ibid., 681–82, 147.

13. Ibid., 100–43.

14. Ibid., 429–31.

15. Ibid., 433–36.

16. Donald Winch offers a brief but good discussion of this point in "Economic Liberalism as Ideology," 290–93.

17. Campbell's Report, November 22, 1808, *WAG*, 1:344; Appleby, "Commercial Farming," 849.

18. Reflections on the Constitution (1788), *PAG*.

19. The relation of Gallatin's thinking to Smith's may be traced in his *Sketch of the Finances of the United States* (1796), *WAG*, 3:75, 108; his Notes on Adam Smith (1809), *PAG*; and his letter to his son recommending *The Wealth of Nations* as the basis for his study of economics, November 11, 1823, ibid. Grampp notes that Gallatin respected Smith "to the point of reverence." *Economic Liberalism*, 1:165. But see above, n. 10.

20. Smith, *Wealth of Nations*, 3–21, 326.

21. Ibid., 353, 403, 460, 506, 645.

22. January 1800, *Annals of Cong.*, 353.

23. Gallatin to Jefferson, August 10, 1801, *WAG*, 1:33.

24. Gallatin to John Badollet, February 7, 1833, *PAG*.

25. Gallatin to William B. Giles, *WAG*, 1:78–79.

26. *NASP: Public Finance*, 32 vols. 2:336.

27. Ibid., 370.

28. March 8, 1808, *NASP: Transportation*, 2:112.

29. Gallatin to Jefferson, February 12, 1808, *WAG*, 1:370.

30. For an overview of the role of two states in this area consult Hartz, *Economic Policy and Democratic Thought*, and Handlin, *Commonwealth*. The state Republican party activities are touched on in Higginbotham, *Keystone in the Democratic Arch*, 220–21, 333; Munroe, *Federalist Delaware*, 247–48; and Young, *Democratic Republicans of New York*, 231, 267.

31. Douglass C. North describes this process, though more in the context of railroads, in *Growth and Welfare in the American Past* (Englewood Cliffs, N.J., 1966), 117–21.

32. Gallatin to Samuel L. Mitchell, April 4, 1808, *PAG*.

33. *NASP: Transportation*, 1:17–39; Carter Goodrich, ed., *The Government and the Economy: 1783–1861* (New York, 1967), 3–5.

34. January 5 and February 23, 1810, *Annals of Congress*, 522–25.

35. Gallatin to Thomas Willing, June 9, 1801, *PAG*.

36. Gallatin to Jefferson, June 18, 1802, ibid.

37. Jefferson to Gallatin, June 19, 1802, ibid.

38. Jefferson to Gallatin, July 12, 1803, *WAG*, 1:129. Jefferson also proposed

keeping "all banks competitors for our favors by a judicious distribution of them." Jefferson to Gallatin, October 7, 1802, ibid., 101–2. This sort of political use of government deposits would have undermined the financial structure of the United States Bank. Gallatin resisted it, as he later opposed Andrew Jackson's efforts to destroy the second bank.

39. Gallatin to Jefferson, December 13, 1803, ibid., 171.

40. Jefferson to Gallatin, December 13, 1803, PAG.

41. Gallatin to John M. Botts, June 14, 1841, WAG, 1:551–52.

42. Gallatin to Jefferson, May 3, 1804, ibid., 191.

43. Gallatin to Willing, June 12, 1802, PAG.

44. Gallatin to Jefferson, April 12, 1804, WAG, 1:184–85.

45. Gallatin to David Lenox, November 5, 1808, PAG.

46. Report on the Bank of the United States, NASP: Public Finance, 21:56–58. The bank was integral to Gallatin's plan for financing a war effort. Gallatin to John W. Eppes, February 26, 1810, WAG, 1:466–75. Alexander Balinky criticizes his fiscal policies by citing the financial chaos of the War of 1812 in his Albert Gallatin: Fiscal Theories and Policies (New Brunswick, 1958), 63. Yet it was the loss of the bank and Congress's refusal to implement Gallatin's fiscal war plans that caused the chaos. Balinky persists in making silly, pseudo-Keynesian criticisms of Gallatin—criticisms which his own exposition of Gallatin's thought refute. Ibid., viii, 63, 185, 194, 217–25.

47. Report on the Bank, 56–58. Twenty years later, in outlining the decisionmaking criteria of the central bank, Gallatin restated its essential character as the highest, nonpolitical arbiter of the economic system. "Independent of every temporary party consideration, there are questions of right and wrong, of what is just or unjust, which must be settled on that principle alone." Gallatin to Robert Potter, December 3, 1830, WAG, 2:440–43.

48. Gallatin to William Crawford, January 30, 1811, PAG. For the debate over recharter see March 1810, Annals of Cong., 615–22. In the Senate the recharter bill was defeated by the tie-breaking vote of Vice President Clinton; in the House it lost 65 to 64. See also Bray Hammond, Banks and Politics, 220–24.

49. Carter Goodrich, "National Planning of Internal Improvements," Political Science Quarterly, 63 (1948), 31–32.

50. See Chapter 6, above, and Wheeler, "Urban Republicans," ch. 9.

51. For the discussion of state aide and foreign policy as an impediment to federal promotion of internal improvements consult Carter Goodrich, Government Promotion of American Canals and Railroads (New York, 1960); Louis Hartz, Economic Policy and Democratic Thought; Oscar Handlin, Commonwealth; Joseph Davis, Essays in American Corporations; and William A. Williams, Contours of American History, 200–223.

52. Gallatin, Autobiographical Sketch (1849), PAG.

53. Jefferson, Sixth Annual Message, December 12, 1806, WTJ, 8:494.

54. Madison, First Inaugural Address, March 4, 1809, WJM, 8:47–49; Seventh Annual Address, June 1815, ibid., 342; and Veto Message, March 3, 1817, ibid., 386–88.

Chapter 9
The Republicans in Power: Political Economy and Foreign Policy

1. See William A. Williams's analysis of the role of foreign markets in the national market system, The Roots of the Modern American Empire (New York, 1969), 47–81.

2. Madison to Clarkson Crolius, December 1819, *WJM*, 9:18.

3. Gallatin to Jefferson, May 1806, *WAG*, 1:287.

4. Jefferson to Madison, September 6, 1808, *WTJ*, 9:18.

5. Clauder, *American Commerce*, 134.

6. Taylor, "Agrarian Discontent."

7. Whitaker, *Independence of Latin America*, 72–85.

8. Ibid., 64–70. America's wartime policy toward Canada was also an extension of commercial coercion. See n. 49 below.

9. Henry N. Smith, *Virgin Land: The American West as Symbol and Myth* (Cambridge, Mass., 1950), and William A. Williams, *Contours of American History*, are two classic studies of this phenomenon. Richard Van Alstyne's *The Rising American Empire* (New York, 1960) and Albert K. Weinberg's *Manifest Destiny* (Baltimore, 1935) also analyze it in great detail.

10. Jefferson to Henry Dearborn, August 17, 1821, *WTJ*, 10:192. The Republican leaders were aware of Malthusian population doctrines and Adam Smith's pronouncement that land was a nation's greatest resource.

11. Jefferson to Robert Livingston, April 18, 1802, *WTJ*, 8:174–76. Madison explained why Spain did not worry the administration: "What is it that Spain dreads? She dreads . . . the growing power of this country, and the direction of it against her possessions within her reach. Can she annihilate this power? No—Can she sensibly retard its growth? No—Does not common prudence then advise her, to conciliate by every proof of friendship and confidence that good will of a nation whose power is formidable to her?" Madison to Pinckney, October 12, 1803, *WJM*, 7:74. For a detailed history of the midcontinent see Arthur P. Whitaker, *The Mississippi Question, 1795–1803* (New York, 1934).

12. Jefferson to Monroe, January 13, 1803, *WTJ*, 8:190–91.

13. Jefferson to Pierre DuPont, February 3, 1803, ibid., 204–7.

14. Madison to Livingston and Monroe, April 18, 1803, *WJM*, 7:41.

15. Gallatin to Jefferson, *WAG*, 1:120.

16. Third Annual Message, October 17, 1803, *WTJ*, 8:267–68.

17. Gallatin to Jefferson, April 13, 1803, *WAG*, 1:121.

18. Jefferson to Meriwether Lewis, April 27, 1803, *WTJ*, 8:194–97, and to André Michaux, January 1793, *WTJ*, 6:158–61. For his settlement plans for the West see Jefferson's Second Inaugural Address, March 4, 1805, *WTJ*, 8:343–47, and his letter to John Jacob Astor, May 24, 1812, *WTJ*, 9:351–52.

19. Second Inaugural Address, March 4, 1805, *WTJ*, 8:343–44.

20. For a detailed account see Isaac Cox, *The West Florida Controversy, 1798–1813* (1918; rpt. Gloucester, Mass., 1967).

21. Madison to Livingston and Monroe, March 2, 1803, *WJM*, 7:16–17.

22. Gallatin to Madison, December 1802, *WAG*, 1:110–11, and to Jefferson, September 5, 1803, September 12, 1805, and August 5, 1803, ibid., 153, 242–49, 399–400.

23. Jefferson to Gallatin, August 11, 1808, *WTJ*, 9:203, and to Madison, August 16, 1807, and September 1, 1807, ibid., 124–25, 134.

24. Madison to Spanish Envoys John Armstrong and James Bowdoin, March 13, 1806, *WJM*, 7:194.

25. Madison to Armstrong, May 22, 1807, ibid., 447–48.

26. Madison to Pinckney, October 30, 1810, *WJM*, 8:121–22; also see Madison to Robert Smith, July 17, 1810, ibid., 105–6.

27. Madison to Pinckney, October 30, 1810, ibid., 121–22.

28. Madison, Special Message to Congress, January 3, 1811, ibid., 131, and

Madison to Monroe, February 18, 1819, ibid., 422.

29. Whitaker, *Independence of Latin America*, 10–12, 23–80.

30. Gallatin to Madison, September 17, 1810, *WAG*, 1:490–91.

31. For a detailed presentation of British, American, and French relations in this period consult Bradford Perkins, *Prologue to War: England and the United States, 1805–1812* (Los Angeles, 1961); Paul Varg, *Foreign Policies of the Founding Fathers*, 178ff.; Reginald Horsman, *The Causes of the War of 1812* (Philadelphia, 1962); A. L. Burt, *The United States, Great Britain, and the British North American* (New York, 1961), 156ff.; and Clauder, *American Commerce*, 59ff.

32. See Lawrence A. Kaplan's analysis in "Jefferson, the Napoleonic Wars, and the Balance of Power," *W&MQ*, 14 (1957), 196–217.

33. See, for example, Gallatin speech in Congress, February 11, 1799, *Annals of Cong.*, 2860–61.

34. Gallatin, Commerce with Great Britain, March 3, 1806, *NASP: Commerce and Navigation*, 2:249–54.

35. Madison to Pinckney, February 3, 1807, *WJM*, 7:401–2.

36. Madison to Pinckney, March 3, 1808, *WJM*, 8:19–20. See also Jefferson's similar comments to Archibald Stuart, August 8, 1811, *WTJ*, 9:326–27.

37. Jesse Lemisch, "Jack Tar in the Streets: Merchant Seamen in the Politics of Revolutinary America," *W&MQ*, 25 (1968), 371–95.

38. Gallatin to Jefferson, April 13 and April 1, 1807, *WAG*, 1:332–33, 335–36; and Jefferson to Madison, April 21, 1807, *WTJ*, 9:47–48.

39. Gallatin to Jefferson, August 18, 1803, *WAG*, 1:144.

40. Madison to Pinkney, May 23, 1810, *WJM*, 8:100.

41. Madison to ?, July 25, 1812, ibid., 203, and his Fourth Annual Message, November 4, 1812, ibid., 230.

42. Jefferson to Lewis, July 17, 1808, *WTJ*, 9:199–200.

43. For a discussion of policy repertoires see Graham T. Allison, *Essence of Decision: Explaining the Cuban Missile Crisis* (Boston, 1971), 78–100, 252–63.

44. Madison to John Armstrong, February 3, 1808, *WJM*, 8:13.

45. Perkins, *Prologue to War*, 140–58, esp. 156–58.

46. Madison to Pinkney, April 30, 1808, *WJM*, 8:25–27.

47. Jefferson's Eighth Annual Message, November 8, 1808, *WTJ*, 9:217–18.

48. Madison to Jefferson, April 3, 1812, *WJM*, 8:185.

49. For clear statement of Madison's reasons for seeking war, see his letters to John Quincy Adams, November 15, 1811, ibid., 167, and to ?, July 25, 1812, ibid., 203. J.C.A. Stagg offers a very good discussion of the consistency in Madison's and the Republican's commercial policy from the 1780s through the War of 1812. In it he integrates the invasion of Canada as an extension of commercial discrimination by closing alternative markets to the British. Stagg, "James Madison and the Coercion of Great Britain: Canada, the West Indies, and the War of 1812," *W&MQ*, 83 (1981), 3–34.

50. Madison, Message to Congress, June 1, 1812, *WJM*, 8:192–201.

51. George R. Taylor has compiled most of these explanations and others in *The War of 1812: Past Justifications and Present Interpretations* (Boston, 1963).

52. See, for example, Perkins, *Prologue to War*, 408–10; Ronald L. Hatzenbuehler, "Party Unity and the Decision for War in the House of Representatives, 1812," *W&MQ*, 29 (1972), 367–90; and Reginald C. Stuart, "James Madison and the Militants: Republican Disunity and Replacing the Embargo," *Diplomatic History*, 6 (1982), 145–167.

53. Rudolph M. Bell, "Mr. Madison's War and Long-Term Congressional Vot-

ing Behavior," *W&MQ*, 36 (1979), 383, 387.

54. Ibid., 378, 387–90.

55. Gallatin to Matthew Lyon, May 7, 1816, *WAG*, 1:700.

Chapter 10
The Republican Triumvirate and Manufacturing: An Overview

1. Peterson, *Thomas Jefferson*, esp. 459, 514–15 and 943; and *Selected Writings of Albert Gallatin*, ed. E. James Ferguson (New York, 1967).

2. Petitions to Congress, January 24, 27, and 28, 1803, *ASP: Commerce and Navigation*, 1:508–9.

3. Petitions to Congress, March 30, 1802, *ASP: Finance*, 1:743–44, and March 24, 1802, *NASP: Manufactures*, 1:90.

4. Petition to Congress, February 2, 1801, *ASP: Finance*, 1:694.

5. Petition to Congress, December 9, 1803, *NASP: Manufactures*, 1:95–98.

6. Petitions to Congress, November 21, 1808, June 1809, and January 22, 1811, *ASP: Finance*, 2:306, 367–68, 465–67; and Petitions to Congress, December 7 and 23, 1811, and January 29, 1812, *NASP: Manufactures*, 1:149, 150, 153. These petitions come from New Hampshire, New Jersey, Massachusetts, Kentucky, and Pennsylvania.

7. Letters and enclosure in Meletiah Jordon to Gallatin, October 1, 1809; John Barnes to Gallatin, October 30, 1809; Thomas Coles to Gallatin, November 13 and 15, 1809; Charles Simmons to Gallatin, November 14, 1809; J. H. McCulloch to Gallatin, November 14, 1809; John Shore to Gallatin, November 22, 1809; and Portsmouth's Collector to Gallatin, December 30, 1809—all in *PAG*.

8. Higginbotham, *Keystone in the Democratic Arch*, 5–6, 22–23, 135, 164–65, 220–21, 326–27, 382n.

9. Munroe, *Federalist Delaware*, 207–13, 220–25, 239–41, 247–48.

10. Coles to Gallatin, November 15, 1809, *PAG*; Taussig, *Tariff History*, 15ff.

11. Burrows, "Albert Gallatin," 114–85. For the Amelung loan debate see June 3, 1790, *Annals of Cong.*, 1630–32.

12. Burrows, "Albert Gallatin," 283–308.

13. Treasury Report, January 1804, *NASP: Revenue*, 29:84.

14. Treasury Report, November 1807, *NASP: Public Finance*, 2:371.

15. Treasury Report, November 1808, ibid., 417–18.

16. Gallatin to Thomas Newton, June 2, 1809, *PAG*. The letter he refers to in the June letter was probably the one dated November 1, 1808, *PAG*.

17. Gallatin, Report on Manufactures, April 1810, *NASP: Manufactures*, 1:130. Gallatin mentioned no specific tariff rates in the report; the rates are taken from his letter to T. R. Gold, March 19, 1816, *WAG*, 1:689–91.

18. Report on Manufactures, 130.

19. For a detailed analysis of Coxe's and Hamilton's reports see above, Chapter 3.

20. June 6, 1809, *Annals of Congress*, 230, 235–36; Murry N. Rothbard, *The Panic of 1819* (New York, 1962).

21. McCoy, *Elusive Republic*.

22. Madison to William Pinkney, April 30 and July 18, 1808, *WJM*, 8:27, 45.

23. Madison, Second Annual Message, December 5, 1810, ibid., 126–27; emphasis added. And see his subsequent message, November 5, 1811, ibid., 163.

24. Fifth Annual Message, December 7, 1813, ibid., 273.

25. Peterson, *Thomas Jefferson*, 514–15.

26. Jefferson to Henry Dearborn, July 16, 1810, *WTJ*, 9:278–79; Jefferson's message to the Democratic Republican Delegates, 1809, Jefferson Papers, Library of Congress.

27. Jefferson to John Langdon, August 2, 1808, and to David Humphreys, January 20, 1809, *WTJ*, 9:201, 226.

28. Louis M. Sears, *Jefferson and the Embargo* (1927; rpt. New York, 1966), 61–65; 108, 125ff.

29. See above, Chapter 6, and Opinion, December 3, 1790, *PTJ*, 18:120–21.

30. Jefferson to DuPont, April 15, 1811, *WTJ*, 9:317–22.

31. Jefferson to John Melish, January 13, 1813, ibid., 374–75.

32. Peterson, *Thomas Jefferson*, 943. Grampp's analysis also confirms this conclusion; see "Reexamination of Jeffersonian Economics," 263–83, esp. 281–82.

33. Gallatin to Jefferson, March 10, 1812, *WAG*, 1:517. Their choice in this respect was between the antirepublican, corrupting influences of constant commercial warfare for foreign markets to vent agricultural surpluses and the development of an internal market for domestic produce through manufacturing, which would lessen the need for foreign outlets and the possibility of conflict. Jefferson reaffirmed the danger of war from commercial conflicts and the use of domestic manufactures to avoid such conflict in a letter to Henry Dearborn, July 16, 1810, *WTJ*, 9:278–79.

34. For a discussion of these mitigating factors see David Montgomery, "The Working Classes of the Pre-Industrial American Cities," *Labor History*, 9 (1968), 3–22; Leo Marx, *The Machine in the Garden: Technology and the Pastoral Ideal in America* (New York, 1967); Lemisch, "Jack Tar," 371–95; and Henry N. Smith, *Virgin Land*. The role of education is mentioned repeatedly in Jefferson's, Madison's, and Gallatin's correspondence and speeches. Gallatin, who lived to midcentury, had the opportunity to witness the working class grow in America. His comment to John Badollet is revealing: "For it appeared to me impossible to procure our democratic institutions & the right of universal suffrage, unless we could raise the standard of general education & the mind of the labouring classes nearer to a level with those born under more favorable circumstances." February 7, 1833, *PAG*.

35. Madison to D. Lynch, June 27, 1817, *WJM*, 8:392–93. Madison further noted that manufactories would absorb emigrant labor.

Chapter 11
Political Economy and Policymaking

1. This is not to say that scholars stressing a random mix of events to explain policy are anti-intellectual. They merely tend to assign relatively equal weight to several causes because they are unwilling to accept a periodization which would allow them to attribute primary and secondary weight to causal factors.

2. In his *Essence of Decision* Graham T. Allison offers a particularly succinct summary with illustrations of this sort of analysis at its best.

3. *Federalist*, no. 51.

4. I am not arguing that slavery was not discussed in this era—particularly during the Revolution; it was. After ratification of the Constitution, however, it was not a major policy issue until the Missouri Compromise debates. In his second volume dealing with slavery in Western civilization, *The Problem of Slavery in the Age of Revolution, 1770–1823* (Ithaca, 1975), David Brian Davis presents a balanced discussion of the issue as it developed in this period.

5. On Indian affairs consult Bernard W. Sheehan, *Seeds of Extinction* (Chapel Hill, 1973), and Edgar B. Wesley, "The Government Factory System among the Indians, 1795–1822," *Journal of Economic and Business History,* 4 (1932), 487–511. There is reason to doubt that even "civilized" Indians would have been free of white settlement pressures. A keen competition for land existed between small, white farmers and Indians seeking property.

6. Madison to William Eustis, May 22, 1823, *WJM,* 9:135–36.

7. Jefferson to Caesar Rodney, December 21, 1800, *WTJ,* 7:472–73; to Gallatin, May 29, 1805, *WAG,* 1:232; and Jefferson's Second Inaugural, March 4, 1805, *WTJ,* 8:343–44.

8. Madison, Special Message to Congress, December 23, 1811, *WJM,* 8:172–73; Eighth Annual Message, December 3, 1816, ibid., 379–80; and Madison to Martin Van Buren, July 5, 1830, *WJM,* 9:381.

9. Gallatin, "Autobiographic Sketch," 1849, *PAG.*

10. The cotton mill figures are from Gallatin's Report on Manufactures, *NASP: Manufactures,* 1:124–30. Tench Coxe also offered an overview of manufacturing which suggests this magnitude of increase in *A Statement of the Arts and Manufactures of the United States for 1810* (Philadelphia, 1814).

11. William Grampp draws this conclusion for Jefferson in his "Reexamination of Jeffersonian Economics," 281–82.

12. William Appleman Williams provides an extensive discussion of the issue of temporal development in American history in his *America Confronts a Revolutionary World, 1776–1976* (New York, 1976). Drew McCoy also touches on the issue of development in space as an alternative to development in time in his book *The Elusive Republic.* McCoy, however, links temporal development in the "world historical" sense, which Williams employs, to economic development of a market system and manufacturing. He concludes, incorrectly, that the Republican leaders opposed economic development because they did not want to become another England. The issue is more complex than whether or not the Republican leaders were willing to tolerate some sort of working class. See the discussion of manufacturing in Chapter 10.

13. Glyndon Van Deusen, "Some Aspects of Whig Thought and Theory in the Jacksonian Period," *American Historical Review,* 63 (1958), 305–22.

14. Jefferson to Gallatin, December 26, 1820, *WTJ,* 10:176–78; Gallatin, *Memorial of the Free Trade Convention* (1831), *PAG;* and Madison's letter of March 1836 and his Advice to My Country, *WJM,* 9:609–11.

15. Gallatin to Badollet, September 3, 1836, *PAG.*

Appendix A
A Note on Commercial Discrimination

1. Madison to Monroe and Pinkney, May 20, 1807, *WJM,* 7:421–45.

2. See Perkins, *Prologue to War,* 146–74; Clauder, *American Commerce,* 139; and, for the influence of the West Indian planters, Eric Williams, *Capitalism and Slavery* (Chapel Hill, 1944).

3. Perkins, *Prologue to War,* 306–21; Clauder, *American Commerce,* 213–16.

4. The conclusions of the Republican leaders concerning repeal are reflected in Madison to Joel Barlow, August 11, 1812, *WJM,* 8:209.

5. Gallatin to Edward Everett, January 1835, *WAG,* 2:492.

Index

ABOUT THE AUTHOR

John R. Nelson, Jr., has worked on public policy for the National Academy of Sciences and the National Opinion Research Center at the University of Chicago. He now holds a corporate management position in New York.

Liberty and Property

Designed by Ann Walston.

Composed by Capitol Communication Systems in Sabon.

Printed by BookCrafters on 50-lb. Sebago Eggshell Cream Offset and bound in Holliston Roxite with Lindenmeyer Multicolor Antique end sheets.